Cathy has a reputation for understanding and gaining the trust of difficult children, and welcomes Reece into her family, despite his troubled past. But it soon becomes clear that Reece has little concept of right or wrong.

Over time Reece responds to Cathy's care, and his behaviour gradually starts to improve. But Reece has a dark secret that is threatening to undo all the progress he's made. Having been sworn to secrecy by his family, he knows he must not tell.

Can Cathy discover the truth before his early childhood corrupts the rest of his life?

Also by Cathy Glass

CATHY GLASS

THE MILLION COPY BESTSELLING AUTHOR

Mommy Told Me Not to Tell

The true story of a troubled boy
with a dark secret

HarperElement
An imprint of HarperCollins*Publishers*
1 London Bridge Street
London SE1 9GF

www.harpercollins.co.uk

1

© Cathy Glass 2010

Cathy Glass asserts the moral right to be
identified as the author of this work

A catalogue record of this book is
available from the British Library

ISBN 978-0-00-821979-6

Printed and bound in the United States of America
by LSC Communications

Find out more about HarperCollins and the environment at
www.harpercollins.co.uk/green

Prologue

'Is he staying with you now?' she bellowed. 'He better be! I ain't 'aving 'im moved again. It's a bleeding disgrace. Them wankers!'

'No, he won't be moved again,' I reassured Tracey.

Reece was pulling on my arm and making a loud hissing noise. 'Stand still, good boy,' I said.

'Do as you're bleeding told!' Tracey yelled, giving him another cuff over the head.

And that was my first meeting with Tracey, Reece's mother.

Certain details, including names, places and dates, have been changed to protect the children in this story.

Chapter One:

Respite

My family and I had said a very emotional farewell to Tayo (the boy whose story I described in my book *Hidden*), our previous foster child, at the end of October, and because we had grown so close to Tayo it seemed a good idea to do some respite fostering, rather than take on another long-term placement.

'Respite' in fostering terms means looking after a foster child (or children) for another carer while that carer takes a much-needed break. Respite fostering doesn't have the same emotional drain or complications as short or long-term fostering: the child or children arrive clean and well fed, with everything they need for their stay, and safe in the knowledge that they will be returning to their permanent carer(s) after the break. Some foster carers only ever do respite fostering, and have a steady procession of children staying with them. The foster carer looks after the child in exactly the same way as they would any fostered child, but the child's time with her (or him) is viewed as a short holiday by all concerned, and the foster carer knows that she cannot become too involved. For this reason respite fostering is said to be 'easier'. While I am always happy to offer respite if I don't have a foster child, I prefer the involvement of longer placements, and the satisfaction of knowing I have, I hope, in some small way helped a child along the difficult path of life.

After Tayo left and before we embarked on the respite fostering we took a week off and had no foster child at all. This gave me a chance to give the bedroom a thorough cleaning and airing, and also me and my family – Adrian, Paula and Lucy – a chance to come to terms with Tayo's departure. Although Tayo had left in the best possible circumstances, there was still a sadness, a gap in the family, which would take time to diminish, and would probably only start to go with the arrival of the next child. Some foster carers take a new placement straightaway for this very reason.

The first child to arrive for respite care at the beginning of November was Jemma, a tiny five-year-old who had been with her carers for six months. She stayed with us for a week. Jemma was developmentally delayed and had the needs of a three-year-old. Paula and Lucy, my sixteen- and eighteen-year-old daughters, were very happy to help with this tiny tot and virtually took over from me when they came home from school and college in the evening. But aware that Paula had a lengthy essay to research and write for one of her A-levels, I thought it was just as well Jemma wasn't staying for longer, as there didn't appear to be much writing going on in the evening but plenty of playing with Barbie dolls. And while I'm sure Jemma enjoyed her week of non-stop activities with my daughters, she was obviously pleased when her permanent carers returned from their break to take her home.

Three days after Jemma left I was asked to take Daisy for two weeks' respite care. She was fifteen. I don't normally foster teenagers – having three of my own is sufficient! And it is thought that a better family balance is achieved if the fostered child (or children) is not of the same age as the child or children already in the family: there is less chance of sibling rivalry, and the foster child's needs can be better catered for. However, the placement was only for two weeks, and I knew that Daisy was considered a 'bit of a handful' and it would therefore be difficult to find respite carers for her. Also, I thought that with Daisy in school and without the high level of needs of a younger child I would have a chance to redecorate the bathroom before I had to start thinking about Christmas.

Daisy was due to arrive at six o'clock with her carer, Kriss, but didn't arrive until 9.30, having not arrived home until nine o'clock. I could see that Kriss was very stressed as she brought Daisy and her suitcase into the hall and kept apologizing for their lateness. I told Kriss not to worry and reassured her that she hadn't inconvenienced us (flexibility and adaptability are essential in fostering), and said that I would take good care of Daisy. Daisy was a slim attractive girl with long fair hair, who obviously liked to dress fashionably, and clearly wasn't happy having to stay with me. I already knew from Jill, my link worker from Homefinders fostering agency, that Kriss was going with a friend for two weeks to Spain. Daisy had been offered the chance to go with them but had refused because she didn't want to leave her boyfriend behind.

'Don't see why I couldn't have stayed at home,' Daisy grumbled as Kriss tried to say goodbye.

'You know why you can't, love, not at fifteen,' Kriss said, looking even more stressed. 'Give me a hug. I must go. My flight leaves in three hours.' Then, looking at me: 'God knows what I'd have done if she'd been any later.'

I reassured Kriss again that Daisy would be fine, and I told her to go.

'Goodbye, love,' Kriss said to Daisy.

'Bye,' Daisy said sullenly, without looking at her and refusing the hug.

'Bye. Have a really good holiday,' I called after her. Closing the door, I wondered if Daisy had been very late returning home with the intention of trying to stop Kriss from going.

'You're a bit young to stay at home by yourself,' I said, smiling at Daisy. 'Anyway we've been looking forward to having you stay.'

'Really,' Daisy said, looking doubtful, but not as doubtful as I was, for she really did have a face on her.

'Yes,' I said brightly. 'My daughters love having other teenagers' company.'

Lucy and Paula were in their bedrooms and I called them down and introduced them. With typical teenage embarrassment, on all their parts, the girls smiled sheepishly, eyes down, and just about managed 'Hi'.

'I need to wash me hair,' Daisy said to me.

'OK, love. Let's get your case upstairs first.'

I helped Daisy heave her very large suitcase upstairs and into what was to be her bedroom. Then I showed her where the bathroom was and made sure she had everything she needed. Lucy and Paula returned to their rooms with the intention of getting ready for bed – with school and college the following day I liked them to be in bed by ten o'clock.

An hour later, Daisy was still in the bathroom and my initial light taps on the door with 'Are you OK in there?' had grown to more insistent knocks, and 'Daisy, please hurry up! We all need to use the bathroom.' I thought it was just as well Adrian was at university and not queuing for the bathroom too, because he had begun spending more time in the bathroom than the rest of us put together.

Daisy finally came out of the bathroom at 11.00 and I wasn't best pleased. Although she was staying with us for only two weeks I needed to set some ground rules, while at the same time making her feel welcome. I made her a bedtime drink – she wanted hot chocolate – and while Lucy and Paula took turns in the bathroom I sat with Daisy on the breakfast stools in the kitchen and gently explained that unlike at Kriss's, where there were just the two of them, there were four of us in this house, and we all had to use the bathroom. Also, that on a school night I wanted her in bed at 9.30, with the light off at 10.00, as she had to be up and out of the house by 7.30 to catch the bus for school. Daisy liked the hot chocolate – she downed it in one go and asked for another – but didn't show the same enthusiasm for my bedtime routine.

'Whatever,' she said sulkily, as in the teenager's 'I hear what you're saying but I don't agree.'

'Excellent,' I said, sanguine as usual. 'I know it's going to be a bit different for you here but I'm sure you will be fine. It's only two weeks and then you will be back with Kriss.'

'Yeah, whatever,' she said again.

I made her another hot chocolate, which she also drank in one go. Then I went with her up to her bedroom and said I wanted her to go straight to sleep and leave the unpacking until morning.

As it turned out, her unpacking was never done. The following morning, I checked she had her bus pass and dinner money, and was dressed in at least some of her school uniform, and then stood on the doorstep and waved her off to school. 'See you later,' I called. But I didn't.

Daisy didn't return from school. I was worried, but not as worried as I would have been with another child, for I knew from Jill that Daisy had a history of disappearing and usually turned up at her boyfriend's. However, I still had to follow the usual guidelines for children who didn't arrive home when they were supposed to and I telephoned the fostering agency at 5.00 p.m. to say Daisy was late. Jill said to give her another hour and then phone again. I phoned at 6.00 to say she still hadn't returned. By that time Jill had contacted Daisy's social worker, who said even though Daisy usually turned up at her boyfriend's I should still report her missing to the police. With Lucy and Paula taking care of dinner, I phoned our local police station and went through the (lengthy) process of completing a 'missing persons', all the while feeling I was probably wasting police time. I was.

Five minutes after I'd finished on the phone and had just sat down to dinner, Jill phoned to say Daisy had phoned her social worker and said she was with her boyfriend at his parents' flat. The social worker had said it was all right for her to stay there. I could hear from Jill's tone that she didn't approve, but it wasn't her decision. I didn't know enough of Daisy's situation to know if it was the right decision or not, but I was disappointed Daisy didn't feel able to stay with us, and regretted the waste of police time.

Daisy popped in after two days to take some clothes from the suitcase that was still unpacked in her bedroom, and accepted a hot chocolate, but she didn't want to talk. Two days after that she reappeared for another change of clothes and a bath; apparently her boyfriend's parents' shower was broken.

'There is only a week before Kriss comes back,' I said, catching her en route from the bathroom to what should have been her bedroom. 'I think it would be really nice if you stayed with us for the week.'

Daisy shrugged, and then asked for the hairdryer and a drink of hot chocolate, which I gave her in the hope it might tempt her to stay. It didn't, and I guessed Daisy had decided from the outset she wouldn't be staying with us. She popped in twice the following week for a change of clothes, a bath and, of course, a hot chocolate but didn't stay long.

I kept daily log notes on Daisy's comings and goings and phoned Jill with regular updates. I have to keep log notes and regularly update Jill with all the children I foster. Jill kept Daisy's social worker informed, and she wasn't unduly concerned for Daisy. Jill and I had to accept that, rightly or wrongly, the social services considered it appropriate for Daisy, aged fifteen, to stay with her boyfriend and his parents. I felt frustrated that I hadn't been able to do my job properly and look after her.

When Kriss arrived to collect Daisy at the end of the two weeks, she wasn't surprised to find that Daisy wasn't with us. Kriss said she would take Daisy's case and then collect her from her boyfriend's parents'. Kriss said she'd been fostering Daisy for two years and because Daisy was 'quite a handful' she took regular breaks, while making sure Daisy also had holidays. She thanked me for my trouble and apologized for Daisy's behaviour, which I assured her wasn't necessary. She added that Daisy often spent the whole weekend at her boyfriend's parents', and after numerous meetings and discussions with Daisy's social worker it had been felt that this was the best arrangement that could be achieved and that at least Daisy had a roof over her head and was safe. The fact that she was sleeping with her boyfriend and presumably having under-age (and illegal) sex had been dealt with by putting Daisy on the pill. Sometimes expectations have to be radically adjusted with teenagers, and a practical working arrangement (with their cooperation) is seen as the better option than trying to impose unrealistic and unworkable goals.

As I helped Kriss load Daisy's suitcase in the car, feeling that I hadn't even had the chance to say goodbye to Daisy, who should appear strolling down the street, hand in hand with her boyfriend, but the young lady herself! When she saw Kriss she dropped her boyfriend's hand and flew into Kriss's arms, really pleased to see her.

'Missed you,' she cried.

'I missed you too,' Kriss said.

I smiled and asked Daisy how she was.

'Good,' Daisy said.

'Yeah, good,' her boyfriend agreed.

Kriss threw me a stoical smile and then opened the rear door of the car for them to get in. I stood on the pavement and saw them off, waving goodbye to the foster child I had never fostered.

After Daisy I had a six-year-old boy, Sam, placed with me for a week. It wasn't respite but an emergency, as his mother, a single parent with no immediate family, had gone into hospital to give birth to her second child. After Sam left, I redecorated the bathroom and then began Christmas shopping in earnest. I knew I wouldn't have any more children for respite care this side of Christmas, as everyone would be involved in their own Christmas preparations, not going on holiday, although I could possibly have an emergency placement. I collected Adrian from university and the four

of us put up the decorations, and also took the opportunity to go to our local rep theatre one evening for a
musical production of *Scrooge*.

On 22 December, three days before Christmas, Jill
phoned and it wasn't just to wish us a Merry Christmas: 'Cathy, we've had a referral for a seven-year-old
boy called Reece,' she said. 'He first came into care just
over a month ago but hasn't settled. He's been with his
present carers a week and they have been persuaded to
keep him over Christmas as long as there is an end in
sight. Will you take him in the New Year?'

Ho ho, I thought, and not the Christmas variety. A
week and he's having to be moved again! 'Thanks, Jill,'
I said. 'Merry Christmas to you too.'

She laughed. 'I'm sure he's not as bad as they say, just
a bit on the lively side. I'll get back to you with more
details and an exact moving date as soon as I have
them.'

'OK. Have a good Christmas.'

'And you.'

I wasn't sure I needed more details, for 'hasn't settled'
and 'persuaded to keep him as long as there is an end in
sight' clearly meant that Reece was causing havoc.

Chapter Two:

A New Record

When Jodie (whose story I wrote about in *Damaged*) had come to live with me, three years before, she had set something of a record in respect of the number of foster carers she'd gone through – I was her fifth in four months. Children who have been badly emotionally damaged by abuse are either terribly withdrawn or, and more usually, angry, defiant, violent and aggressive, lashing out at everyone and everything around them in a bid to vent their pain on a cruel and confusing world. Not only is this type of behaviour very difficult for the foster carer to deal with, but it is also frightening and upsetting to watch, and emotionally draining for the whole foster family. Foster carers want to do their best for the child they are looking after and hope to see some improvement in the child's behaviour, as well as keeping everyone in the family safe. Sometimes the situation becomes impossible to manage, if the child's behaviour is extreme and completely out of control, so the foster carer has to admit they can no longer look after the child. This is called a placement breakdown. While everything is done to avoid such breakdowns, sometimes there is no alternative and the foster child has to be moved to another carer.

On Wednesday 2 January, the first day most people were back at work, Jill phoned shortly after 11.00 a.m. We skipped briefly through the pleasantries of 'Did you have a nice Christmas and New Year?' before Jill said: 'I'm afraid Reece has been very unsettled over Christmas. Are you able to take him tomorrow?'

'Yes. What time?'

'I'll find out. Cathy, apparently he's been in care six weeks and is on his fourth carer. You'll be his fifth.'

'What! That's ridiculous.'

'I know, although one carer had him for only two nights, because her mother was taken ill, so it wasn't Reece's fault.'

'No.' If she really was taken ill, I thought, rather than it being an excuse in a desperate situation. I was starting to feel decidedly uncomfortable and also under pressure. The number of carers a child has been through can often be an indicator of just how 'challenging' the child's behaviour is.

I felt under even more pressure when Jill said: 'I've reassured his social worker you can cope and he won't be moved from you until everything is sorted out. I've got some more details here. I'll read them out. "He's seven and a half. His birthday is in August, and he has been on the 'at risk' register for three years. He is white Caucasian and has five half-brothers and -sisters, all of whom are in care. There was another sibling but sadly she died as a baby. Reece is of medium build with brown hair and eyes. He eats well and sleeps well, and there are no immediate health concerns, although he does wet the bed and soil himself sometimes." He came into care on an interim care order. It says here the reasons were: ongoing concerns about the high level of violence within the family home, very poor hygiene in the home, emotional and physical neglect of Reece, the father's possible sexual assault on his stepdaughter, mum's assault on Reece and men coming into the house with criminal history, including suspected paedophiles.' And as if that wasn't bad enough there was more to come. 'Oh yes, and he has learning and behavioural difficulties and doesn't appear to be in school.' Little wonder he has behavioural difficulties, I thought, having to contend with all that at home.

'Will mum know where he will be staying?' I asked.

'No. Mum is very angry and has a history of assault. The family is well known to social services and has been since the eldest daughter was taken in care eighteen years ago. Oh yes,' Jill added, 'and Reece likes to be called Sharky.'

'Really? That's a strange nickname.'

'Perhaps he likes sharks – you know, the way some boys like dinosaurs. I've also managed to get some details on why the placements broke down. Would you like to hear them?'

'Yes, please. Forewarned is forearmed.'

Jill gave a small laugh. 'The first family were experienced carers, but they had a child of a similar age to Reece and the two didn't get along. Reece hit the boy with a plastic sword and he needed stitches. The second

placement was with a new carer. It was her first placement and she didn't feel able to cope. I think Reece
took his anger out on the furniture, because she's put in
a claim for a new sofa and coffee table. Reece was then
moved to another female carer: that was the one whose
mother was taken ill. He was then moved to his present
carers, a couple called Carol and Tim. They are experienced carers but Carol works part time. With Reece
not being in school, it has put a lot of pressure on her
and the family.'

'I see,' I said, feeling that possibly it wasn't as bad as it
had first appeared: jealousy of the other boy causing the
first placement breakdown; an inexperienced carer out
of her depth the second; (possible) illness for the third;
and work commitment for the fourth. 'Why isn't he in
school?' I asked.

'It doesn't say and the duty social worker didn't
know. Perhaps it was because of all the moves. Reece's
social worker is Jamey Hogg but he is on extended
leave until the end of February. I'll give the team
manager a ring and see if anyone can tell you more.
I'm going to a meeting shortly, so I'll ask them to
phone you direct.'

'Thanks, Jill.'

'You're welcome. I'm sure Reece will settle with you.'

As we said goodbye I thought the same as Jill would
be thinking, that Reece was going to have to settle with
me because one thing was for certain: he couldn't have
another change of carer. I would have to make sure he
settled, for without a stable home life there was no hope
of getting his behaviour back on track.

Half an hour later the phone rang again and Karen introduced herself as a colleague of Jamey Hogg, working in the same team at the social services. She was phoning to give me some more details, and these weren't good news.

'I know Reece's family,' she began. 'I was their social worker for a while. Reece was brought into care at the same time as his half-sister, Susie. She is ten and with another local carer. They couldn't be placed together, as none of the carers available had two free bedrooms. Although Susie and Reece have different fathers, they are the closest of the siblings. There are four older half-brothers and sisters but they were removed from home years ago. The eldest, Sharon, is eighteen now. Reece has witnessed a high level of violence in the family home, and goodness-knows what else. His father, Scott, has served time in prison for assault, among other things. While he was inside he made some pretty undesirable friends who have become regular visitors to the house, including at least one paedophile.

'I see,' I said slowly, not liking what I was hearing.

'When I was on the case I found a very poor level of hygiene in the house,' Karen continued. 'Susie and Reece were very dirty and smelt of stale urine. Mum is very loud and aggressive and the whole family shout at the top of their voices the whole time in order to be heard. Reece seems to have spent most of his waking hours in front of the television. When I last visited, although I was expected, he and Susie were watching an X-rated horror movie. Mum couldn't see anything wrong in that and refused to switch it off. Reece is large for his age, heavily built, and he is developmentally delayed. He's functioning at a pre-school level in many respects. Oh yes, and Reece bites. Mum nicknamed him Sharky some years back and it has stuck.'

'He's called Sharky because he bites?' I asked, astonished.

'Yes, I know, appalling, isn't it? Mum and dad have indulged his behaviour. They seem to find it amusing, and even actively encourage it. They laugh at him when he bites, and throw food in his direction, which he tears apart with his front teeth. He also bites objects and people. One of the reasons for his exclusion from his previous schools was biting.'

I was silent, trying to take in what I'd just heard.

'He has been excluded from two primary schools to my knowledge,' Karen continued, 'and he has had very poor school attendance since he first started school. The education department has been informed that Reece will be coming to you, so they will be looking for a school for him near you.' Karen paused. 'What else can I tell you?'

'Contact? Will he be seeing any of his family?'

'Yes. He'll be seeing his parents and his half-sister Susie each week at supervised contact. He may also see some of his other half-brothers – it hasn't been decided yet. I don't know yet where the contact will take place. We were using the Headline Family Centre but mum has been banned from there. She has also been banned from the other family centre, Kid-Care. She's a very aggressive woman.'

'She must be. I've never heard of anyone being banned from both the family centres before.'

'No, neither have I, but believe me, her behaviour merited it. Reece has obviously seen a lot of violence at home, and when he is frustrated he resorts to aggression. There have been no boundaries at home, no discipline at all. My feeling is that he and Susie should have been removed years ago.'

'So why weren't they?'

Karen sighed. 'I don't know. Unfortunately there have been a lot of changes of social worker, and mum is very good at getting what she wants and controlling people. She shouts and threatens, and with her volatile and erratic behaviour most professionals who have dealt with her just seem pleased to get away in one piece. When we removed Reece and Susie, there were two social workers and three police officers present, and there was only mum and the two children at home. You can't reason with her: it's impossible. She often comes into the council offices and we have to have security remove her. She was in again this morning, demanding to know where Reece was being moved to. We didn't tell her, obviously.'

Good, I thought, and please make sure my contact details aren't accidentally disclosed, as had sometimes happened in the past with previous placements.

'From what I know of Reece,' Karen said, trying to finish on a positive note, 'he's not really a bad kid. I'm sure his aggression is learned behaviour from home.'

'Yes, it usually is,' I agreed.

'Can you think of anything else I can tell you that might help?'

'Not at present. Thanks, you've been very helpful.'

'Thank you for taking Reece. We were getting desperate,' Karen said.

That evening when Lucy and Paula were home and we'd eaten, I took the opportunity to tell them of our new arrival before they started their homework or television watching. Lucy and Paula were fully aware of the implications of fostering a child with 'challenging behaviour' and, knowing they had a well-developed sense of humour, I decided to take a light-hearted approach.

'Ladies,' I said, as we loaded the dishwasher, 'you know what a quiet time we've had over the last couple of months – just doing the respite fostering?' They looked at me cautiously, suspiciously almost. I smiled. 'Well, I thought it was time for a change, something to liven us up a bit.' I smiled again. 'Tomorrow a boy called Reece will be coming to stay with us. He is seven but has learning difficulties, so functions at a much younger age. Although he shouts, bites and hits people when he is frustrated, I'm sure with all our help he will soon change. What he needs more than anything is stability and boundaries—' and I was about to continue with a few reminders on how we would achieve this when there was a chorus of:

'Can't someone else have him?'

I looked at them sombrely. 'They have. We will be his fifth carers in six weeks.'

Another chorus: 'You're joking!'

'No.' And I could tell by their expressions they were shocked and knew, as I did, that whatever Reece threw at us, physically or emotionally, he couldn't have another move, and would stay with us until the court made its decision on his future, which would take the best part of a year, or longer if the case was complicated.

Chapter Three:

sharky

Jill phoned at just gone 11.00 the following morning and I felt my stomach tighten. I'd had a night to sleep (or rather not sleep) on all that I'd heard about Reece and, despite years of fostering, my nerves were starting to get the better of me. Supposing his behaviour was as bad as had been reported and I wasn't able to help him? Supposing this was the one child I had to give up on? I pulled away from that thought.

'A male social worker, Imran, will be bringing Reece,' Jill said. 'At about one thirty. I'll aim to be with you half an hour before – at about one.' Jill tried to be with me when a child was placed, partly to make sure the paperwork was all correct and also for a bit of moral support.

'OK. Thanks,' I said.

'And I believe Karen phoned you yesterday.'

'Yes, she was very helpful.'

'Good. She worked with Reece's family for a while. It's a pity she's not still on the case. She's very practical and down to earth.'

'Yes.'

We said goodbye and I returned upstairs, where I was putting the finishing touches to what would soon be Reece's room. With Lucy and Paula at school and college, and Adrian away at university, I was alone in the house and it seemed very quiet. Not for long, I thought. In a couple of hours I'd have Reece to entertain me! I finished putting the Batman duvet cover and matching pillowcase on the bed, and then I glanced around the room. I hoped Reece would like it. I'd put posters of *Star Wars* on the walls, and jigsaws and puzzles in the toy box; and, mindful that Reece was functioning at a much younger age, I'd included a poster of Winnie-the-Pooh, two soft cuddly toys and a wizard castle with play people.

I always try to make the child's bedroom suitable for their age and gender, with things that are likely to appeal, based on the information I have on the child. If the child comes with a lot of their own personal possessions, then I pack away what they don't want of my things and put up theirs instead. It's so important for the child to have their possessions around them: it helps them to settle and makes them feel secure.

As I had been doing respite fostering for three months, the theme in the room had changed repeatedly and as a result there were little nests of drawing-pin holes where posters and pictures had been up and down. I'd filled them with a quick coat of paint, a pot of emulsion being another essential tool for good fostering.

At twelve noon I was about to have a bite of lunch when the phone rang. It was Jill.

'Sorry, Cathy, will you be able to manage alone this afternoon? I've been called into our south county office. One of the workers has gone home sick.'

'Yes, don't worry. I'll be fine.'

'Phone my mobile if you need anything. Otherwise I'll phone you later after Reece is placed.'

'All right, Jill.'

Jill being unable to attend when a child was placed had happened before and I wasn't unduly concerned. I'd been fostering long enough to know the procedure and Jill knew that. Had I been new to fostering another worker from Homefinders would have come in her place, but I could cope – so I thought!

By 1.30 I was as prepared as I was going to be for Reece's arrival. I wandered in and out of the front room, glancing up and down the street from behind the net curtains. Nerves were starting to get the better of me again, and I wished Reece had arrived as an emergency placement as Sam (and others before him had done); then I wouldn't have had this build-up. But I reminded myself that if I was feeling anxious, goodness knows what Reece must be feeling, on his way to his fifth new home in six weeks.

At just after two o'clock, when there was still no sign of Reece, I began thinking about giving Jill a ring to make sure everything was going according to plan. I gave one final glance through the front room window and as I did a silver car drove up and stopped outside the house. I looked out from my vantage point behind the nets and saw a boy who'd been in the rear of the car scramble over the top of the passenger seat, fling open the passenger door and leap out on to the pavement. Aged about seven, heavily built with a shaved head, he began jumping up and down, yelling at the top of his voice: 'Beat you! Beat you out! Beat you out the car, slag!'

Reece had arrived.

As I watched, a woman, who I assumed must be a social worker, jumped out of the driver's seat, ran on to the pavement and grabbed his hand. 'Don't do that!' she cried, anxiously. 'It's dangerous. You should have waited until I got out.'

Reece, oblivious to her caution, continued jumping up and down, still shouting: 'Beat you! Beat you, slag!' Then he tried to head-butt her. I flinched as he narrowly missed her nose.

I began towards the front door, making a mental note that when Reece was in my car I would have the central locking down, rather than just the child locks, until he learned to stay in his seat until I opened his door. I also made a mental note to keep my head up as I greeted Reece, for clearly head-butting was another of his accomplishments.

'Hello,' I said, smiling, as I opened the front door and they came down the path. 'I'm Cathy, and you must be Reece?'

The social worker was holding Reece's wrist to stop him from running off – he clearly didn't want to hold her hand. As they came into the hall she transferred his arm to me and sighed.

'Hello, Reece,' I said, not bending to his height. He didn't look at me but stared and then lunged down the hall. I kept hold of his arm and he pulled against me.

'Leggo! Leggo of me,' he yelled.

Placing my free hand on his shoulder, I tried to turn him round to face me so that I could make eye contact with him and gain his attention. 'Reece, listen,' I said, kindly but firmly. 'Listen to me.' He was still pulling and refusing to look in my direction. I didn't want to bend forward to make eye contact, as that would leave me in exactly the right position for a well-aimed head-butt. 'Reece, we are going down the hall now and into the back room. There are some toys there already set out for you.'

'Leggo! Leggo of me!' His voice was rasping, guttural, like an old man's, and so loud it filled the air and obliterated any other sound.

'OK. Let's go down the hall together,' I said calmly but firmly. I knew if I let go of him now in his heightened state of alert he would be off like a free radical, charging around the house, doing damage to himself and anything that got in his way. Later I'd show him round, but for now I just needed to get him calmer and establish some form of control.

With Reece still pulling against me – and he was very strong with his weight behind him – I began steadily, if not a little jerkily, down the hall and towards the back room, which is our living room.

'I'm Veronica,' the social worker called from behind me, closing the front door.

'Nice to meet you,' I returned over my shoulder.

'Slag!' Reece shouted.

Once we were in the living room I let go of Reece's hand and closed the door. As I'd hoped he would, he went straight to the selection of games I'd arranged in the centre of the room; the rest of the toys were in cupboards in the conservatory that acts as a playroom.

Veronica sank gratefully on to the sofa, happy to transfer the responsibility for Reece to me, while I remained casually standing in front of the door. It wasn't obvious to Reece, but I was blocking his exit in case his interest in the toys vanished and he made a dash for it.

'Sorry we're late,' Veronica said. 'Imran was supposed to bring Reece but it became impossible.'

I glanced at her questioningly as Reece continued overturning the toys, tipping them from their boxes but not actually playing with them. 'Imran is Asian,' she said, and then nodding at Reece, mouthed: 'He's racist.' She looked anxiously from me to the framed photographs of my children on the walls, where there were some of my adopted daughter Lucy, who is part Thai.

'Don't worry,' I said. 'I'll deal with it.' For while some carers would refuse to look after a child who is deemed racist, I had found that children of Reece's age will have learned such behaviour from home, and it can be unlearned pretty quickly. I was more concerned about Reece's apparent ADHD (Attention Deficit and Hyperactivity Disorder), which hadn't been mentioned by Jill or Karen but was very obvious now. His continual agitated and jerky movements, his short quick breaths as though he was hyperventilating and his heightened state of alert, which stopped him from focusing on anything for longer than a second, suggested hyperactivity. I needed to get him calmer before I could offer Veronica a coffee, let alone address the paperwork, which she was now taking from her briefcase.

Reece had finished turning out all the boxes of puzzles, jigsaws and toys, and they were now in a colourful mountain in the centre of the room. I slowly moved away from where I was standing by the living-room door and went over, squatting on the floor beside him.

'Reece,' I said, trying again to make eye contact, 'choose a game for us to play with and we'll put the rest away.'

He didn't so much as glance in my direction. His brain seemed so busy firing off in random directions it had blocked out almost everything and everyone around him, or any logical thought. I lightly touched his hand and he glanced towards me, but I didn't think he'd actually seen me. 'Reece, shall we play with these building bricks?' I suggested. 'I bet you are good at building things.' I put two pieces together but Reece was already on his feet, going straight over to the book-case, where he began pulling books off the shelves. By the time I was at his side he had cleared one shelf and was starting on the next. 'Reece, would you like me to read you a story?' No reply, and no response, just more books thrown on the floor.

'Right, Reece. Here's a nice book,' I said more loudly. I stooped and retrieved a large colourful counting book from the ever-increasing pile on the floor. 'Let's read this one. It's a counting book, with lots of pictures, and all the numbers to a hundred. I wonder if you can count to ten?'

The books suddenly stopped raining down and he turned to look at me properly for the first time since arriving. I noticed what lovely brown eyes he had but what unusual front teeth. His front four teeth at the top were very large, overlapped each other and had prominent serrated edges. It crossed my mind whether this had contributed to the 'Sharky' tag his mother had given him, in which case it was unbelievably cruel.

'Well?' I said, making direct eye contact. 'Can you count to ten, Reece?'

He grinned broadly, which highlighted even more the unusual configuration of his teeth. 'Of course I can, you silly bugger!' he said. 'I can count to a hundred.' He grabbed the book from my hand and, throwing himself on the sofa, sat expectantly, waiting for me to read. I wasn't worried about being called a 'silly bugger' or his snatching the book, for at last he was calmer and I had his attention.

I sat beside him on the sofa as Veronica began sorting through her paperwork. Reece moved closer into my side and then placed the book in my lap. I opened it at the first page, which showed a huge three-dimensional number 1 on the left-hand page with a corresponding picture of one large white cuddly rabbit on the right-hand page.

'So what is this number?' I asked.

'One!' he yelled.

'Good. Well done. But there's no need to shout. I'm sitting next to you.' I turned the page to reveal a large three-dimensional number 2 and an accompanying picture of two rag dolls.

'Two!' Reece yelled.

Veronica now had the placement forms and relevant paperwork ready on her lap. Between turning the pages and reading the numbers I began answering her questions, first about my doctor's contact details where I would register Reece, and then my mobile number, which the social services didn't have.

'I would offer to make you coffee,' I said to her, 'but I think it would be wise to keep this book going for a while.'

'Absolutely,' she said. I continued turning the pages as Reece shouted out the numbers, and Veronica asked questions and made notes. By the time Reece and I had arrived at number 15, Veronica had all the additional information she needed, and the placement agreement form was ready for me to sign. She leaned forward and passed me her pen and the form. I signed with my right hand, while turning the page of the book with my left. Veronica separated the copies and put one copy on the coffee table for me.

'I would normally go through the essential information forms with you,' she said, glancing at Reece, 'but I'm not sure that's a good idea at present.' The essential information forms contained the full names, addresses and ages of the child's immediate family, and details of his and their ethnicity, any religious, dietary or medical needs, the type of court order granted to bring the child into care and any special conditions the child had such as behavioural difficulties.

'No,' I agreed. 'I'll look at it later when I have the opportunity.' I turned the page to the number 20 and a picture of twenty little elves.

'I don't think it contains any more than you've already been told,' Veronica said. 'The contact arrangements haven't been finalized yet.'

I glanced up from number 24, which was twenty-four small white mice. 'All right. Fine.'

Reece nudged me to continue, which I did. Then I paused and said: 'Reece, you've been a very good boy. You've sat here very nicely. I'm so pleased you like books, because I do too.' Number 25 was twenty-five red tulips. Reece yelled out the number and I turned the page again.

'Well, unless there is anything else you can think of, I'll leave you to it,' Veronica said, placing the set of essential information forms on top of the placement forms.

I stopped turning the pages and looked at Reece, still calm beside me. 'Reece,' I said. 'I will continue reading this in a minute after we have said goodbye to Veronica. All right?'

He jabbed the open page with his forefinger. 'No, read!' he demanded. 'I want the book.'

'Well, in that case, if you are not going to say goodbye, you can look at the book by yourself for a moment while I see Veronica to the door.'

I moved the book, now open at twenty-eight twinkling stars, from my lap to his and stood up. Reece immediately jumped up beside me, jettisoning the book on to the floor. 'What about me fings?' he yelled at the top of his voice.

Veronica and I looked at each other and smiled. In all the kerfuffle of Reece's arrival we had both forgotten about Reece's belongings, which would be in Veronica's car. Learning difficulties Reece might have, but he wasn't going to be left without his possessions!

'Well done,' I said to him. 'We can't let Veronica go without giving us your things, can we?'

He grinned his toothy grin. 'You silly buggers, you forgot!' he shouted, giving me a hefty whack on the arm. He shot out of the living room and down the hall towards the front door. I went straight after him, leaving Veronica putting away her paperwork.

'Reece, don't open that door!' I called.

He was already grappling with the front doorknob, which fortunately sticks, trying to turn it to get out and to the car for his belongings. I arrived beside him and gently put my hand over his on the doorknob. 'There's a busy road out there,' I said. 'You must always wait until I open the door. We don't want you getting hurt.'

My left hand was lightly on top of Reece's hand, and both of them were on the doorknob, which was level with his head. Before I realized what he was about to do he'd brought his mouth forward and sunk his teeth into the back of my hand.

'Ow!' I cried, and immediately withdrew my hand as Reece continued to yank on the door. I pressed my foot against the bottom of the door so it wouldn't open and looked at the back of my hand. His front teeth were clearly imprinted in my flesh, but fortunately it wasn't bleeding. I took hold of him lightly by the shoulders and, turning him away from the door and towards me, I tried to make eye contact.

'Reece,' I said firmly, 'that was naughty. You don't bite. It hurts. It's not a nice thing to do.' But his eyes were darting all over the place and I knew he couldn't hear me even if he'd wanted to. 'Reece,' I said more loudly, still holding his shoulders, 'Reece, look at me. You don't bite.' Still not looking at me, he brought his chin down on to his left shoulder and tried to bite my hand, which was resting there. Then he turned his head quickly and snapped at my other hand, but both were fortunately out of his range.

'No!' I said again. 'Don't bite. It's cruel. You will stop that now!'

He snapped again at both my hands, and then wrenched free of my hold and charged up the staircase.

Veronica was beside me now. 'Cathy, are you all right?' she asked.

We both looked at my hand, which still bore the perfect impression of Reece's front teeth.

'Yes,' I said. 'It hasn't broken the skin.' I glanced anxiously up the stairs. I could hear Reece charging around the landing. I certainly didn't want him up there alone.

'Veronica,' I said. 'Could you bring Reece's belongings in from the car while I go up and settle him?'

'Of course,' she said. I quickly propped the door open so that she could get in and out, and then I went upstairs.

I found Reece in my bedroom, bouncing up and down on the bed for all he was worth. The springs bonged unhappily.

'Off now!' I said. He continued bouncing, turning away so that his back was towards me. 'Reece! Get off that bed now!'

He ignored me, so I moved forward. I leant over the bed and, taking hold of him round the waist, I drew him down on to the bed and into a sitting position. I sat behind him and encircled him with my arms, with him facing away from me. My hands covered his and were out of reach of his teeth. He laughed at being held, and then struggled, laughing some more, before finally he gave up and relaxed.

'Good. That's better,' I said. I held him for a moment longer; then I took my arms from around his waist and took hold of one of his hands. I led him off the bed. 'Reece, this is my bedroom,' I said. 'It's private. It's just for me. You don't come in here. I'll show you your bedroom when we've said goodbye to Veronica.'

'Want to see it now,' he yelled.

'And I want you to stop biting, Reece. Look at my hand.'

I raised the hand he had bitten to his line of vision while holding on to him with my other hand. Had I let go of him I had no doubt he would have shot off straight into another bedroom. 'Look at those marks,' I said, needing to make the point about biting. 'Your teeth did that and it's not good.' In truth the physical damage was small, but biting is a nasty habit and I had to stop it straightaway. If he had broken the skin it would have been far more serious, for all types of infections including hepatitis and the HIV virus can be passed through blood drawn by a bite.

Reece now seemed to be focusing on my hand and I left it in his line of vision while remaining alert to any sign that he might strike again. 'People don't bite each other,' I emphasized. 'And you mustn't.'

'I'm not a people. I'm a shark,' he said.

I turned him round to face me squarely, and searched again for eye contact. 'Reece, you are not a shark. You are a little boy, and boys don't bite.'

'Yes, they do. I'm Sharky boy.'

'You're not Sharky. You are Reece and you will stop biting. Do you understand?'

He didn't say anything and his eyes once again ran over the room, looking at everything except me.

'Have I got a telly in me room?' he asked suddenly.

'Yes, you have. And it's a special treat to have a television in your bedroom. As you can see, I haven't got one in my bedroom.' I would be using the television in his room – as I had with other children who liked television – as a reward for good behaviour and its removal as a sanction for bad behaviour. 'OK, Reece,' I said, taking his left hand in mine and leading him from my bedroom, 'we'll look at your room now and I'll show you the television.'

Springing along beside me, with his hand in mine, we went round the landing and into his bedroom. I heard Veronica downstairs make another trip into the hall with Reece's belongings.

'I want it on now,' he yelled, making a lunge for the remote control, which lay on top of the television.

I intercepted and took it. He glared at me. 'Right, Reece,' I said, trying to make eye contact again, 'having a television in your bedroom is a very special treat. You will be allowed to watch it for short periods if you are good. Being good means not biting and doing what I ask you to. Do you understand?'

He nodded, and briefly looked in my direction.

'Excellent. Now, you can sit on this beanbag, and I'll see if there are any children's programmes on.' It was just after three o'clock, so I thought there would be. He did as I asked and sat on the beanbag. I turned on the portable television at the plug, and then flicked the remote until I came to a pre-school children's cartoon.

The change in Reece's behaviour was instant and dramatic. He was immediately transfixed, as he had been earlier by my reading a book. His limbs stopped their frantic and continuous twitching and his breathing regulated; all his attention was on the bright cartoon images chasing across the screen. Although his calmness was welcome, it was also odd because children with true ADHD often can't relax even in front of a television. I could see that carefully controlled television watching together with story reading were going to be useful strategies in managing Reece's behaviour. Leaving Reece on the beanbag, completely absorbed in the programme, I went downstairs to Veronica, who had just finished offloading Reece's belongings into the hall. She was now waiting for me.

'OK?' she asked hopefully.

'Yes. He's watching children's cartoons and is much quieter.' I glanced at his luggage – a large suitcase, a couple of rucksacks and two toy boxes, which was about what I would have expected to come with a child who had been in care for just over a month.

'Well, I hope you have a good evening,' Veronica said. Then she took a folded piece of paper from her pocket and passed it to me. 'His previous carer asked me to give you this. It's the food he likes.'

I unfolded the paper and read: '*Reece likes most things but his favourites are Chicken Dippers, fish fingers, tinned spaghetti hoops and Wall's sausages. He is used to drinking a lot of fizzy drinks but these make him hyperactive. He has been having milk, juice and water with me.*' Very sensible, I thought, because research has shown that diet can play quite a large part in children's behaviour, particularly if they are sensitive to additives, which many children with behavioural problems are.

'Thanks,' I said to Veronica, refolding the paper.

'And I should keep him off the E numbers,' she said with a smile.

'Absolutely,' I agreed.

After Veronica had left I took the bags and boxes up to Reece's room. I told him I would start unpacking his clothes and he could help me if he liked, or he could continue watching his programme. He didn't answer or turn in my direction, but remained absorbed in the colourful cartoon, which was designed for children aged about four. I opened the suitcase and began taking out his clothes, folding and hanging them as I put them into the wardrobe and drawers. As I worked I repeatedly glanced in Reece's direction. He remained relaxed but oblivious to my presence. His eyes followed the rapidly moving cartoon figures, which were now on an adventure in a park. Occasionally he made little noises, sometimes grunting his approval at something that was happening on screen and repeating the odd word as the story unfolded. It crossed my mind that Reece seemed to relate far better to the television than he did to people, probably as a result of all the years he'd spent in front of the television that Karen had mentioned. And I thought that while television might be a useful tool in managing Reece's behaviour his viewing was going to have to be very carefully regulated. I wanted him to engage and interact with people, not a screen.

When Lucy and Paula arrived home just before 4.00 they did not, as they had expected, enter a house heaving under the strain of an out-of-control child, but one that was quiet, with a child sitting serenely on a bean-bag, watching television, while I unpacked.

'Up here,' I called as I heard the front door go.

Leaving their bags and coats in the hall they came straight up. They knocked on the bedroom door, which we always do before entering a bedroom other than our own, and came in.

'Hi,' I said. 'This is Reece. Reece, these are my daughters, Paula and Lucy.'

The girls said 'Hi' and 'Hello'. Reece grunted what could have been an acknowledgement while not taking his eyes from the screen.

'I'll finish unpacking this case,' I said to them. 'Then I'll think about dinner. Have you had a good day?'

'Yes,' Paula said.

'Not bad,' Lucy added.

The girls looked from Reece to me and back again. I knew what they were thinking: that the child who was sitting so contentedly and now smiling at *The Basil Brush Show* couldn't possibly be the one I'd told them to expect. However, I also knew, given what I'd previously seen of Reece's behaviour, that things could revert very quickly.

Chapter Four:

Toilet Training

With Reece being entertained by the television and before I began making dinner, I took the opportunity of mentioning to the girls that they should be a bit careful, as Reece could and did head-butt and bite. They nodded, but I could tell they weren't convinced. We had fostered children before who'd come to us with appalling records of bad behaviour but had never shown it to us. 'Just be careful,' I said. 'I don't want any injuries.'

I also took the opportunity of interrupting Reece's television for five minutes to show him where the toilet was and explain the rules regarding other people's bedrooms: that our bedrooms were our own private space and we never went in to anyone else's without being asked. Reece compliantly agreed because he knew the television awaited once I'd had my say. I knew I would have to repeat the bedroom rules because children of Reece's age (even those without learning difficulties) are impulsive and tend to be in a room in search of someone before they have remembered to knock and wait.

At five o'clock while I was making dinner, Reece left the television, stood at the top of the stairs and yelled at the top of his voice: 'Cathy! I need a pooh!' I heard him clearly from the kitchen, which is at the opposite end of the house, so great was the volume in his voice. Aware that Reece had a history of soiling himself, I immediately left peeling the potatoes and went upstairs.

'Good boy,' I said. 'Straight into the toilet, then.' I turned him round and steered him along the landing, and opened the toilet door. Completely unselfconsciously he pulled down his joggers and pants and sat on the toilet. I held the toilet door to and waited outside. Presently a none-too-pleasant smell wafted out, followed by, 'Cathy! I've finished!'

'Good boy,' I said from the other side of the door. 'Now wipe your bottom and wash your hands.'

I remained waiting outside because I wanted to make sure Reece did wash his hands, and properly, for so many children come to me having never been taught basic hygiene. I waited some more but couldn't hear the toilet roll being used; it was on the back of the door and rattled on its fitting when pulled.

'Are you OK?' I asked.

'I've finished!' he shouted back.

'Yes, now wipe your bottom, flush the toilet and then wash your hands.'

More silence and I repeated the instructions again. Then I said, 'Reece, are you wiping your bottom?'

'No.'

I eased open the toilet door and looked in. He was still sitting happily on the toilet, joggers and pants round his ankles, elbows resting on his knees as though he was in a deck chair on the beach, and making no attempt to clean himself.

'Come on,' I encouraged. 'If you have finished, get off and wipe your bottom.'

'Can't,' he said.

'You can't wipe your bottom?'

'No.'

Although I was surprised that a child of his age, even with learning difficulties, hadn't been taught to wipe his own bottom, I wasn't going to make an issue of it; but neither was I going to do it for him, which was presumably what had happened in the past. His abilities and coordination, although delayed, were quite adequate to master this skill: if he could count to a hundred I felt sure he could learn to wipe his own bottom.

'All right. I'll show you what to do. Now watch me carefully, Reece, then you can do it. First you tear off three sheets of toilet paper, like this.' I tore them off. 'Then you fold them like this, and wipe yourself like this.' I turned slightly away from him and ran the folded toilet paper over the outside of my trouser where he should wipe. 'You only use it once. Then you throw it down the toilet and tear off the next few sheets.' Obvious though it may be to most of us, you'd be surprised at the number of children who have never been taught this and try to reuse the paper by turning it over and end up with excrement all over their hands.

'Now you do it,' I said. I passed him the folded tissue paper and he made a clumsy effort at trying to get it round to his bottom while still seated. 'You'll have to stand up to do it,' I said.

He wriggled off the toilet and, standing ungainly, made a brave attempt at wiping his bottom. Then he sat down again.

'Right, the next piece. Watch carefully,' I said. I tore off another strip of paper, folded it and passed it to him. Again he tried to wipe his bottom, still sitting down. 'Remember to stand up to do it,' I said.

'Can't you do it?' he grumbled.

'I could, but I want you to learn. You will feel very clever being able to wipe your own bottom, won't you?'

He shrugged, unconvinced, but accepted the next folded sheets of paper, stood and managed reasonably successfully to use them. And so we continued, with me tearing off the sheets of paper and him wiping, until he was clean.

'Well done,' I said. 'Now flush the toilet.'

He did that successfully first time, presumably used to flushing a toilet after going for a wee. Then he pulled up his pants and joggers.

'Good. Now before you touch anything you need to wash your hands very well in hot water and soap.'

Reece stood helplessly as I put the plug in the basin and ran the hot water. I then squirted soap into the palms of his hands and plunged them into the water.

'Who wiped your bottom at home?' I asked as he rubbed his hands in the water.

'Don't know,' he said, and laughed.

'What about when you were at school? Who did it there?'

'I never did a pooh at school.' Which didn't surprise me, because children who have never mastered toilet skills will wait all day, until they have returned home, before relieving themselves. There's little alternative if you aren't going to be seriously embarrassed. It is for the child's self-respect as much as anything that we teach these self-care skills early.

'Now you will be able to use the toilet at school. Well done.' I smiled. 'Shake the water off your hands and then dry them on the towel.' Reece was very enthusiastic about shaking the water off his hands and it sprayed everywhere. I directed his hands to the towel and waited until he had finished drying them. He nipped back into his bedroom while I opened the toilet window.

I looked in his room on my way past. He was seated on the beanbag again in front of the television.

'Reece, you can finish watching that programme,' I said. 'Then we will switch it off and you can come and play downstairs. Understand?'

He nodded, although I wasn't convinced he'd heard me, for he was now completely engrossed in *Blue Peter*, which would be the last of the children's programmes before the adult ones took over and his television went off.

I had just returned to the kitchen and the half-peeled potatoes when I heard Reece again on the landing shouting, 'Cathy! I need a pooh!' There was an urgency in his voice and I shot back upstairs as he rushed into the toilet and sat down just in time.

'Don't worry,' I said. 'You've got a bit of an upset stomach. I expect it's because you have been a bit worried about coming here.'

I waited until he'd finished, and then went through the ritual of tearing off and passing him the folded toilet paper again, until he was clean. I ran the water in the basin and supervised his hand washing, before opening the window wider.

Two minutes later when I had just returned downstairs and to the potatoes there was another cry: 'Cathy! I need a pooh!' I went back upstairs and through the whole process of toilet paper tearing and folding, and hand washing, again. By the time I'd finished peeling the potatoes I had been summoned twice more, and the girls were now asking what the strange smell was permeating round the landing and into their bedrooms, or words to that effect.

At 5.25 I knew *Blue Peter* had finished, and with the dinner cooking, I went upstairs and explained to Reece that the children's programmes had come to an end, and that he had watched enough television. I asked him to switch it off. He didn't, so I asked again; then I switched it off.

As soon as I pressed the button on the remote it was as though a button had been pressed on Reece. An hour of sitting still in front of the television had recharged his batteries and he fired off like a rocket. In his own world and oblivious to us, he charged round the landing, up and down the stairs, in and out of all the rooms including the bedrooms, making loud and unrelated zooming and whooping noises. Paula, who tried to catch him as he made another lap of her bedroom, narrowly missed a head-butt as he collided with everything and anyone who happened to get in his way. Reece was hyped up and out of control. I knew the only way to make him calmer was to do a more controlled release of some of his pent-up energy. In the summer I encourage all children into the garden, where they can run and make whooping noises to their hearts' content. But it was the middle of winter, cold and dark, so I decided to use my other strategy of going for a brisk walk.

'Could you keep an eye on the dinner?' I said to Lucy and Paula, who were standing on the landing watching Reece unwind like a coiled spring. 'I'll take him for a short walk. I'll only be twenty minutes, but it should do the trick. He probably hasn't had much exercise today.'

It was no good trying to catch Reece because he would see that as a game and enjoy the chase, and that in turn would make him even more hyperactive. So I went down the hall, unhooked my coat from the hall stand and began putting it on, while calling: 'Come on, Reece. You and I will go for a walk before dinner.'

He was still zooming around, up and down the hall, in and out of the front room and the living room, now yelping for all he was worth. I wasn't sure if it was imaginative play and he was pretending to be something like a Boeing 727 or a pterodactyl, but it was dangerously out of control. He had his arms out either side of him like wings but the accompanying noise was more like that of a wolf than a plane or prehistoric bird.

'Come on, Reece,' I said again. 'Let's go for a quick walk before dinner.'

'No!' he yelled at the top of his voice, zooming past me and narrowly missing my arm with his outstretched wings.

I knew there was little point in insisting he come with me because it would have led to a confrontation, so I tried a different ploy: one of feigned indifference, which can work with younger children. 'No problem,' I said lightly. 'I'll go for a walk by myself. You can stay here with Lucy and Paula. They will look after you very well.' I would never have left a child on their first night with my daughters babysitting, let alone one who had Reece's problems – it would have been far too much responsibility for them – but Reece didn't know that. I slowly put on my shoes and then concentrated on buttoning up my coat, while Reece had a chance to think about what he was going to miss. He had slowed down now and was watching me from the far end of the hall. I didn't look at him but nonchalantly turned towards the front door, calling out, 'See you all later.' My hand was on the doorknob, ready to turn it.

'No! I want to come!' he yelled, charging the length of the hall and straight into me.

'Steady,' I said, lightly holding his shoulder and looking at him. 'Are you sure you want to come? You don't have to.'

'Yes! Take me! I'm coming for a walk!' He was already trying to get his trainers on.

'OK, if you're sure.'

All children like to feel they have some control and responsibility for their own lives, and this is even more so for children who have been brought into care, as they had no choice when being removed from home. By giving Reece the choice I had allowed him to feel he had made the decision. Sometimes there isn't a choice – for example, when having to get dressed for school at a certain time – but so often if a child feels they have a say in the matter they can be eased into doing something to which they would otherwise have put up fierce resistance. It's not rocket science, just a useful little ploy, which most parents use without realizing it.

I helped Reece into his coat, did up his trainers and took hold of his hand as we went outside. It soon became obvious that Reece hadn't the least idea how to walk safely along the pavement. He hopped and jumped all over the place and tried to pull away from me while gyrating his free arm in large circles.

'Stay away from the kerb,' I said, as he kept trying to jump into the gutter. Then I swapped hands so that he was on the inside and well away from the road and passing cars. As we walked he repeatedly tripped, over nothing, and had I not been holding his hand he would have gone heavily, knees first, on to the pavement each time he stumbled. Although I was retrieving him before he hit the ground and he wasn't hurt, he yelped and cursed the pavement as if it was to blame. 'Watch it!' he threatened. 'I said watch out!'

I was walking briskly to burn off some of his energy, but my pace wasn't excessive and shouldn't have caused him all the problems it did. Apart from stumbling and tripping he was very soon puffing and panting, completely out of breath.

'Aren't you used to walking?' I asked, slowing slightly.

'Don't know,' he said.

'Did you walk when you were with your other carers?'

'No, in the car.'

'What about at Mum's? Did you have a car there?'

'Don't know.'

It wasn't important; I was trying to make conversation more than anything, and it was pretty obvious he wasn't used to walking and was very unfit. What I was also starting to notice, as I had done previously at home, was that any question about Mum or home was met with 'Don't know'. I never question children about their life at home beyond a general enquiry, unless of course they are trying to tell me something about an abuse they have suffered, when I would gently draw it out of them. But what I was finding with Reece was that even the most innocuous enquiry like 'Did you have your own bedroom at home?', which I'd asked earlier when I'd shown him his bedroom, was met with 'Don't know'. Reece had only been in care six weeks, so it was unlikely he'd forgotten all about home and the seven years he'd spent there, particularly in relation to quite significant details like having his own bedroom or his parents having a car. I was starting to wonder if he'd been warned off saying anything about his home by his parents. He wouldn't be the first child I'd fostered who'd been threatened into silence. So a question like 'Which cereal would you like for breakfast?' was answered without any problem, but 'Did you have this cereal at home?' was met with no reply or 'Don't know'. The child, rather than trying to sift through what they were allowed to answer and what was a 'secret', found it easier to say 'Don't know' to everything.

Fifteen minutes later, with my right arm now a good inch longer than my left from having it continually wrenched by Reece tripping up or pulling, we completed our circuit and headed for home. I swapped sides so that Reece was again away from the roadside, because he was still all over the place and would have happily walked in the gutter and under a car if I'd let him. I was still trying to make conversation, but although Reece could talk in short sentences he didn't seem able to converse. If I made a statement like 'It's cold, isn't it?' either he didn't answer or he supplied an unrelated statement like 'That car's got lights.' If I tried to pick up the thread by saying, 'Yes, the headlights let the driver see the road in the dark,' he would say something else unconnected, which was now increasingly about his feet aching, or his legs hurting, and how much further was it?

By the time we reached the house and were going up the path Reece was telling me, 'I ain't walking no more. You use the car.'

'We probably will use the car tomorrow,' I said, putting my key into the lock and opening the front door.

'Silly cow, you should have used it now,' he said. And although his comment was related to his previous comment, which I supposed was progress, it wasn't a comment I appreciated.

'Reece don't say that, please. It's rude.'

'Silly cow,' he said again louder, running off down the hall.

I wasn't convinced the walk had had the desired effect, for Reece seemed to recharge the moment we entered the house. It took me five minutes to persuade him out of his coat and shoes. Then, abandoning my attempt to get him interested in some of the games and puzzles, I called up to the girls for a volunteer to read Reece a story while I finished cooking the dinner.

'I've got homework,' Paula called.

'I'm on the phone,' Lucy said.

'Well, put it this way, girls,' I called up, above the noise of Reece's imitation Boeing/pterodactyl, 'if you want to eat then someone needs to read to Reece.'

They immediately appeared from their bedrooms and came down, and I felt guilty for my terseness. 'Thanks,' I said. 'It's impossible for me to do anything with him zooming around like this. Reece!' I said loudly, above the noise of what could have been a plane landing on reverse thrust or a pterodactyl swooping on its prey. 'Go into the living room and choose a book. Lucy and Paula will read you a story.'

The mention of the words 'book' and 'story' was like the off switch being pressed again. Reece dived into the living room and on to a sofa, where he sat quietly waiting for the girls with a book open on his lap. I waited as Lucy and Paula sat either side of Reece and began taking it in turns to read the pages of Shirley Hughes's *Alfie's Feet*. Reece sat mesmerized. It seemed that when he was absorbed in something visual his mind and body were able to switch off and relax, but the second the visual stimulus stopped, hyperactivity kicked in, big time. Whether this was the reason for him watching a lot of television while at home, or the result of, I obviously didn't know, but one thing was for certain: I was going to be reading a lot of books, particularly with him not being in school.

Fifteen minutes later I called through to say that dinner was ready. Reece appeared first. 'This is your place,' I said, showing him to his seat at the table. 'Lucy will sit here' – I patted the chair beside him – 'and Paula opposite.' Reece sat where I had shown him and the girls took their places. I served a chicken casserole, explaining to Reece what it was. He looked at it, and then up at me with a huge appreciative grin.

'Cor, this looks nice,' he said.

'Thank you, love,' I said. 'That was polite.' I took my place at the end of the table and felt that things were looking up.

Reece picked up a piece of chicken with his fingers and popped it into his mouth. 'Hmm, yummy,' he said, chewing loudly.

'Good,' I said, 'but try to use your fork. It's better than fingers for this meal.' He looked at the fork and then at me and popped another piece of chicken into his mouth with his fingers. I picked up his fork, stabbed a piece of chicken and laid the fork on his plate, ready for him to use. Somewhat clumsily he gripped the fork in the palm of his hand like a spoon and pushed the meat into his mouth. Then he resorted to using his fingers again.

'Reece, have you never used a knife and fork before?' I asked lightly. The girls looked up.

'Don't know,' Reece said.

I skewered another piece of chicken on to his fork and left him to take it to his mouth, which he did. Then he attempted to use his fingers for the boiled potatoes.

'Would you like a spoon?' I asked, for I could see the peas and gravy were going to cause him a real problem. Reece nodded. I fetched a dessert spoon, which he used quite successfully, so I guessed that that was what he had been used to. 'That's better, isn't it?' I said, smiling.

He grinned back. 'I use me fingers for Chicken Dippers and burgers.'

I nodded and thought that here was another child who had never had to master a knife and fork because they had only ever eaten 'finger food'. I'd recently read a newspaper article which had highlighted the number of 'well brought up' children from good homes who didn't know how to use a knife and fork properly because so much of their diet hadn't required one.

Reece had a very healthy appetite and wanted seconds. Although he was heavily built, he wasn't so much fat as solid, and as he was a growing boy I gave him a second helping, and a yoghurt and piece of fruit for pudding. Considering that he obviously wasn't used to sitting still at the table and using cutlery he had done very well and I praised him. However, as soon as he'd finished the last mouthful of banana he was up and off, zooming around and yelping at the top of his voice. Lucy and Paula read him another story while I cleared the table and loaded the dishwasher. Then I read him a story before explaining it was time for his bath.

'Don't want one,' he said and was off the sofa and chasing around again. Paula came out of her room and tried to take hold of his arm, narrowly missing a head-butt.

'Reece, don't do that,' I said. Then to Paula: 'Let me. I'll call if I need help.'

I waited until he was doing a return lap of the landing and caught hold of him lightly by his arm. I encircled him as I had done before to get him off my bed. He struggled briefly before laughing and relaxing against me. I gave him a cuddle; then, with a mixture of cajoling and promises of a bedtime story, I managed to run the bath and get him into it. Reece wasn't able to undress himself (another skill I would have to teach him another day) so I did it, and as he sat in the bath pretending to be a shark, I realized that neither had he the first idea about washing himself. It would have been helpful if the previous carers had written down some of this detail so that I could have anticipated and better accommodated Reece's needs in the first few days. As it was, apart from knowing about his love of burgers and Chicken Dippers, I was working in the dark. I showed him how to lather the soap on to the sponge and then encouraged him to run it over his body. Although I was happy to wash his back and neck it was important to teach him to take care of most of his washing, particularly his private parts. This is another example of giving a child responsibility for his or her own body and nurturing self-respect.

'Wash your feet and knees,' I encouraged, 'and between your legs. Do you have a name for your private parts?'

'Willy,' he responded with a laugh. 'Sharks have willies but no legs.'

'Well, wash your willy and your legs.'

I waited while he squashed the sponge on various parts of his body, which would be sufficient for now. Then I ran the sponge over his shaved head – there wasn't enough hair to shampoo. Letting out the water, I wrapped him in the bath towel.

A mixture of more cajoling and repetition saw Reece into his pyjamas, and after another bedtime story, for which he sat on the beanbag with me squatted beside him, I eased him into bed.

'I want Henry,' he said, snuggling down and obviously finding comfort in being cocooned beneath the duvet. I guessed Henry was a soft toy he took with him to bed and that he would be in either the rucksacks or the toy boxes, which I hadn't had a chance to unpack yet.

'What does Henry look like?' I asked, as I undid the first rucksack.

'A hippo,' Reece said.

I smiled. 'Henry Hippo, that's a good name. Did you call him that?'

'Don't know.' So I thought that Henry Hippo was probably an old favourite and had come with all the other 'Don't knows' from home.

I began rummaging through the first rucksack, which contained an entire school uniform, hardly worn, and presumably from one of the schools Reece had been excluded from. At the bottom of the bag my fingers alighted on something soft and furry, and I pulled it out.

'That's not it!' Reece yelled.

'No.' It was a soft toy but in the shape of a shark.

I began on the second rucksack, which contained some new books. As I took them out and placed them on the bookshelves in the recess of his bedroom, I saw that they were all about sharks, or ocean creatures including sharks. 'Who bought you all these?' I asked.

'Carers,' Reece said.

I wasn't sure it was a good idea to indulge Reece's love of sharks, given his biting, but doubtless the carers had acted with the best of intentions by giving Reece something he liked. Further down this bag were some large-piece jigsaws, the pictures on the front of the boxes showing underwater scenes with fish and sharks. The boxes were new, so I guessed a well-meaning carer had bought these too. I pulled out a couple of short-sleeved T-shirts emblazoned with pictures of sharks, but there was no sign of Henry Hippo.

'Do you know where Henry is?' I asked, dearly hoping that Henry had been packed. I took the lid off the first toy box.

Reece didn't answer. He was lying in bed, watching me intently. Although the toy box was new, it contained lots of old small toys, many broken, so that I guessed the contents had come from home. As I rummaged through I saw that the theme of sharks dominated here too. There were models and toys of sharks in plastic, rubber and cardboard, in various poses of swimming, all with their mouths open, displaying rows of barbed white teeth. They had clearly been well used, for many had been chewed and had bits missing. One particularly nasty creature, which was a model of a shark's head about ten inches across, had half its teeth missing but the grin on its face said that it was still capable of doing real damage and enjoying it. When social workers take a child into care they always try to bring as many of the child's clothes and favourite toys as possible so that the child feels comfortable with what they know around them. Usually these things are loaded into carrier bags, so I assumed one or more of the previous carers must have bought the new toy boxes, rucksacks and suitcase. Reece was still looking at me carefully, not saying a word; clearly these toys were poignant reminders of home.

'Well, it's not here,' I said.

I shuffled over on my knees and took the lid off the second toy box. To my great relief and Reece's delight, at the top lay a grubby, well-chewed, but clearly much-loved hippopotamus soft toy.

'Henry!' Reece cried.

I smiled and tucked Henry in beside Reece. Then I had a quick glance at the toys that had been under Henry in the box. It was no great surprise that the shark theme dominated again, together with McDonald's. The fast-food chain must have been giving away small plastic models of sharks and aquatic creatures in their children's Happy Meal boxes, for this toy box was full of them. Putting the lid back on the box, I stacked it, together with the rucksacks, on one side of the bedroom, to be sorted out the following day.

"Night 'night,' I said to Reece, kissing his forehead. His face was buried deep into Henry's soft fur, the toy's familiar smell welcoming and secure.

"Night,' came the muffled reply.

I went to the bedroom door. 'Would you like your light on or off?' I asked, as I ask all children on their first night. It is essential the child sleeps as they are used to and feels comfortable.

'On,' came the muffled response.

'OK, but I'll dim it a little so it doesn't keep you awake.' I turned the knob on the light switch down so that the room was lit but not startlingly bright. 'And Reece, do you want your door open or shut, love?'

'Shut,' Reece said.

'All right. See you in the morning. Sleep tight.' Only the top of his head was visible as his face snuggled into Henry. 'See you in the morning,' I said again and came out and shut the door.

I waited on the landing, for given how hyperactive Reece had been during the day, coupled with it being his first night in a strange bedroom, I was expecting him to be out of bed the moment I left the room, in which case I would keep resettling him until he finally dropped asleep. But five minutes later, when there had been no sound from his room, I gently eased open the bedroom door and found him fast asleep. He was exhausted and so was I. Closing the bedroom door again, I went downstairs, where Lucy and Paula were in the kitchen making a hot drink.

'He's asleep.' I said. 'Thanks for all your help. It's much appreciated.'

'Mum?' Paula said, pouring milk into her tea. 'What's the matter with Reece's front teeth?' Lucy looked at me too.

'I don't know. I'll ask the dentist when I take him for a check-up. I'm sure it's something that can be corrected by an orthodontist when he's older.' I hesitated. 'I know this sounds odd but Reece has the nickname Sharky. I think it could be because of his teeth and that he bites.' They both looked at me. 'His toys and books are all about sharks. It was a label that began at home and they encouraged him to behave like a shark and bite. He bit me when he first arrived earlier, so please be careful. And obviously we all have to work towards getting rid of that ridiculous nickname.'

They nodded and I could see from their expressions that they didn't know whether to laugh or cry, because who on earth calls their child Sharky and encourages him to bite?

'We'll get him interested in something other than sharks,' I said. 'Something that doesn't bite, like cars or aeroplanes.' And it occurred to me then that perhaps all the zooming around the house Reece had been doing with his arms outstretched wasn't a plane or prehistoric bird but a shark skimming through the water in search of prey. 'Anyway, thanks again. You were both a big help.'

They smiled and handed me a very welcome mug of tea. 'Oh yes,' Lucy said, 'I nearly forgot. Jill phoned while you were out and asked how we were doing. I said we were all fine.'

Chapter Five:

safer caring

I went to bed early that first night, at ten o'clock, expecting to have a very broken night's sleep; children, unsurprisingly, are often unsettled for the first few nights, in a strange bed and a new house. But Reece must have been exhausted, for I wasn't woken until five o'clock. Then it was with a vengeance!

I was just starting to surface, with my eyes flickering open, when I heard Reece's door fly open with a loud bang, followed by the sound of Reece in full flight. His feet thumped along the landing and he was making a high-pitched yeooowing noise, banging on the walls and bedroom doors as he went. He had done a full circuit of the landing and was on his way downstairs before I was out of bed. I threw on my dressing gown and went after him. Apart from stopping him from waking the girls (if they hadn't already been woken), I needed to start to get him into the routine of staying in his bedroom and amusing himself until I was up and dressed.

I caught up with Reece downstairs, where he was trying to get into the living room, which I locked at night for security. 'Reece,' I said over the noise of his yeooowing. 'Reece, sshhh, quietly, love.' I placed my forefinger to my lips and, with my other hand lightly on his shoulder, turned him to face me.

'Yeooooow,' he went at the top of his voice.

'Ssshh,' I said again.

'Yeoooow,' he continued. Then, bringing his chin down towards his shoulder, he tried to bite my hand.

'No,' I said firmly. 'No, you mustn't bite. It's naughty.' He snapped again at my hand, which was safely out of reach. 'No, Reece, don't bite.'

'I can bite, I'm Sharky.' Which I had guessed and ignored. 'Want to get in here,' he said and, pulling away from me, he thumped on the living-room door with his fist.

'No, Reece,' I said. 'Now quietly. We are going back to your bedroom, where you can play until it's time to go downstairs. It's too early. It's not morning yet.' I knew there was no point in suggesting he went back to sleep, as he had clearly had enough sleep and was now completely recovered from the previous day's exhaustion.

He thumped on the living-room door again; then, with his mouth wide open, he tried to sink his teeth into the metal doorknob. The resulting sound of his teeth on metal set my own teeth on edge, and I thought it would do nothing for the enamel on his.

'No, Reece,' I said. 'Don't do that. You'll hurt yourself. Come back to your bedroom.'

He turned and, breaking free from my light hold on his shoulder, was off down the hall, and then up the stairs. I caught up with him on the landing and, taking him by the arm, went with him into his bedroom, where I closed the door.

'Yeoooow! Crunch!' He went at the top of his voice. 'Yeooow! I'm Sharky.'

There was a great temptation to say, 'Well, Sharky had better play quietly with his toys,' but I didn't. 'Reece,' I said, again taking him by the shoulder and trying to get him to look at me. 'Reece, I need you to be quiet, love.'

'Yeck! Yeck! Crunch!' he went.

Not letting go of his arm, I took the lid off one of the toy boxes and drew him down, so that we were both sitting on the floor. 'Here, look at all these lovely toys. Let's play with them,' I encouraged.

Reece pulled in his cheeks to make his mouth narrow, which highlighted his front teeth. He then began making loud sucking noises, which I guessed were supposed to be an impression of a shark. I ignored it and continued sifting through the toys, hoping to gain his attention.

Half an hour later I was still there, seated on the floor of Reece's bedroom in my dressing gown and trying to engage him in the toys and books. Reece whooped and yelped, snapped his jaws at invisible passing fish and every so often tried to jump on the bed or leave his room. It was imperative that I kept going until I had achieved what I had set out to: Reece remaining in his room and playing until I had washed and dressed and was ready to go downstairs. If I gave in now, it would set a precedent for all the future mornings and would be harder to change at a later date. As with so many behaviour issues, retraining relies on consistent and firm boundaries – i.e. endless repetition of the expected behaviour.

'I need you to play in your bedroom until I say it is time to get dressed,' I said over and over again, while picking out another toy or book, or starting a jigsaw.

Eventually, after another fifteen minutes, when Reece was probably as bored as I was with the sound of my voice repeatedly saying the same thing, he started to dive into the box of small McDonald's toys of his own accord and began playing with them. I stayed for another five minutes, and then said: 'Good boy. Now you carry on playing while I get dressed.' I came out and closed the door.

I waited on the landing. A minute later Reece flung open his bedroom door and was about to zoom off again. I lightly caught hold of his arm and led him back into his room, where I resettled him with the toys. I told him again what I wanted him to do – to play quietly while I got dressed – and I came out and closed the door.

I waited on the landing and a minute later Reece appeared again in what I took to be full shark attack, snapping and yelping at the top of his voice. Again I returned him to the toys in his bedroom and, restating what I wanted him to do, came out. He reappeared and I resettled him, time and time again, doing what I had anticipated having to do the night before when I'd put him to bed.

Finally at 6.30 a.m., an hour and a half after Reece had first woken and got out of bed, he was playing with his toys in his bedroom, and I had the time I needed to shower and dress. He wasn't particularly quiet – he was making noises which sounded as though they could be part of the pretend play – but at least he was doing what I'd asked. I knew I would probably have to repeat the resettling process every morning for a week or more, but the investment of time and effort now would reap rewards later, when Reece would wake and automatically play with his toys until I told him it was time for him to dress and come down for breakfast.

It was Friday, and a school day, so I woke the girls at seven (being teenagers, they had managed to go back to sleep despite all Reece's noise). Then I knocked on Reece's door and went in. He was seated, as I had last left him, cross-legged on the floor, now surrounded by the entire contents of both toy boxes. I told him he was a good boy for playing nicely in his room; then I said that although it was still early, he could get dressed and come down if he wanted to, or he could stay and play with his toys.

'Telly?' he asked. I hesitated. I wasn't sure I wanted him watching television at this time in the morning. It could become a habit, which certainly couldn't continue when he started school.

'OK, but only for a little while.' I switched on the television and found some children's programmes on BBC2 which Reece recognized, presumably from having watched the series before. He immediately fell quiet, completely transfixed and absorbed by the screen. I could see only too clearly the great temptation of leaving Reece in front of a television for longer periods than were good for him.

Half an hour later, with the girls washed, dressed and having had their breakfasts, I knocked on Reece's bedroom door and went in. He was, as I suspected he would be, still seated in the same position on the bean-bag and riveted to the children's programmes.

'Good boy, Reece,' I said. 'I want you to switch off the television now, get dressed and come down for breakfast.'

He didn't answer, so I repeated the instructions; then, taking out clean clothes from his wardrobe, I repeated the instructions again. He still didn't answer, so I explained again what I wanted him to do. Then I switched off the television. As soon as the screen went blank Reece jumped up from the beanbag and began stamping on the piles of small toys that littered the entire floor.

'No, Reece,' I said. 'You will break them.' I knelt down and, taking him gently by the arm, drew him down beside me. 'The first thing we are going to do is put these toys back into their boxes so they don't get broken,' I said, and I began putting them away. Reece was beside me watching. Then as I leant forward to retrieve another toy, hoping he would follow suit, he cuffed the back of my head with his open hand. 'No, Reece,' I said. I took hold of his hand and directed it again to the toys on the floor.

'Want me breakfast now!' he yelled.

'You will have breakfast as soon as we have cleared away and got you dressed,' I said.

'Want it now,' he yelled and went to cuff my head again. I took his hand and drew it once more towards the toys.

'You will have breakfast as soon as we have cleared up and got you dressed,' I repeated.

Eventually he realized I wasn't going to give in and that if he helped me to clear away it would complete the task and get him what he wanted that much quicker. Suddenly he started grabbing handfuls of toys and throwing them into the boxes, so that very soon the floor was clear.

'Well done,' I said. 'Excellent! Now get dressed. Then we can have breakfast.'

I had already taken out clean joggers, sweatshirt, vest, pants and socks, and placed them on the chair ready for him to dress himself.

Reece looked at them. 'No!' he yelled. 'Can't!' which I had more or less guessed.

'All right, I'll teach you how to dress yourself, and won't you feel good when you can?' I smiled bravely, knowing that achieving this task was probably going to be no easier than the last of clearing away his toys, or any other task, come to that. It seemed that Reece was so used to not doing things, either because he couldn't or didn't want to, that his first response to any request was either 'can't' or 'won't'.

'No,' he yelled again. 'Can't!'

'I'm sure you can,' I said evenly. 'You are very clever. And, Reece, try not to shout, love. I can hear you just as well when you talk quietly. OK, love?' There were so many issues with Reece that I was having to address them one at a time. Certainly, while the continuous shouting, or rather 'voice modulation' as it's correctly termed, needed to be addressed, it wasn't as much of a priority as his biting, head-butting or running berserk around the house.

'Now, take off your pyjama bottoms,' I encouraged, 'and put on your pants.' I held up his pants ready, but he stood helplessly waiting for me to do it.

'Can't,' he said with slightly less volume, now sulking.

'Try,' I said. 'I'm sure you can.'

'Can't,' he said again and made no attempt. 'You do it, cow!'

'Reece,' I cautioned, 'please don't use that word. It's rude.'

'Cow,' he said again. He crossed his arms and stood glaring at me defiantly.

I remained where I was, a short way in front of him, still holding his pants. 'Take off your pyjama bottoms and put on your pants.' I repeated. 'Do you want me to leave the room while you do it?' I didn't think it was modesty that was stopping him, for he hadn't been self-conscious at bath time the night before.

He shook his head. There was an impasse for a good two minutes when Reece continued with his arms folded and glowered at me menacingly, while I stood relaxed and outwardly at ease, holding his pants out ready for him, as though waiting for Reece to get dressed was of no great importance and I had all the time in the world. For as the evening before when I had wanted him to go for a walk, if he saw my request was important to me, his refusal could easily become a tool for trying to manipulate me. But I had already been there, done that and 'got the T-shirt' many years ago when I had first started fostering. Eventually Reece would do as I asked and see that if he cooperated he would win my approval and feel happier in himself, but not yet. Now he hated me and wanted to do exactly what he had always done, which appeared to be nothing, or exactly what he felt like doing.

Five minutes later Reece pulled roughly on his pyjama bottoms and then, using his feet, stamped them to the floor.

'Well done,' I said, 'although next time it might be easier to use your hands.' He snatched the pants from me and, sitting on the bed, put them on without too much trouble.

'Good,' I said. 'Now take off your pyjama top and put on your vest.'

He had real problems trying to get his arms out of his pyjama top, so I helped him, showing him how to do it, and then gave him his vest, which he got into first time. Next I helped him on with his sweatshirt.

'Excellent,' I said. 'Now the socks.'

Aware that putting on socks is difficult for young children, particularly those with poor coordination, I told him to sit on the bed again and I would show him how to put on one sock and he could do the other.

As I knelt in front of him, he tried to cuff me over the head again and I guessed this regular cuffing had probably been done to him. 'No, you don't do that,' I said, moving my head out of reach. 'Do you understand?'

He nodded. I showed him how to put on one sock

and passed him the other. 'Who used to dress you before?' I asked casually as he struggled to get his toes into the sock.

'Carers.'

'And at home?'

'Don't know.'

He had made a reasonable attempt at putting on the second sock and I helped him to complete the task. Praising him, I took his hand and we went downstairs together. Lucy and Paula were in the hall, putting on their coats, ready to leave for school and college. I hadn't seen them properly that morning because I had been so occupied with seeing to Reece.

'Bye, loves,' I said. 'Have a good day.' I kissed them both.

Reece pursed his lips, wanting to kiss them goodbye also. Lucy and Paula smiled and, bending towards him, offered their cheeks. He gave them a nice little kiss each.

'Goodbye,' they both called to us. I saw them out and closed the door. Reece was beside me, his hand still in mine.

'Cor, that was nice,' he said, grinning. 'I'd really like to give them one.'

I paused in the hall and looked at him, my heart sinking. 'Pardon, Reece? What did you say?'

He grinned again, leering almost. 'I want to give them one,' he repeated. He dropped my hand and clamping his left hand on to his right arm he brought up his fist in the crude pumping gesture of wanting sex.

'I'm not sure what you mean,' I said, knowing only too well. 'But it's not a nice thing for a boy of seven to say. And please don't do that with your arm.'

'My dad does to my sister,' he said and stopped, aware that he had committed the ultimate sin of saying something about home.

'Does he?' I asked lightly, while assured of Reece's reply.

'Don't know. I want me breakfast now. You said it was time.'

I followed Reece into the annexe off the kitchen, which we call the breakfast room. I knew from Reece's history he'd seen a lot of inappropriate behaviour, possibly even sexual abuse, but I was still shocked and saddened. I also knew that Reece had been sworn to secrecy and wasn't about to say anything more. Later I would talk to the girls and remind them of our 'safer caring policy' – the guidelines all carers follow. They had just left with Reece giving them a kiss on the cheek like any younger brother, but Reece had laden it with sexual connotations and for all our safety we were going to have to be very careful.

The 'safer caring policy' is a document drawn up by all foster carers detailing how they keep everyone in the household safe. It is not just about strapping children under seatbelts in the car or making sure there are batteries in the smoke alarms. It is also about how we treat foster children who have come from inappropriately sexual explicit homes, or have been sexually abused, and have therefore developed feelings and attitudes that are inappropriate and beyond their age. I

knew already from what Karen had told me on the
phone that there was a suggestion that Reece's father
had sexually assaulted Reece's half-sister, and that a
paedophile had been going into the family home. What
I didn't know, and what the social worker, Jamey Hogg,
would I hoped tell me when he returned from holiday,
was whether Reece had witnessed or been included in
any paedophile activity in the home. I also knew that
Reece had been allowed to watch adult videos, which
could account in some way for his viewing the girls in
sexual terms, but without further details we would have
to assume the worst and act accordingly. For if Reece
did view Lucy and Paula as objects of sexual desire
instead of older sisters, as his comment had suggested,
then his behaviour would reflect that. Not only would it
be very unpleasant for the girls but it could easily lead to
Reece interpreting any affection from the girls towards
him in sexualized terms. The whole subject of sexual
abuse is sickening and sad but it is something that has to
be dealt with by foster carers all too regularly.

Although I had written up my daily log notes the
night before, detailing Reece's first day with us, I had
been too tired to look at the placement forms. Now I
wondered if they contained any more information on
Reece's background that I should be aware of. Settling
Reece at the table with the two slices of toast and jam
he had asked for, I quickly went into the front room,
unlocked my desk and took out the placement forms;
then I returned to sit opposite him at the table. I read as
Reece ate, eating being another activity that appeared
to keep him quiet for its duration.

As I turned the pages of the placement forms, I saw
there was nothing on his background beyond what I
already knew, apart from Reece's parents' address,
which came as something of a surprise. His parents
lived in a flat on an estate no more than half a mile
away. I hoped the social services had noted this, for it
was a little too close for comfort, given that his parents
wouldn't be told our address. It was quite possible that
we used the same high-street shops, which meant there
was a risk of us bumping into each other. Not a problem
if the child's parents were cooperating with the social
services, and were allowed to know where the child
was, but clearly that wasn't the case with Reece. I'd had
experience of 'impromptu' contact before – in the shops
or outside the school gates – and it's a difficult and
embarrassing situation for all, not to mention intimidating if the parents are angry and blame the foster carer. I
would mention my concerns and Reece's attitude to the
girls to Jill when she phoned again – not that I thought
for one moment the social services would move Reece
because of where his parents lived, but it was something
they needed to be aware of, if they weren't already.

I returned the placement forms to my desk as Reece
finished his breakfast. Although he had been focused
and concentrating while eating, as soon as he'd finished
he was out of his seat, zooming around and streaking
jammy fingers along the walls.

'Come on, Reece,' I said. 'We'll give you a wash and
do your teeth; then we're going out in the car.'

The mention of the car seemed to please him, because
he ran straight up the stairs and into the bathroom,

with his arms outstretched and yelping at the top of his voice. I showed him how to squirt toothpaste on to his toothbrush and watched as he made a good attempt at brushing his teeth; then I ran warm water into the sink and, wringing out his face flannel, helped him to wash his face. I asked him if he needed the toilet before we went out, and he said he didn't. I took his hand and we went downstairs and into the hall, where I passed him his coat and shoes. He made a good attempt at putting them on and I was pleased he hadn't just stood there helplessly as he had done the night before – this was already a small improvement and I praised him immensely.

I assumed Jill would be phoning at some point during the day, so before going out I switched on the answerphone and dropped my mobile in my handbag. It took me some while to settle Reece on the booster seat under his belt in the rear of the car; he didn't appear familiar with the procedure, which was surprising given that yesterday he'd said he was used to being in a car rather than walking. First he wanted to ride in the front passenger seat, which I explained wasn't legal at his age; then he didn't want to sit on the booster seat, which I explained was a legal requirement. I secured his seatbelt over his shoulder, but he kept tucking it under his arm, which would have not only rendered it useless in an accident but also badly hurt his stomach if it had suddenly tightened.

Fifteen minutes later I reversed out of the drive with Reece making brumm-brumm noises at the top of his voice. I stood it for as long I could, for I realized he was only doing what a lot of boys do, imitating the car engine noise, but very loudly.

Then I said, 'Reece, I need you to be quiet in the car so I can concentrate on driving.'

'Brummmm! Brummmm!' he yelled, louder.

'Would you like some music on?' I asked. 'I have a sing-a-long CD here.' Although Reece's singing would doubtless break the sound barrier (everything he did was at such a volume) it would be preferable to the exploding sound of his brumms, which were making me jump each and every time they erupted.

'Brummm! Brummm!' Reece yelled, his lips trembling with the vibration of the brummm. I inserted the CD in the hope he might join in, but five minutes later, when the brummms had increased in volume and intensity and were drowning out the sound of 'The Wheels On The Bus', I switched it off again.

'Reece, you will have to try and sit quietly,' I said. 'I can't concentrate on driving when there is a lot of noise.'

'Bruummm! Bruumm!' Then, 'Yeoooo crunch crunch,' which I wasn't sure represented a car, a plane or even a shark attack, but whatever it was the noise was deafening. Then he started kicking the back of the passenger seat.

I indicated, and drew into the kerb. Putting the car into neutral and the handbrake on, I turned in my seat to look at Reece. He was now yelping and kicking the seat in a frenzy.

'Reece!' I said. 'Reece, listen to me.'

He didn't.

'Reece, I need you to be quiet and sit still.' I tried again, raising my voice so it could be heard over the relentless yelps. 'Reece, quiet, and please stop kicking that seat. We don't kick anything other than footballs.'

He didn't stop, so I switched off the engine, got out and went round to the pavement and opened his door.

'Reece,' I said firmly. 'Sit still. Now, please!' I placed my hand lightly on his legs to quell the kicking. 'Sit still and be quiet. Then we can go to the supermarket and you can push the trolley.'

He continued with the yelping and kicking for another few seconds; then suddenly he stopped the noise and became still.

'Can I?' he said, looking at me suspiciously. 'Can I push the trolley?'

'Yes,' I said, smiling. 'Would you like to help?'

He nodded furiously, his head bobbing up and down. All Reece's movements were accentuated when he was in a hyperactive state. 'I've never pushed a trolley before,' he said. 'Can I really push it?'

I smiled sadly. The poor kid: while he had been party to goodness knows what in the adult world at home he had missed out on the simple childhood pleasure of pushing a supermarket trolley and helping mum to shop.

'All right, Reece, now listen to me,' I said, looking at him carefully. 'You can push the trolley as long as you sit quietly while I drive to the supermarket. OK?' It wasn't bribery, just positive reward for good behaviour, and he nodded furiously. I returned to the driver's seat and drove to the supermarket at the edge of town with no more than a 'wow' when I had to brake quickly as the car in front suddenly pulled into the kerb without signalling. And I thought that pushing the trolley was going to be another strategy for encouraging Reece's good behaviour, so that together with reading a lot of books I was also going to be doing a lot of shopping, which was fine because we consumed a lot of food.

Reece pushed the trolley remarkably well, controlling the speed to an acceptable 5mph, once I'd explained there were elderly people in the store who couldn't get out of the way in time if he went any faster or tried to run them over. Reece's biggest problem in the super-market was curtailing his enthusiasm. I had asked him, as I ask all foster children, to choose some of his favour-ite food. We already had Chicken Dippers, tinned spaghetti hoops and Wall's sausages in the trolley in abundance, but would also have had, had I not returned them, five cartons of chocolate ice-cream (I kept one), six packets of Jammie Dodger biscuits (I kept two) and twelve tubes of brightly coloured sweets (I put them all back because of the additives and replaced them with milk chocolate bars). I praised Reece for the way he steered the trolley and helped me, and he glowed from achieving the task successfully. He was also pretty patient at the checkout, considering the length of the queue, and I only had to remind him a couple of times not to shunt the trolley into the back of the man in front.

Once it was our turn at the checkout Reece's enthusi-asm for shifting all the food from the trolley on to the belt knew no bounds. The items were jettisoned with such force that they found their way to the cashier without the need of the moving belt. I held back the box of eggs and put them on myself. I paid, and then Reece helped me push the trolley out of the store and through the car park, missing most of the cars. I strapped him into his seat while I packed the bags in the boot – it was safer than having him hopping around in the car park. Once all the shopping was in the boot I returned the empty trolley to the trolley park close by and got into the car. Before inserting the keys into the ignition I turned and looked at him. 'Good boy,' I said. 'Thanks for helping me.' Then I noticed he was chewing something.

'What are you eating?' I asked, for certainly I hadn't given him anything. I had said he could have one of the iced buns when we got home.

'Sweets,' he said, producing a packet of fruit pastels from his coat pocket.

'Where did you get those?'

'From the shop.'

I stared horrified. 'But I didn't buy them.'

'No, I tooked them,' he said, popping another one into his mouth.

'But Reece, that's stealing. I didn't pay for them.'

He gave a shrug. 'No worries. The police can't do me. I'm under age.'

I stared at him, dumbfounded, as he chewed loudly, unashamed by his admission. Clearly Reece had no idea that stealing was wrong but was well aware he was below the age of criminal responsibility and therefore couldn't be prosecuted even if he was caught.

'Who told you that?' I asked.

He shrugged. 'Don't know.' So I could guess.

'Did you used to steal things when you lived at home?'

He didn't say anything, but popped another pastel in his mouth and grinned. I certainly couldn't let him enjoy the spoils of his theft. I opened my door and got out. I went round to his door.

'Reece,' I said leaning in and taking the pastels. 'You have taken these without paying for them, so they are not yours. It's stealing. We have to pay for the things we want: we don't just take them.'

'But they're mine!' he yelled, making a grab for them.

'No. They are not, Reece. They belong to the shop. They only become ours if we pay for them.'

If the item had been of any greater value I would have taken it back to the store, but returning a half-eaten tube of fruit pastels was going to cause more trouble than it was worth, particularly as I would have to take Reece with me and he was now erupting with force.

'Mine!' he yelled, kicking the back of the seat in a frenzy. 'Mine! Give me them! Thief!' which I thought was choice.

'No, Reece. You won't have these sweets. They are not yours, they are the shop's.' I dropped them into my coat pocket to throw away later.

'Mine,' he screamed. 'Mum gives me the sweets when I help her.'

'Help her do what?' I asked over the noise.

'Take things,' he said. Then he stopped.

'You stole things for your mum?'

He stopped screaming and looked at me. 'Hate you,' he said and poked out his tongue, which was bright green from the pastels.

The return journey from the supermarket was more eventful than the one going when Reece had sat quietly in his seat with the promise of pushing the trolley. Now he screamed, yelled he hated me and kicked the seat relentlessly. I had to stop three times to resettle him and return him to under his seatbelt. After repeated warnings, I told him he had lost thirty minutes' television time that evening because I couldn't have him distracting me while driving, as it was dangerous.

'I'm watching television,' he yelled defiantly as we finally entered the house.

'No, you are not, Reece. You can help me to unload the car or you can play with some toys.'

'I'm watching telly,' he yelled again, sticking out his tongue.

I ignored it and began unloading the car with the front gate bolted so that he couldn't run out into the road if he had a mind to. Each time I carried the bags of shopping into the house I checked on where he was and what he was doing, which was zooming around, arms outstretched and making whooping noises, so at least I knew where he was.

Once I had all the bags in the hall I began carrying them through to the kitchen. 'Would you like to help me?' I called to Reece, but he was in no mood for cooperating. By the time I had all the bags in the kitchen Reece had done a dozen laps of the house and was demanding lunch.

'You can have lunch, yes,' I said, glancing at the clock. 'It's twelve o'clock. But say "Can I have lunch?" rather than "Give me". Sit at the table and I'll make you a sandwich.'

The promise of food settled Reece and I quickly made a ham sandwich, which he ate while I unpacked the food into the cupboards and fridge-freezer. As soon as he'd finished he was out of his seat and orchestrating one of his plane landings or shark attacks. I made a hasty sandwich for myself, took it into the living room and ate it while reading Reece some stories. He was quiet again and the incident of the sweets had now been forgotten. I wouldn't say anything more about them now, but next time we went shopping I would remind him that things in the shops only became ours when we paid for them.

Sadly, Reece wasn't the first child I had come across whose parents had primed their child to thieve as though they were modern-day equivalents of Fagin. Sometimes it had been out of necessity – there was no food in the house and the benefit money wasn't due until the following week. Sometimes it had been for more expensive items like iPods, jewellery and CDs, where the easiest option was to take the item rather than save up for it as socialized parents teach their children to do. I didn't know enough of Reece's home situation to know whether it was from necessity or greed he had been trained to steal and then rewarded with sweets, but clearly I would have to be more alert in future, because I still had absolutely no idea when he had slipped the sweets into his coat pocket. His technique had clearly been well designed and I suspected well practised.

The afternoon passed with me reading Reece more books and then with me beside him, painting and Play-Doh. This was interspersed with him zooming around when there was a break in the activity. Reece repeatedly asked if he could have his television on and I repeatedly explained that he had lost half an hour of his television time for his behaviour in the car, and that he could have it on at four o'clock instead of 3.30 when the pre-school programmes began.

When Lucy and Paula returned, I briefly took them aside and, having asked them how their day had gone, told them of Reece's comment that morning after he'd kissed them goodbye. I didn't need to say anything more: they knew the implications of having a sexually aware child in the house, and they also knew the guidelines we all had to follow. We followed the 'safer caring' guidelines anyway, with any fostered child, but if there were issues over possible sexual abuse or even inappropriate television watching which had made the child sexually aware, we were even more careful. So, for example, bedtime stories were read downstairs, not in the child's bedroom, and kisses and cuddles were given downstairs, with the child at our side, not on our laps or face to face. It's sad, really, because we naturally hug and kiss our own children without a second thought, but with a child who has been sexually abused, or has come from a highly sexualized and inappropriate home life, even the most innocent of hugs or kisses (like those the girls had allowed Reece that morning) can be misinterpreted. Reece would still be having his hugs and kisses – he was after all a little seven-year-old – but there would always be someone else present and we would be just that bit more careful so that nothing could be misconstrued by him.

Jill phoned just after 5.00 p.m. and I updated her, and before I went to bed I wrote up my log notes. That night I lay in bed contemplating and worrying over the day's events, and I wondered how well I had handled everything that had happened – from Reece's hyper-active behaviour, to the stealing, and of course his comments about giving the girls one. Foster carers are plagued by analysing and self-doubt, even more so than when raising one's own children; for when all is said and done what greater responsibility is there than bringing up someone else's child?

Chapter Six:
Kids in Care

On Sunday evening, as we were approaching the end of our first weekend together, I was feeling quite positive. Although it had been hard work, with Lucy and Paula home for the weekend the three of us had been working together and continually reinforcing the expected standards of behaviour. Perhaps it was my imagination, but Reece now seemed to be cooperating more readily than he had done during the first couple of days. I was still having to resettle him regularly in the morning, but it was taking only half an hour rather than the hour and a half when he'd first arrived. He slept well each night and because Lucy and Paula had helped, the task of caring for Reece's many needs had been split three ways and hadn't been so draining on me. We'd had only a couple of incidents over the weekend when he'd tried to head-butt and none of him biting.

It was seven o'clock. Reece had had his bath and hair wash and was downstairs in the living room in his pyjamas, dressing gown and shark-shaped slippers.

Paula was reading him some bedtime stories. We had all been sitting together in the living room to begin with; then Lucy left to watch a television programme in her bedroom and I slipped into the kitchen to clear up. I had purposely left the living-room door open – this was one of our safer caring policies – and I was standing in the kitchen waiting for the kettle to boil.

Suddenly I heard Paula squeal, and then shout: 'No, Reece! That's naughty! Don't do that!'

Paula is the most quietly spoken and placid of my three children and it was so unlike her to raise her voice, let alone cry out in alarm, that I was instantly out of the kitchen and into the living room. Reece was still sitting on the sofa, now grinning from ear to ear. Paula was on her feet and looked flustered and alarmed.

'What is it?' I asked her.

'Don't know,' Reece said.

I looked at Paula, who, while not crying, was quite clearly upset and embarrassed.

'I'm talking to Paula,' I said to Reece. I looked again at Paula.

She came up close to me and, with her back to Reece, said quietly: 'Mum, he grabbed my breast and tried to put his hand up my skirt.'

'Reece!' I said, turning and glaring at him.

'So?' he said and shrugged, clearly seeing absolutely nothing wrong in his behaviour.

'Stay there,' I said to him. I drew Paula out of the living room and into the hall so we couldn't be over-heard. I wanted to speak to Paula first and find out exactly what had happened before I spoke to Reece.

'Are you all right?' I asked. It was an unpleasant thing for a grown woman to have to deal with, let alone a self-conscious teenager.

'Yes,' she said, still acutely embarrassed. 'I was just reading him a story and he suddenly grabbed my breast. Then he tried to put his hand up my skirt and kiss me on the lips.'

'Dear me!' I said, appalled. 'I'll talk to him now.' Paula knew it was no good me simply telling off Reece, because he had seen nothing wrong in his lewd behaviour and therefore wouldn't know what he was being told off for. If he had come from a home environment where it had been the norm for people to grope each other, then he was probably copying what he had seen without any moral judgement or principle.

I desperately needed more information on Reece's background to know what exactly I was dealing with in terms of the level of abuse at home. No one had phoned from the social services on Friday and when Jill had phoned she didn't have any more information. I would phone her first thing on Monday and ask her to find out more. I wasn't having my family abused because of simple lack of information. It is a sad fact that foster families are abused by the children they look after – physically, mentally and, even as had just happened to Paula, sexually. However, I could minimize the risk by knowing more, and it was a sign of how mature my family had become with fostering and having to deal with this type of behaviour that Paula wasn't more distressed by the incident.

'I'm sorry,' I said to her, blaming myself for not being more vigilant. 'Are you sure you're OK?' I gave her a hug.

'Yes,' she said. 'I know it's difficult. He didn't think he was doing anything wrong, Mum.'

'I know, but he is going to start to learn, and now.'

Paula went upstairs to her room while I returned to the living room. Reece was still sitting on the sofa and looking at the book, not zooming around as he normally did if we left him alone for a minute, so that I wondered if he was subdued because part of him knew what he had done was wrong and he was expecting to be told off. How naïve I was!

'Isn't she gonna read the story?' Reece asked as I went over and sat beside him on the sofa.

'No, Paula isn't going to read. She is upset and I have to tell you why.'

He didn't look up but turned the page of the book. I took it from him and, closing it, set it to one side. I wanted his full attention.

'Reece,' I said, searching for eye contact. 'I need to talk to you about how you just touched Paula. It wasn't nice and little boys don't do that.'

He glanced up at me and shrugged. 'I wanted to feel her cunt. Ain't nothing wrong in that.'

I looked at him, and felt sickened to the core. Whatever had he been party to at home to acquire that type of language? He said it so easily and matter-of-factly that he clearly believed there was absolutely nothing wrong in it. As foster carers we become used to hearing all types of crude language but never before had I heard it so blatant and in one so young.

'Reece,' I said, deathly serious. 'What you did to Paula was very wrong. You touched her private parts, and they are private. We don't touch anyone there. You have private parts which are different from a girl's, and they are private too. Private means they are only ours. We can touch or look at our own private parts but no one else can. Do you understand?'

He shrugged again. It was a difficult conversation to have with a child of seven, even one with an average IQ, but it was so much harder to explain to a child who had learning difficulties, so I tried to explain further.

'Reece, do you know where your private parts are? The places that only you can touch?'

'Yeah,' he said, grinning.

'OK, point to them.' He jabbed a finger towards his crotch. 'That's right,' I said. 'But it's a wider area, all round here.' Without actually touching him I ran an imaginary band round him, below his waist. 'It includes your willy and your bottom,' I said. 'Those are a boy's private parts. Now a girl's private parts are down here too' – I drew my hand across the lower part of my stomach – 'and round here.' I patted my bottom. 'But girls have another area that is private, here.' I ran my hand round my bust line. 'This is also private and you never touch a girl in either of these places. Do you understand?'

'Yeah,' he said, grinning. But I wondered how much he was actively taking in, and how much of what he had seen and learned at home could now be corrected by my lecture. I paused.

'Why did you do it, Reece?' I asked after a moment. 'Why did you touch Paula there?'

He shrugged. 'Dunno. Felt like it. Felt like touching her up.'

'Well, don't,' I said firmly. 'Ever again. Do you understand me?'

His language and attitude suggested he had assumed his behaviour was completely acceptable, the most natural thing in the world, and that I was making a fuss over nothing. I shuddered at the possibilities of what exactly had been going on at home and what he had seen and heard. I was also somewhat angered that when Reece had been placed with me the social services hadn't told me more. The family had been 'known' to them for years, so someone in the offices must have a good idea of what had been going on.

It is a continual and justifiable complaint of foster carers that we aren't given enough information when it is available and known to the social services. We are told things about the foster child (or children) on a 'need to know' basis, and sometimes the social services' interpretation of what we 'need to know' is very different from the foster carer's. Not only does this mean that we can't cater for the child's needs as best we might, but in the worst-case scenario foster families have been put at risk, and even had their own children abused because vital information has been withheld. There have been cases brought by foster carers against the social services where the judge has found in favour of the foster carers and awarded damages against social services, so attitudes should have changed.

Without wishing to labour the point, a friend of mine who fosters recently had a two-year-old boy placed with her whose parents were intravenous drug users and were known to be HIV positive. The child had been given a test for the HIV virus the year before, and although the test result was known to the social services, they refused to pass it on to the carer. They said if she was practising good hygiene then she and her family wouldn't be at risk and so she didn't need to know if the child was HIV positive.

I repeated to Reece what I had already told him about private parts meaning exactly that. Then, without finishing the book Paula had been reading, I took him upstairs to get ready for bed. He was still unrepentant, which was understandable, as he appeared to genuinely not know that he had done anything wrong, but as with all his unacceptable behaviour we had to try to help him unlearn it, and change what he was used to; otherwise his future was mapped out, and it wasn't good.

After I'd settled Reece in bed and said goodnight, I checked on Paula in her bedroom. With years of experience as the daughter of a foster carer, she showed resilience and understanding.

'It's OK,' she said, raising a smile. 'It was more a shock than anything.'

'All right, love,' I said, kissing her cheek. 'But I want you to put some distance between you and Reece for the next few days. It will help him to understand what is acceptable if he feels your disapproval.'

* * *

First thing on Monday morning, with Reece settled in the living room in front of a DVD of the Walt Disney *Aladdin*, I telephoned Jill and updated her. She appreciated the seriousness of what I was saying and said she'd phone the social services, try to get some more information and then get back to me asap.

True to her word, half an hour later Jill phoned, having spoken to Karen, who was standing in for Jamey Hogg while he was on leave. Disappointingly Karen hadn't been able to add much beyond what she'd already told me, but had said again that she'd seen Reece watching a sexually explicit adult video when she'd visited the family, and that there were concerns about Reece's father's sexual behaviour towards Susie, Reece's half-sister. This, together with neglect, had been the basis for bringing Reece and Susie into care. Karen had said that as soon as Jamey Hogg returned he would contact me.

I thanked Jill and asked if she could find out what was happening about contact arrangements, and also Reece's schooling, as I hadn't heard anything about either. She said she would and that she would visit us the following morning. I spent the rest of the day keeping Reece constructively occupied, reinforcing the boundaries for good behaviour and praising him at every opportunity. By the time the girls returned from school I was exhausted and dinner was late, but I felt I was making some progress.

When Jill visited us the following morning she was able to witness all aspects of Reece's behaviour first hand, from flying around in a prehistoric bird or shark attack (when she first arrived), to sitting quietly absorbed in a book which Jill read to him while I made us coffee. She also heard his defensiveness about anything connected to home.

'That's a smart sweatshirt,' Jill complimented him. 'Did mum buy it?'

'Don't know.'

'Susie sends her love. You'll be seeing her before too long.'

'Don't know.'

'Secrets,' Jill said quietly to me when I saw her out. 'He's been sworn to secrecy.' And I agreed, but the worrying thing was about what?

On Wednesday at lunchtime as Reece and I were having some soup and a roll, the phone rang. I answered the extension in the kitchen, where I could keep an eye on Reece, although he was absorbed in eating. It was a social worker called Melissa, who said she was trying to arrange contact between Reece and his mother, and as many of the siblings as possible. She said Reece's mother, Tracey, had been into the council offices threatening them with legal action because she hadn't seen Reece since he'd been moved to me the week before, and the court order said that she was supposed to see him twice a week. Whatever Tracey may or may not have done, she was right about this. Melissa was in a panic now, trying to arrange contact and comply with the judge's court order.

'It's going to be between six and seven thirty tonight,' she said. 'Are you able to take and collect Reece?'

'Yes,' I said, aware that it is a requirement that foster carers take their foster child (or children) to, and collect them from, contact when appropriate. 'Where is it being held?' I asked.

'Here, at the council offices. Tracey has been banned from the family centres. They've already given her a second chance, so they won't budge. I'm arranging for two social workers and a security guard to be present. Don't worry: you won't have to meet Tracey. All you have to do is to phone when you arrive in the car park and someone will come down and collect Reece.'

The arrangements were unusual, to say the least. I'd never heard of contact taking place at council offices in any county, and the mention of the security guard, plus the reassurance that I wouldn't 'have to meet' Tracey, was adding to my disquiet. Normally, not only would I meet the child's parents at the start and end of contact, but I would actively try to build a working relationship with them – it benefits the child if we can all work together – but it now sounded that I was being saved from this for my own protection.

'I'll give you the phone number of the duty social worker,' Melissa said. I reached for a pen, wrote down the number and read it back.

'Thanks,' Melissa said. 'It's a nightmare trying to arrange this contact. Tracey's kids are with foster carers all over the area, and some are well outside the county. Hopefully we will be better organized by next week. Good luck.'

With Reece still eating, I went to my desk in the front room and took out the essential information forms to look up the names and ages of Reece's extended family. Although it appeared I wouldn't be meeting any of them, I needed to have some idea of who Reece's half-brothers and -sisters were so that I would know who he was talking about after he had seen them at contact. I had briefly scanned the forms when Reece had first arrived but now I looked at them more carefully. Reece had two half-brothers – Brad and Sean, aged sixteen and fourteen respectively – and three half-sisters. Apart from Susie, aged ten, who had been brought into care at the same time as Reece, there were Sharon, aged eighteen, and Lisa, twelve. They all had different surnames, none of them being Tracey's; only Reece had the same surname as his father, so that I assumed Reece was the only child of Scott and Tracey.

The forms also listed the contact details of the siblings and other important family members, as it is usual for the child to keep in touch with the extended family as much as possible. As I looked at the names and addresses of the carers where the children were living, I could see the problem Melissa had been having in trying to bring them together. All of them but one had addresses outside the county. Susie had been placed with foster carers in a neighbouring county about 20 miles away; the two half-brothers, Brad and Sean, were together in the opposite direction, about 15 miles away. Sharon, at eighteen the eldest, was in a teenage residential unit within the county, while Lisa, who it appeared had been brought up by an aunt since the age of two, was in a town which I guessed was over 80 miles away.

When children are first brought into care the social
services usually try to place them with their own 'in
house' carers inside the county, but if there are no
places available, they place them with an agency carer,
either within the county or as close to it as possible.
Occasionally children are purposely placed out of the
area: for example, a teenager who has got into trouble
with the police and needs a fresh start. I noticed from
the information that all the children in the family,
apart from Reece and Susie, had been in care for many
years, and were with permanent long-term carers. I
therefore assumed that the reason for them being so
widespread was that when the social services had
matched the children to suitable permanent families,
the best match could only be found outside the immediate area. I also noticed, as I read down the page, that
the children had been taken into care at different times,
beginning fifteen years previously with Sharon when
she had been three. Susie and Reece had been the last
to go.

Before returning the forms to my desk I made a note
of the birthdays of Reece's mum, dad and all the
siblings, so I could arrange for Reece to send or give
them a present and card on their birthdays, as is normal
for foster carers to do. I could hear that Reece had now
finished his lunch and, having swooped into the sitting room, was jumping up and down on the sofa. I
returned the forms to my desk and went through to the
living room.

'Come on, off the sofa,' I said. 'We sit on sofas, not
bounce on them. Would you like to go to the park?'

I guessed he did, for with a flying leap he was off the sofa and down the hall, fumbling to get his trainers on while yelling, 'Park park,' in a good imitation of a strangled parrot. I quickly joined him in the hall, where I put on my coat and shoes and then helped Reece with his coat zip.

'You're going to see your mum tonight,' I said, as we left the house, 'and maybe some of your brothers and sisters too.' It was then I realized that since he'd arrived Reece had not once asked when he would be seeing his parents, which was very unusual. Reece had been living with his parents for over seven years and should have formed a strong enough attachment to be missing them badly, particularly as he'd been in care and away from them for only six weeks. I'd found in the past that most children, even those who had been neglected and abused, pined for their mothers (and fathers if they were in contact with one) for months. They eagerly awaited contact and asked repeatedly when they would be seeing their mums again. In my experience only the worst cases of abuse, for example Jodie (of *Damaged*), had resulted in the child having no bond or attachment with their parents and never mentioning them. I also realized, though, that Reece had had an awful lot on his mind with all the moves, and had probably had enough to cope with without the added burden of fretting for his parents.

'Are you looking forward to seeing your mum?' I asked as, hand in hand, we walked up the street and towards the park.

'Dunno,' he said.

'Do you remember when you last saw her?' I asked, for I realized that I didn't know, and hadn't thought to ask Melissa. Melissa had said that the judge's order had set contact at twice a week, so I assumed it had been complied with, apart from in the disruption of Reece's move to me.

'Dunno,' Reece said again, hopping along beside me and hissing at a cat.

'Did you see your mum when you were with your other carers?' I asked.

'Yes.'

'What about your brothers and sisters? Did you see them?'

'Think so.'

'OK, love, I just wondered.' It wasn't of any great significance, other than that it helped me to gain a better idea of what had been happening.

We spent an hour in the park, which gave Reece a chance to burn off some of his energy, and arrived home again just before the girls returned from school and college. When they came in I explained I would be in and out with contact that evening, and that I would plate up the dinner and they could have theirs when they wished. Reece didn't mention contact or that he was going to see his parents.

At five o'clock I gave him an early dinner and then persuaded him into some fresh clothes so that he would look smart for contact. I also persuaded him into the bathroom, where I ran a flannel over his face. Contact is an 'occasion' and I like the children to look their best; this also gives the parents less reason to complain. So often the child's parents are angry about their child being taken into care, and they direct their anger at the carer and seize on anything and everything – from a small mark on an otherwise clean top to a tiny skin blemish for which the carer could be held responsible. Not all parents do this but a sizeable proportion do, and I can see only too clearly the reasoning behind it, although this doesn't make it any easier to deal with. In having their child removed the parents have lost virtually all control over the child's upbringing, and have effectively been told that their parenting wasn't good enough. Human nature being what it is, it therefore makes some sense for them to retain what little control they still have in their child's upbringing by criticizing the carer and wanting things done differently. Also, trying to show that the carer is doing a less than perfect job in some way minimizes their own shortcomings and failings.

However, I have worked with plenty of parents who recognize that, for whatever reason, they were not able to raise their children and want to work with me. This makes life so much easier for all concerned, particularly the child, who isn't subjected to divided loyalties between the parent and the carer. Given that Tracey had all her children in care, and that had been so for fifteen years, I hoped she'd come to terms with this and would therefore view me as an ally and not an enemy, for the benefit of Reece.

* * *

With Reece at last settled under his seatbelt in the car, and with a couple of books to keep him amused, I headed for the council offices, which were on the other side of town. I had allowed half an hour for the journey, which would get us there in good time. Contact started at six o'clock, so I had allowed an extra ten minutes for parking and then phoning and waiting for the duty social worker to arrive. I had entered the duty social worker's number on my mobile, which was now in my handbag on the passenger seat.

Reece was pretty quiet in the car, not looking at the books but peering out of his side window at the brightly lit shops, which were just closing. He was making a low humming noise which, although mildly irritating, was considerably less distracting than the jarring sounds of planes and cars crashing which had accompanied our previous car journeys. I had explained to Reece what was going to happen – i.e. that we would park in the council offices' car park, and a social worker would come to the car and then take him to see his mother in a room in the building.

'Why aren't you taking me?' Reece asked.

'I don't know which room you will be in,' I half-truthed, 'so they thought it would be easier this way.' I could hardly say his mother was considered dangerous.

It was 5.50, and I was waiting for a gap in the traffic so that I could turn right into the council offices' car park. As I glanced across I saw that the car park, which flanked two sides of the six-storey building, was virtually empty. By this time most of the council employees would have left work, so I guessed that apart from a few employees working late – the social workers, security guard and cleaners – the building would be deserted, like the car park. I knew the building was normally closed and completely in darkness by 7.00 because I'd driven past it on a couple of occasions on my way to see a friend, but clearly they would be keeping part of it open tonight for Reece's contact, which wasn't due to finish until 7.30.

I made the right turn and slowly drew across the car park so that I could park beneath the one lamp that lit the otherwise dark parking area. I nosed the car up to the dwarf wall that skirted the car park and nearly jumped out of my seat as Reece bellowed 'Mum!' at the top of his voice.

I looked over and saw a lone figure come out of shadows of the building and begin towards us. I felt my heart start to race. Pulling up the handbrake, I turned off the engine.

'Mum!' Reece yelled again, releasing his seatbelt.

'Stay there until I let you out,' I said firmly. I looked at the woman, who was now about 10 yards away. I wondered what the hell I was supposed to do. I could hardly sit in the car with Tracey outside while I phoned the duty social worker as I had been told to do: it would have been rude and also impractical. Reece was now clamouring at the window and bellowing, 'Mum! Mum!'

I took the keys from the ignition and my mobile from my handbag, and got out. I went round and opened Reece's door and took hold of his hand.

'Sharky!' a deep woman's voice boomed from behind us. 'Sharky, me boy!'

With Reece now beside me, I locked the car and, holding his hand so he couldn't dash across the car park, I turned to greet Tracey. About 5 feet 8 inches tall, and very overweight, she was dressed in nylon jogging bottoms and a short-sleeved nylon Liverpool football club T-shirt, despite the cold night air. Her hair was drawn severely back in a tight ponytail that just touched the top of her broad shoulders. She came towards us with one hand thrust into the pockets of her jogging bottoms and in the other hand she held a packet of cigarettes and a lighter. For all intents she looked like a wrestler.

'Sharky, me lad!' she shouted again, continuing towards us. Coming right up she cuffed Reece over the head. 'Good to see ya, Sharky.'

'Hello, Tracey,' I said, smiling. 'I'm Cathy, Reece's carer.' It wouldn't necessarily be obvious to Tracey who I was, as escorts are sometimes used to take children to contact if the carer can't. As I introduced myself and saw her face fully illuminated by the lamp of the car park, I noticed how much Reece looked like her. He was her spitting image, from the pale skin to the brown hair and eyes, and even the prominent upper serrated teeth, which were less pronounced in Tracey but still evident. He was so similar to his mother he could have been cloned.

'He wants a bleeding 'air cut,' Tracey said. She went to cuff him again over the head but Reece automatically ducked. Then she stood looking at me.

Although Reece's hair was little more than stubble, Tracey's wishes had to be adhered to, as Reece was on an interim care order (ICO). On an ICO the parents retain parental responsibility and have a say in the child's upbringing. This remains so until a full care order has been granted by the court, when the social services take full control. Hair is often a contentious issue and carers do what the parents wish.

'Perhaps you could tell me what you normally do with Reece's hair,' I said, hoping this might be the starting point for a working relationship with Tracey, for while this meeting shouldn't have taken place, now that it had I could try to use it for the best.

'Shave it,' she said. 'Number two all over. His dad done it at home, every week.' I could see where Reece had got his shouting from, for Tracey's normal speaking voice was very loud, almost shouting.

'OK, fine,' I said. 'I'll see to it, although I'll have to take him to the barber's, so it won't be every week.'

''As he been good?' she boomed, changing the subject. Before I could answer she'd turned to Reece and, with another cuff which Reece also missed by ducking, shouted affectionately at him: 'You been good, Sharky? You little bugger, I bet you ain't!' She laughed loudly and her chest rattled, so I guessed she was a heavy smoker. I was about to say that Reece was settling in well but I didn't get a chance. 'He's been moved four times 'cos of his behaviour, and it ain't good!' Tracey yelled. 'I'm in court next week, and when I talk to the judge he'll be having that bleeding social worker. I ain't 'aving me kid pissed around.'

Again I was about to open my mouth to speak and say something conciliatory but I didn't get the chance.

'Is he staying with you now?' she bellowed. 'He better be! I ain't 'aving 'im moved again. It's a bleeding disgrace. Them wankers!'

'No, he won't be moved again,' I reassured Tracey. Reece was pulling on my arm and making a loud hissing noise. 'Stand still, good boy,' I said.

'Do as you're bleeding told!' Tracey yelled, giving him another cuff over the head, which met its target this time. Reece immediately stopped the hissing and stood quiet and still, her method of child control apparently effective, if not recommended.

'You seen his social worker yet?' Tracey demanded.

'No, not yet,' I said. 'I understand he is away at present.'

'Fucking 'ell, them bleeding social workers are always on holiday. All right for some! He should be 'ere, sorting me bleeding kids out, not on 'oliday. Do you know, I've got all me kids in care?' she added as though it was something to be proud of. 'All except Lisa, and she's not being fostered, she's with me sister. Ain't seen 'er for years, but I'm gonna be changing that. I'll tell the judge! Lisa's bright, yunno.'

I nodded and thought that now I had met Tracey and talked to her I had better do as I'd been instructed and phone the duty social worker, for I had the feeling that this conversation could go on for ever. Tracey obviously had a lot of grievances and needed a sympathetic ear.

'Would you like to hold Reece's hand while I phone the duty social worker?' I asked. 'I don't want Reece to run around the car park.'

'Yeah, good on ya. That's sensible.' I breathed a sigh of relief and transferred Reece's hand to hers. 'I reported them other bleeding carers to the police for not looking after me Sharky,' Tracey said. Then she looked at me carefully, her eyes narrowing (just as Reece's did some-times). 'And I'll do the same to you if I 'ave to. Nothing personal, you understand, but me kids are important, and I want the best for 'em.'

'I hope you won't have any reason to complain,' I said, pressing the duty social worker's number on my mobile.

'I'll take Sharky up,' she said. 'I know where they are. Me other kids are already there. They was early.'

Oh dear, I thought. It was supervised contact, and I couldn't let her take Reece without a social worker present; nor did I want a confrontation in this deserted and dimly lit car park. Reece had started hopping up and down again, chanting, 'Susie, Susie, want to see Susie!'

'Quiet, Sharky!' Tracey boomed, clipping his ear. He fell silent.

'Tracey,' I said, throwing her a smile. 'If you don't mind, could we wait here for the social worker? I've been told to phone him and wait here, and I'll get into trouble if I don't.' I had the phone pressed to my ear and could hear it ringing.

'Yeah, go on then. I know what they're like. Don't want you getting into trouble.'

Another couple of rings and the phone was answered. 'Hello,' I said. 'It's Cathy Glass, Reece's carer. I've brought Reece for contact. I'm in the car park with Reece's mum, Tracey.'

'Right,' he said, understanding the urgency. 'I'll be straight down.'

'He's coming.' I smiled at Tracey and dropped my mobile into my pocket.

'You coming as well?' Reece asked me, or rather shouted, for being here with his mother and hearing her shout had undone all I had achieved in the past week and returned the volume of his voice to what it had been.

'No,' I said. 'I'll be back to collect you at the end of contact.'

'May as well 'ave a fag, while I'm waiting,' Tracey said. Dropping Reece's hand, she opened the packet and, lighting one, offered the packet to me.

'No thank you,' I said.

'Good. I don't want Sharky breaving in smoke. It ain't good for his asthma.'

'Has he got asthma?' I asked. 'I didn't know.'

'Summink else they 'aven't told you. Fucking useless, them social workers. Wait till I get 'em in court.' She dragged heavily on the cigarette while I took hold of Reece's hand.

'Reece's chest has been quite clear since he has been with me,' I reassured her, 'but I will keep an eye on it.'

'He was bad at 'ome,' she said. 'Social worker said it was 'cos his dad and me smoked in the flat. Cheeky buggers!'

I didn't say anything, for very likely the social worker had been right, and clearly Tracey has absorbed some of his message, given her comment to me about not wanting Reece breathing in smoke. She drew heavily again on the cigarette while Reece hopped up and down again yelling, 'Susie! Susie! Reece seeing Susie.' Clearly he had missed Susie, his half-sister, although he hadn't said so to me.

'Hush, you little bugger,' Tracey said, grabbing his hand from me. Taking another drag on the cigarette, she looked at me suspiciously. I prayed the social worker would get a move on, for I had the feeling the conversation could deteriorate from here on.

'You wiping Sharky's bum?' Tracey asked.

'No,' I said. 'He can do it himself now.' I glanced at Reece and smiled proudly.

'Can he?' she asked surprised. 'What about his dick? He can't do that. You cleaning his dick for him?' Foster carers get used to being questioned by the parents about how they are looking after their children, but never in over twenty years of fostering had I had a question of this nature put to me at the first meeting, and put so crudely. I was shocked, although I didn't show it.

'No,' I said. 'I run Reece's bath and he washes himself. I do wash his back and hair, but he washes his private parts.'

'Private parts!' she boomed and laughed loudly, her chest rattling. 'That's a joke. Nuffing private about Sharky's dick, I can tell you. He used to 'ave it out all over the place. Even showed it to a social worker once. You should 'ave seen 'er face.' Dear me! I thought, and Reece was listening to this! 'You gotta clean his dick for 'im. He can't do it 'imself!' Tracey insisted. 'I always did it.'

'I'm afraid I can't do that,' I said, 'but I will make sure Reece cleans himself properly. As Reece's carer I have to be careful about these things. It's different for you: you are his mother. I'm sure you understand.'

Perhaps it was the conciliatory tone in my voice, or the fact that I was acknowledging I was only the carer and she, as his mother, had a higher status, but Tracey's tone softened.

'Yeah, OK, I can see that,' she said. Then, looking down at Reece: 'You make sure you clean your dick, boy. You don't want an infection like last time.'

I was saved from any more of this by the arrival of the duty social worker, a tall slender man in his late twenties who hurried anxiously out of the main entrance and across the car park.

'Sorry,' he said as he approached us, looking at me. 'Is everything all right?'

I nodded. Reece was now dragging his mother towards the main entrance, happy to be going to see Susie at last. 'I'll collect Reece at seven thirty, then?' I confirmed with the social worker.

'Yes. You didn't have a problem just now?'

'No, not really.'

'Sorry, I'll make sure it doesn't happen again. We didn't realize she was outside.' He hurried quickly after Reece and Tracey, who were now entering the building, while I unlocked my car and got in, reeling from my first encounter with Tracey.

Chapter Seven:

Chaos

Driving home, I thought about Tracey and what she had said in the car park. Although I was shocked by her language and what she had said, I had to admit she was a character, to put it mildly! I mused on how much Reece looked like her: he was identical, and I could now see where a lot of his (defiant) mannerisms had come from. When I arrived home it was 6.30. I called up to the girls to say I was home; then I ate my dinner and made a cup of tea, with my ears still ringing from the sound of Tracey's loud and demanding voice.

I tried not to sit in moral judgement on Tracey, although I did feel she should show Reece more respect. All that cuffing around the head, talking about his private parts to me in front of him and calling him Sharky hardly helped his behaviour or self-esteem. I also thought that she clearly viewed the social services and the carers as enemies, which was going to make working with her very difficult unless she could be won over. It was likely Reece would be with me for a year or more while all the assessments and reports were written and then filed in court for the final court hearing, when the judge would make his (or her) decision on where Reece would live.

I had no doubt I would be bumping into Tracey again before (and perhaps after) contact, and there might be meetings that she and I, together with the social worker and other professionals, would attend. She said she had reported Reece's previous carers to the police, but for what? I couldn't begin to imagine. It seemed unlikely that one, let alone all of them, had been negligent or abusive in their care of Reece, so I wondered if Tracey had made it up to intimidate me. In which case she had partly succeeded, for without doubt while I had been alone with her in the car park and waiting for the social worker, I had felt more than a little intimidated. She was a very large woman, and her manner, even before she had spoken, was threatening and aggressive.

With some trepidation, at seven o'clock I got back in my car and drove to the council offices to collect Reece. I had been told to wait in the car park for Reece to be brought to me at the end of contact, so I parked again under the one lamp and cut the engine. The building was now in darkness, save for the main entrance and two rooms on the second floor, which I assumed were being used for the contact. I switched on the radio and sat back to wait.

A few minutes passed and another car pulled into the car park and parked on the far side. The driver, a woman, didn't get out but sat waiting; I wondered if she was another carer who had come to collect one of Reece's half-siblings. Five minutes later a large Range

Rover bumped into the car park and parked a few spaces away from me; the male driver stayed inside.

At 7.35, over and above the music now playing on my radio, and despite my car windows being closed, I heard Tracey's voice coming from inside the building. It grew louder and louder as it came closer, together with other voices, male and female, and excited children's voices, all shouting to be heard.

I switched off the radio and looked towards the main entrance. I still couldn't see them, but the voices were becoming more distinct as they approached, presumably coming down the stairs that led into reception. I could now make out Reece's and Tracey's voices above the others. The driver's door of the Range Rover opened and the driver got out and stood by his vehicle. I got out, and the woman in the other car did likewise. The man glanced in my direction and nodded; I smiled back. The woman standing by her car on the far side looked over, but she was too far away in the dark to see us properly. Clearly we were all waiting to collect the siblings. The approaching voices grew louder; then the group began to appear through the glass revolving doors of the main entrance, and I saw the lights go off on the second floor.

Tracey came out first, shoulders back and strutting defiantly down the steps to the edge of the car park. She was shouting something over her shoulder at the throng following her. She seemed angry, despite having just spent an hour and a half with her children. It was impossible to make out what she was saying over the noise the others were making.

Two large strapping lads, whom I took to be Brad and Sean (aged sixteen and fourteen), were immediately behind her and came out 'play-fighting', cuffing each other over the head with their open hands, then ducking and cuffing again. Behind them was a uniformed security guard and behind him came a large woman who had a similar profile to Tracey, but whom I couldn't identify. Directly behind her were two smartly dressed women, whom I took to be the supervising social workers. One of them was holding a little girl's hand; I assumed she was Reece's half-sister Susie (aged ten). Beside Susie came Reece, leaping and bobbing and yelping, completely hyperactive and out of control. There were nine altogether, led by Tracey, who, while still shouting at them, was now surveying the car park as though deciding which of the carers to approach first. The noise level rose further as the play-fighting of the two lads, Brad and Sean, developed into a free-for-all, which quickly saw the pair of them rolling on the tarmac in a mock wrestling session while making deep ouching and groaning noises and swearing at each other.

'Get off 'im!' Tracey bellowed at Brad, who was the elder and larger, and was now straddled on top of Sean.

'I can't fucking breathe,' Sean yelled from underneath.

'I told ya to bleeding get off,' Tracey yelled again. Then she went over and cuffed Brad over the head.

Reece was leaping up and down, shouting at the top of his voice, 'Fight! Fight!'

'No, it ain't,' Tracey yelled. 'Not if he bleeding well knows what's good for 'im.' She cuffed Brad again, and then tried to pull him off his younger brother.

I saw the man standing beside his Range Rover to my right make a move towards them, so I thought he was probably the boys' carer, but he took a step and stopped, clearly unsure whether he should intervene or not. One of the two female social workers said something to the boys but understandably didn't physically intervene. Then the other one who was holding Susie's hand spoke to the security guard, who quickly went over and lifted Brad off his brother.

Tracey immediately turned on the security guard. 'Get your fucking 'ands off 'im!' she yelled. 'I'll sue you for assault!'

I stayed where I was by the side of my car, as did the other two carers, while the scene before us quickly developed into mayhem. Sean, now released from under his brother, retaliated by walloping Brad in the middle of his back. Brad yelled and, turning, hit his brother in the chest and the play-fighting escalated. Tracey was still shouting at the security guard and the social workers that she was going to 'fucking do 'em all for assault'. I wanted to get Reece into the car as quickly as possible, for I could see he was beside himself, jumping up and down, shouting at the top of his voice and imitating his mother, 'Do 'em, do 'em for fucking assault,' he yelled. I wondered how long it was going to be before he joined in the fighting with his older brothers. It was not for me to intervene – not with two social workers and the security guard present.

The chaotic throng slowly moved forward into the centre of the car park. Tracey looked at us again, still undecided about whom she was going to approach first. I cowed and hoped it wouldn't be me. The social workers followed her while the security guard tried to break up the boys again. The noise reached a new level, with all Tracey's family now bellowing at each other. Even little Susie had begun imitating her mother: 'Sue 'em, fucking sue 'em!'

As they drew closer, under the light, I could see more clearly the faces of Reece's siblings. What struck me was that they all looked the same. Brad and Sean, who were now making a haphazard approach to their carer's Range Rover, were, given their age difference, identical – older versions of Reece. And I now saw that the other woman whom I hadn't been able to place when she'd first come out of the building was in fact a younger version of Tracey. I guessed it was Sharon, her eighteen-year-old daughter.

Sharon's red bloated face and heavy hips and thighs maligned her youth, giving her the appearance of a middle-aged woman. She wore nylon jogging pants and a Liverpool T-shirt, and her hair was pulled straight back in a severe ponytail exactly like her mother's. It wasn't just her appearance that was the same as Tracey's: when Sharon shouted to Reece to 'shut up', it was Tracey's voice that came out. I looked at little Susie, who had dropped the social worker's hand and was now dancing up and down beside Reece and imitating his whooping noises. She had the same features – the pale skin, brown hair and eyes and unusual prominent and serrated front top teeth. It was weird and quite unsettling to see such a starting likeness in all the children, particularly as they all had different fathers. Clearly Tracey's must have been the dominant gene and it crossed my mind it was a pity that fate hadn't been kinder to them, for without doubt they appeared a strange bunch.

It had now become obvious to the social workers that the most pressing need was to get the two older boys, Brad and Sean, into their carer's car first. The social workers were trying to herd them in that direction, while the boys, fists up, circled each other as if in a boxing match. Their carer took a step forward into the approaching throng and said forcefully, 'Brad, Sean, in the car now, please.'

The boys glanced at him and continued the play-fighting, smacking each other around the head with their open palms. 'Brad, Sean,' the carer said again. 'Say goodbye to your mum and get in the car. It's time to go now.'

One of the social workers repeated this, with no greater success. The boys continued slapping each other while at the same time gradually inching towards the Range Rover. The carer opened the rear door and waited patiently as they made their halting approach. He was as impotent to do or say much as the other carer and I. When foster children are with their parents, the carers have to stand back and allow the parents a chance to perform the role of parenting, and clearly Tracey wouldn't have appreciated intervention.

I looked at Reece and tried to make eye contact with him, hoping he might come to the car and get in of his own accord. I even opened the rear door ready, but it had no effect. Reece was having a great time leaping up and down and hollering, possibly aware I had little authority now. Susie then took off, and began circling the car park.

'No, come here, Susie. Good girl,' one of the social workers called.

''Ere, now!' Tracey bellowed, and Susie did return.

'Please get in the car, boys,' the male carer said. Sean and Brad were close now, near the bonnet, but still slapping and throwing punches at each other. I wondered if they behaved like that at home with their carers; probably not.

'Why ain't Brad been in school?' Tracey yelled, going right up to the boys' carer and jabbing a finger in his face. 'He says he ain't been in school for a week.'

'He has been excluded,' the carer said evenly, taking a step back. 'The social services have been informed and we are looking for another school.'

'Social services ain't gonna do nuffink,' she hollered. 'I want me boy in school. I'm seeing the judge next week and if he ain't in school by then, you'll all be in for it!'

'We're doing our best,' the carer said calmly, while still holding open the car door for the boys. It would be doing nothing for the boys' respect for their carer to hear him being spoken to like this, and I thought his job was probably difficult enough without his having his authority undermined.

'Well, make sure you do,' Tracey finished, prodding her finger at his shoulder. 'I want me kids educated. No good 'aving kids in care if they ain't educated.'

Five minutes later, with a mixture of repetition and the promise that dinner was ready and waiting at home, the boys were in the Range Rover being driven out of the car park. With the boys gone, Tracey turned her attention to me. So too did Sharon, in a mirror image of her mother.

'Why ain't Sharky in school?' Tracey glared at me.

'Why ain't Sharky in school?' Sharon repeated.

'He was in school when he was wiv me,' Tracey added.

'I understand the education department is looking for a school,' I said to Tracey. 'I'll phone the department next week and see if I can speed things up.'

'Yeah, you do that. I want 'im in school on Monday,' Tracey snapped. I thought that was highly unlikely, given it was Wednesday evening now, but I also knew I wouldn't be saying that to Tracey. I just wanted to get Reece into the car. He was going frantic, and I knew he would be very upset later.

The other carer, who'd been waiting by her car, now came over and Sharon looked at her. 'We need to be going,' the woman said to Sharon, so I guessed she was a carer from the residential home where Sharon lived. The woman was only in her mid-twenties and no match for Tracey.

'She'll go when I say she's ready!' Tracey barked at her. 'And I want a word wiv you. I ain't pleased about Sharon's care.'

At that moment another car drew into the car park. We all looked over as it pulled to a halt a few yards away.

'It's Marie,' Susie yelled, and I realized that up to that point, there hadn't been anyone to collect Susie and take her home.

'She can wait! I ain't finished yet,' Tracey hollered.

Marie got out of the car and came over. 'Sorry I'm late,' she said. 'There was an accident on the motorway.'

Tracey ignored her, returning her attention to me. 'And why ain't Sharky wearing a vest? He'll catch 'is bleeding death.'

Reece was actually well wrapped up, with a T-shirt under a zip-up fleece and his winter coat on top, but I wasn't going to argue. 'He can wear a vest if you wish,' I said. 'It's not a problem.'

'Make sure he does,' Tracey returned. 'It's bad for 'is chest if he ain't wearing a vest. He always wore one wiv me.'

I nodded and said nothing, thinking that not wearing a vest wasn't as bad as breathing in her smoke.

'We must go,' Sharon's carer said again. 'It's gone eight.'

'She will go when I say,' Tracey hissed at her and I saw the carer take a step back.

I looked to the social workers and I could see from their expressions that they were as exasperated as we were, but reluctant to do any more than placate Tracey and hope the children would eventually find their ways into the cars as the boys had done. The situation was

ridiculous; it was bedlam. I cringed at the thought that
contact had been set at twice a week.

'Reece, come and say goodbye to your mum,' I called,
but Reece was making so much noise I doubted he had
even heard me.

'Time to go, Susie,' Marie called to her as Tracey's
attention was diverted by barking at the social
workers.

'Sharky ain't been in school for months,' she yelled at
the social workers, starting to wave her fist. 'What you
doing about it? Bleeding nuffin'!' The security guard
took a step closer to Tracey. 'And you can bog off,' she
yelled at him.

'Tracey, it's getting very late,' the social worker said
eventually. 'Reece and Susie should be in bed by now. If
you come into the office tomorrow we can discuss it
then, and I'll try to find out what's happening.'

This seemed to defuse Tracey slightly and spark some
cooperation. 'Sharky!' she bellowed. 'Get in that bleeding car now!'

'Sharky,' Sharon yelled in a direct imitation of her
mother. 'Get in that bleeding car now!'

'Shut up, will ya,' Tracey yelled at Sharon. 'I ain't
asked ya!'

Reece took no notice. He was still yelping and whooping and jumping up and down, out of control and
oblivious to everyone, even his mother.

'Sharky! Get in the bleeding car now!' Tracey yelled
again. Then she went over and, grabbing him roughly
by the arm, brought him to my car.

'Get in, good boy,' I said quietly. 'I'll put your belt on.'

Reece got in and then Tracey stuck her head in. 'You got the right belt in 'ere?' she yelled at me over her shoulder.

'Yes, I'm very particular about car safety,' I reassured her.

'Good, 'cos I can sue you if you ain't. I'm not 'aving me kids' lives put at risk like that last bleeding carer.'

Tracey pulled her head out of the car and I fastened Reece's seatbelt.

'Mum! Mum!' Reece yelled.

'What is it, boy?' She stuck her head back in. I glanced at the social workers, who met my gaze with resigned frustration.

'Bring me Nintendo next time,' Reece yelled into his mother's face, 'and me games, all of 'em.'

'OK, Sharky. Don't you worry, I will,' Tracey yelled back. Pulling her head out of the car, she turned to me. 'Ain't you got no Nintendo for 'im to play wiv?'

'No, but we've lots of other toys,' I said tersely, because I was coming to the end of my patience. 'If you would like to bring Reece's Nintendo, it would be nice for him to have that too.'

'I'll bring it, Sharky!' she yelled towards the open car door. 'Don't you worry, your mum will see to it.'

I had my hand on the car door, ready to shut it as soon as the opportunity presented itself. 'Say goodbye to your mum,' I said, and began to ease the door to.

'Goodbye, Mum!' Reece yelled, but Tracey wasn't listening. She had her back to him and was now bellowing at Marie about Susie's hair.

I quickly closed Reece's door, went round to my door and got in, pressing the central locking system.

'Mum,' Reece screeched. 'Mum! I want me games! All of 'em!' He was banging on the window now, screaming, 'Mum, Mum!'

But Tracey was oblivious, shouting at Marie and gesticulating at Susie's hair. There was nothing to be gained by staying, so I quickly started the engine and pulled to the exit.

'Mum, don't forget me games!' Reece screamed again, banging his fists even harder on the window.

Once out of the car park, and a little way along the main road, I turned into a side road. Parking, I got out and went round to settle Reece. He was beside himself, screaming that his mum would forget the games and also just screaming. I climbed into the back seat and sat next to him. With my arm around him I gently talked to him and stroked his head for over quarter of an hour until he had calmed down.

By the time I arrived home it was after nine o'clock. Lucy and Paula met me in the hall, looking worried.

'What happened?' Lucy said.

'Don't ask.'

'We thought you were just going to collect Reece from contact,' Paula said.

'I was! I'll explain later.'

I took Reece straight up to the bathroom and helped him have a quick wash and clean his teeth; then I helped him into his pyjamas and into bed. He was emotionally exhausted, as I was. He fell asleep as soon as his head touched the pillow. I came out and went downstairs. Then I did something that I only normally do at Christmas, New Year and on my birthday: I poured myself a drink.

I sat in the living room with a glass of white wine and rested my head back on the sofa. My ears still buzzed from all the noise, and my forehead throbbed with tension. It had been an absolute nightmare and I doubted it had done the children much good either. Reece had been hysterical and I knew the other carers would have their work cut out calming their children down too. Contact is supposed to give the children quality time with their parents and siblings, not generate chaos, with all of them shouting and hitting each other. If it had been like that during the actual contact session, then I would have thought the supervising social workers would have something to say about it in their reports.

Yet, despite the chaos and Tracey's aggressive and highly critical manner, part of me felt sorry for her. She obviously had learning difficulties herself and when all was said and done, she'd had seven children and hadn't been able to parent any of them. I wondered if all her shouting and threats was a lot of hot air – a desperate woman trying to cling to the last vestige of responsibility. Only time would tell.

Chapter Eight:

'school'

The improvement in Reece's behaviour temporarily disappeared and in the following days returned to what it had been when he'd first arrived. I suspected this was a result of being with his mother and having his 'old' behaviour reinforced. He woke at five o'clock in the morning and it took me a long time to resettle him. Then he spent most of the day charging around the house banging into things, throwing things, making loud noises, swearing and telling us to 'fuck off' if anyone tried to stop him. He would only become calmer if either Lucy or I sat with him and read a story. Paula was still keeping her distance after the incident of Reece touching her sexually. She talked to him, obviously, but wasn't playing with him, as this would have put her in close physical proximity to him.

Apart from Reece's aggression and hyperactivity we also had a number of instances of him trying to head-butt Lucy and me, and two of him biting, one of which had resulted in teeth marks in Lucy's hand. I told Reece off and stopped some of his television time, which produced a full-scale tantrum. He kicked everything within reach and screamed at the top of his voice that he 'fucking hated' me, so he lost more television time.

I wasn't surprised Reece had taken a step backwards after contact. Apart from having his 'old' behaviour reinforced, there was the reminder of the home he had left. All children become a bit unsettled after contact and if the child already has behavioural problems then they tend to escalate as he or she expresses their feelings of confusion in the only way they know how. I knew Reece would settle again and continue with the progress he had already started, until the next contact, when he would take another step back. Eventually, as the weeks passed, and he got used to the routine of contact and adapted to the change, the 'fallout' after-wards would, I hoped, be less. However, there would always be some reaction afterwards as he struggled to bring the two halves of his life together and come to terms with everything that had happened.

Current social work policy dictates that children should see their natural parents in all but a very few exceptional circumstances. Many foster carers would challenge how much good ongoing contact is for the child if there is no hope of them ever returning home. But as in many areas of fostering, we have to do as we are told and just pick up the pieces afterwards by giving the child lots of hugs and reassurance.

By Monday Reece was settling down again and as he wasn't going to school, I decided the days ahead, until he was found a school, needed some structure. I would ask Jill and the social services what was happening about Reece's schooling when we next spoke, but I knew from experience it could take weeks, sometimes months, to find a school willing to take a child who had been excluded. So after breakfast I explained to Reece we would do some reading and writing for a little while – pretend he was at school – and then have a break with a drink and a snack; then we would do a little bit of maths work. The rest of the day would be play. He liked the idea of 'playing schools'. We would also be going out for a while each day, for apart from the practical issues of my having to shop etc., Reece needed the release of energy that a trip to the park or even a walk would, I hoped, effect.

I'd no idea what stage Reece was at with his learning, so I got out a selection of early learning books from the cupboard, which included first- and second-level reading books, and some work sheets. I'd photocopied the work sheets from those of a tutor who'd visited another child I'd fostered who hadn't been in school. The books and work sheets began at the most basic reception school level and were very appealing, designed to capture the child's interest, with big words and pictures for the child to colour in.

But before I started I needed a better idea of where to begin, for if I pitched the work too low Reece might see it as 'babyish' and reject learning out of hand. A copy of his statement of special educational needs would have been helpful and would have detailed the level he was at, his progress and his difficulties, but I hadn't received this statement yet. So to gauge his level I decided to show him some 'key word' cards, which I had also photocopied from the tutor's work sheets, and then mounted on brightly coloured cards. Each card contained a simple word beginning with the words a child would learn first, such as 'he', 'she', 'the', 'we', 'so', 'cat', 'dog' and 'go', gradually going on to more difficult words like 'where' and 'because'.

I began showing Reece the very basic words, passing the card to him and asking him if he knew what it was.

'Mmm, not sure,' he said to each, rubbing his chin thoughtfully.

'OK, so we'll put them in this pile,' I said, placing the cards on the table. 'These are the words we will learn first.'

By the end of the first twenty very basic words, I stopped. Reece had recognized only one word – 'a'. He was seven and a half and appeared to have a sight vocabulary of one word, which was a single letter. The average child of the same age would have had a sight vocabulary of about 150 words; brighter children would have been reading Harry Potter.

'Can I do me reading now?' Reece asked eagerly.

I opened the most basic of the books and began. It was from a structured reading scheme I had bought years before to help a child who had just started school and was struggling. Each page contained a large picture with a single word describing the picture printed underneath – for example, dog, cat. Of course with Reece having no sight vocabulary, I had to tell him each word, which he then happily repeated. We went through the first book twice.

I then opened the second book in the series, which repeated the words in the first book and was supposed to consolidate what the child had learned. But because the pictures had changed in the second book, although the words were the same Reece couldn't recognize them: he had memorized the sound of the word with the picture, and not the sight of the word, which is what reading is. I returned to the first book and, covering up the pictures, went through the words again. Then I did the same with the second book, repeating the word over and over again.

Although this was very repetitive for Reece and he had some difficulty sitting still in his chair, he was very happy with what we were doing and appeared to want to learn. After about fifteen minutes of this word recognition I put away the reading books and said we would do a little bit of writing, and then have a break. I gave him a pencil and paper and asked if he could write his name.

'Yeah,' he yelled excitedly. 'Of course I can. I ain't stupid!'

'No, you're not. You are doing very well.' I smiled and he planted a big kiss on my cheek.

'I like it here,' he said. 'I like you.'

'That's nice,' I said. 'I am pleased. We like having you here.'

He looked surprised. 'Do you?'

'Yes. Very much, Reece. I'm pleased you have come to stay with us.'

He beamed from ear to ear. 'Good, 'cos I ain't bein' moved again. It's a bleeding disgrace.'

I had to smile, for although Reece had learning difficulties he had remembered word perfect what his
mother had said in the car park the previous Wednesday.
There was certainly nothing wrong with his hearing!

Reece could only write his first name, and the letters
he formed were large and poorly drawn, equating to
the average child's first use of a pencil at about the age
of three and a half. I wrote Reece's surname in large
letters, and then made a series of little dots in the shape
of the letters, which he joined together to form his
name. I did the same with some other basic 'key words',
and he enjoyed doing this very much.

'I'm writing!' he screamed with excitement right in
my ear.

'Yes, you are, but try to talk a bit more quietly, Reece,'
I encouraged, as the girls and I did constantly. But I
knew only too well where all the shouting had come
from, and seven years of shouting to be heard at home
wasn't going to be altered in weeks or even months.

We had a short break after the writing, when Reece
had a banana and a glass of milk and I had a cup of
coffee. Then we completed the morning's 'school work'
with some very basic number work, using more photocopied activity sheets. After that we went out, via the
park, to the shops. I bought the bread, fruit and vegeta-
bles we needed, and then we headed back, Reece helping me carry the shopping.

When we got into the hall I saw that the answerphone
was flashing with a message. I pressed play: 'It's Mary
Smith, Jamey's team manager. I'm in the office until
two. Could you call me back please on this number ...'

Eureka, I thought. At last! The team manager would have more information and be able to answer my questions. Aware that I might be talking to her for some time, and it was already lunchtime, I quickly made Reece a sandwich, let him choose a packet of crisps and left him eating while I used the phone in the hall so that I couldn't be overheard. I dialled the number Mary had given and she answered immediately.

'It's Cathy Glass, Reece's carer,' I said.

'Good. Thank you for calling back. How are you?' I could tell from the urgency in her voice she had a lot to say and wanted to get on with it.

'We're doing all right,' I said.

'Contact,' she began. 'I understand it was a fiasco last week, so I have decided to split it. Have you got a pen handy?'

'Yes.' I reached for the pen and paper I keep beside each phone. Mary sounded very efficient and I was relieved.

'I've read the contact supervisor's reports,' she continued, 'and I don't want a repeat of last Wednesday. I shouldn't think you do either.'

'No,' I said with a light laugh. 'It took quite a while to resettle Reece.'

'I can imagine. I've heard from the other carers as well, so I'm separating contact. Reece will be seeing his parents on Tuesday and Friday, same time and place. Will you be able to take and collect?'

'Yes,' I said as I wrote. 'So he will be seeing his father as well?'

'Yes. We couldn't have Scott there last Wednesday because of Susie being there. There's a police investigation in respect of Scott's alleged sexual abuse of Susie. But Tracey insisted she wanted to see all her kids together. She knows her rights, as you probably found out when you saw her, but it's Reece's rights I'm thinking of here, and he has a right to see his father.'

'Yes,' I agreed. 'Absolutely.'

'I'm arranging for the other siblings to see Tracey on another evening, because they are not Scott's children. Scott is only the father of Reece.'

'Yes,' I said again.

'Reece has no relationship with any of his half-brothers or sisters, apart from Susie. He hadn't seen any of them for years before last week's meeting. We're in court again next week, so I'll be able to tell the judge that we tried to bring them all together, but that it isn't in any of the children's interests to repeat it regularly. I anticipate bringing all the siblings together once a year, but I would like Reece to see Susie regularly. He does have a relationship with her.'

'Yes, he does,' I agreed.

'So I was wondering, Cathy, if I give you Susie's carer's telephone number, could you arrange between yourselves to meet up every so often, so that Reece and Susie can spend some time together?'

'Yes, of course. How often would you like?'

'Every three weeks?'

'Yes, that would be nice for them. I'll arrange it.'

'Good. Susie's carer is Marie. I think you met her briefly on Wednesday in the car park.'

'I saw her but that was all. There was too much going on for us to speak.'

'So I understand. Sorry about that. It shouldn't happen again. If there are any problems with the contact when there is just Reece and his parents, we will have to rethink the arrangements for taking and collecting him and maybe use an escort.'

'Fine,' I said, impressed. Clearly this team manager was on the ball. I wrote down Marie's telephone number, which Mary now gave me, and read it back.

'So how is Reece settling in?' Mary asked.

I told her of the progress he was making – that I thought he was calmer and was accepting the boundaries I had put in place for controlling his behaviour. 'But it would help,' I said, 'if I had some more background information. We've had one incident of sexualized behaviour, and I've very little to go on. Also I haven't heard anything about his schooling. What's happening with that?'

I thought I heard a little sigh before Mary said, 'I know. Tracey has been in this morning. I've promised to look into his education, when I get a minute. The position is this, Cathy. James has taken over the case but is away at present. I haven't got access to his files – I think he might have taken them home or away with him. His computer is password protected, so I don't really know what stage he's at with this. I do know that the education department has been informed that Reece is with you and I understand they are looking for a school in your area. Can I ask you to be patient until Jamey gets back? It's only ten days now, and I'll ask him to get in touch with you as soon as he returns. He'll be able to give you a clear picture and also get things moving with education.'

'OK,' I said, aware that ideally things needed to be moving now, but my carping on wasn't going to help. 'Do you know what happened at Reece's last school?' I asked, 'and how long he has been out of school? Tracey seems to think it is months.'

'I think she could be right. Reece was a poor school attender when he was with her. Despite the emphasis she now places on educating her kids she didn't take him to school regularly, I know he was excluded from two schools. Jamey will be able to fill you in when he returns. Also he'll be the best person to give you more background information. But I do know that sexualized behaviour was an issue at one of the previous carers, and also at school. So I should practise your safer caring policy.'

'We do,' I said.

'Was there anything else?' Mary asked.

'Jamey will be in touch as soon as he's back?' I confirmed.

'Yes, and thanks for all you are doing, Cathy.'

We said goodbye and I hung up.

While I could have hoped for more information, I appreciated that without access to the files the team manager was not easily going to be able to supply it, and ten days weren't going to make much difference. Individual social workers carry a huge workload, with fifteen or more families to look after, all requiring home visits, meetings, court appearances and paperwork.

How much greater was the team manager's workload, as they oversaw all the cases of all the social workers in their department?

I was pleased that Mary had taken on board one of the most pressing concerns – that of contact. For if Wednesday's 'fiasco', as she had put it, had continued twice a week indefinitely, not only would it have undermined Reece's chances of settling, but I doubted my own nerves would have stood it. Reece seeing his parents by himself seemed a much better solution all round. He would get the benefit of one to one with his mum and dad, and doubtless the beginning and end of contact would be much less fraught, or so I thought. My only real concern about contact now was meeting Reece's father, Scott. For while I didn't have all the details, knowing that Scott was under investigation for a sexual assault on his stepdaughter, Susie, who was only ten, I baulked at the thought of having to meet him, although it was a situation I had been in before. I reminded myself that Scott was only under investigation and that he hadn't been found guilty yet.

I checked on Reece, who was still eating his lunch, and took the opportunity to phone Marie, Susie's carer. She was expecting my call, the team manager having phoned her earlier with the details of her new contact arrangements. Susie was attending school, so we decided the best time for us to meet would be a Sunday. Marie was busy the next Sunday, so we made an arrangement for the following one, which was the last Sunday in February. Marie lived in a neighbouring

county about 20 miles away, so a children's park halfway between us seemed like a good idea. We said we
would phone nearer the day to confirm which park and
what time, and said our goodbyes. I made a note in
my diary with a reminder to phone Marie to confirm
arrangements. When Reece had finished his lunch I
explained about the new contact arrangements, both
the ones with his parents and with Susie. He liked the
idea of the outing with Susie very much.

Normally when a child first arrives in care, the carer
makes appointments for the child to see a dentist, an
optician, and the doctor for a medical. With so little
information, and the files not being available, I didn't
know if this had happened or not at his previous carers'.
I asked Reece if he had been to the dentist recently or
had his eyes tested but he couldn't remember. I would
have to leave it until the return of the social worker,
who would also issue the consent form for the medical
if Reece hadn't had one.

Reece didn't mention seeing his parents again until he
was getting ready to go to contact the following day,
Tuesday. I had made dinner early and given Reece his
at five o'clock, leaving the girls' dinner plated up. This
would become part of our contact routine; foster carers'
households revolve around contact.

'Am I seeing me dad?' Reece asked as we stood in his
bedroom and I passed him clean jogging bottoms.

'Yes,' I confirmed. 'It will just be your mum and dad
this time.'

'I like my dad,' he said.

'Good. I expect you will have a nice time then.' He had one leg in his joggers and was now hopping around trying to get the other leg in. 'Try sitting down to do it,' I suggested.

He didn't, but managed to get his leg in anyway. 'I like me dad more than me mum,' he said.

'Do you?' I asked lightly. 'Why is that?'

'Don't know,' he said; then after a thoughtful pause: 'I think it's 'cos he's nicer.'

'I see,' I said. 'Nicer in what sort of way?' He was struggling into his vest and I helped him get his head in the neck hole rather than the armhole.

'Don't know,' he said again. 'I don't like vests.'

'No, but your mum wants you to wear one because she's worried about you catching cold.'

'OK, but I ain't wearing it on the other days. Only Tuesday and Friday for contact.'

'All right.' I smiled, impressed, for again Reece had shown, despite all his learning difficulties, that he had remembered not only when contact was but also how to placate his mother. I was beginning to find that when Reece wasn't consumed by hyperactivity, with his brain randomly firing all over the place, it was surprising what he could remember, having heard it only once. I would build on this as much as was possible. Perhaps he found it easier to remember things when he heard them rather than saw them. Children learn in many different ways and it was a matter of finding out which way best suited Reece.

* * *

Drawing into the dark council offices' car park at 5.50 p.m., I parked as close to the lamp as I could and switched off the car's engine. There were more cars here than on Wednesday, presumably because more council employees were working late, and as I glanced up at the building I saw that many of the offices were still lit. I pressed my mobile to call the duty social worker.

A different male voice answered: 'I'll tell the supervising social worker you're here,' he said. 'She will collect Reece from the car.'

'Thanks,' I said. Then I turned to Reece in the back. 'They won't be long,' I said. 'A social worker will be down to collect you soon.' He was looking out of the side windows, obviously looking to see if his parents were in the car park. Apparently they weren't, and five minutes later one of the social workers who had been supervising contact on Friday appeared. Smiling, she came over. I got out and opened Reece's door.

'Hi, Reece, Cathy,' she said. 'Mum and dad are waiting inside.'

It all seemed a lot better planned and organized than last week. I was able to say goodbye to Reece and wish him a nice time in a calm atmosphere. I waved until he entered the building and then got into the car and returned home, where I ate my dinner and drank a mug of tea, before returning to collect Reece at 7.30. I was hoping that perhaps Reece would say goodbye to his parents inside the building, which is what happens at the contact centres. The child says a calm goodbye in the controlled atmosphere of the supervised contact and then leaves with the carer, quiet and less fraught. But there was to be no such luck here.

At 7.40 I heard Tracey's voice shouting something unintelligible some while before she appeared in reception. Then she came through the revolving doors. Reece was behind her, with a tall thin man whom I took to be his father. They came out play-fighting with their fists up, lightly boxing each other on the arm. Every so often Scott picked up Reece by his legs and, turning him upside down, shook him for some moments before setting him down again. Reece's screams of fright and delight reverberated around the car park and doubtless beyond. Behind Reece and his father came the two supervising social workers and the security guard. I got out of my car and waited as first Tracey, and then Reece and his father, made their way across the car park towards me, the social workers and security guard following.

Tracey came straight over to me and I knew by her manner even before she spoke that she was angry and was going to complain. But I knew it couldn't be about Reece's vest because he was wearing one.

'When ya gonna cut 'is bleeding 'air?' she demanded. 'I told ya last week to cut it.' It was still only stubble but I knew that wasn't the answer.

'We've been rather busy,' I said. 'I could get it cut tomorrow if you like.' In truth I had been so occupied dealing with Reece's behaviour that I had forgotten all about having his hair cut.

'Yeah. And that top he's got on,' she continued, moving swiftly on to the next complaint, 'it stinks, and it's filthy. I want me kids in clean clothes. I'll report ya if ya don't.'

'Tracey, the sweater was clean on before we left,' I said, feeling hurt after I had gone to so much trouble to make sure Reece looked smart.

'Well, it ain't now. It's got Coke all down it.' I failed to see the logic in this, as the Coke must have come from her, but I wasn't going to argue. I was more concerned to hear that Reece had been given Coke to drink; I hoped, but doubted, it was the caffeine-free variety.

The two social workers had now joined us and were standing a little to one side, watching and listening, and I trusted ready to intervene if it became necessary. Reece was now involved in an amateur wrestling match with his father in the centre of the car park and was shrieking every so often as his father turned him upside down. Although I would rather they had engaged in a calmer activity, I could see, as could the social workers, that this was obviously how father and son related to each other. I knew the social workers wouldn't stop it unless it got out of hand and became dangerous.

'You been hitting Sharky?' Tracey suddenly demanded, jabbing her finger at me.

'Of course not! I—'

'How did he get that bruise on 'is leg then? It's a thumbprint! You must have done it!' The social workers were now looking at me, and while Tracey's accusation was so preposterous as not to merit a response I felt under pressure to defend myself.

'I would certainly never hit any child, Tracey,' I said firmly. 'And I resent your suggestion.' I looked her straight in the eyes and could have said a lot more, but stopped myself. I wasn't even aware Reece had a bruise, and if he had it was probably from playing in the park. It couldn't be very big because I would have noticed it when he'd changed his joggers just before we had left.

'Just you watch out in future,' she barked in the same threatening manner. 'I'll be checking him all over, like I did tonight. If I find anyfing I'll report you to the police. I 'ope you're not like those other bleeding carers. They was 'itting 'im as well.'

The woman was impossible. 'Tracey, I would never hit any child,' I repeated, 'and I doubt the other carers did either.' I stopped and looked towards the social workers. 'I think it's time we left,' I said.

They nodded and called to Reece. 'Time to go home, Reece.' Reece and his father took no notice. They were still dancing round each other, now aiming punches at each other's arms. 'Time to go home!' they tried again.

'And what about Sharky's school?' Tracey now demanded. 'What ya bleedin' playing at? I told you I wanted him in school but he ain't!'

'I really don't know, Tracey,' I said, exasperated, although of course Tracey had a valid point. 'You'll have to speak to the team manager and ask her.'

'I will, don't you worry! I'll be down 'ere and 'ave her first thing tomorrow. Stuck up little tart.' Which I assumed referred to Mary.

'Reece,' I called, but he didn't answer. 'Reece!' Having had more than enough, and not wanting a repetition of last week when Reece was wound up to the point of hysteria, I left Tracey and went over to Reece and his father.

'Hello, Mr Williams,' I said, offering my hand for shaking. 'I'm Cathy, Reece's carer. It's nice to meet you.' He stopped the play-fighting and shook my hand. I smiled. 'Do you think you could bring Reece to my car now, please? It's nearly his bedtime.'

'Yeah, sure,' he said, amicably. 'Reece, lad, come on, time to go.'

'Thank you,' I said. Not only was I relieved to have Scott's cooperation but I was also pleased he hadn't called Reece 'Sharky'.

He led Reece past Tracey and to my car. I opened the rear door and Reece got in. 'Thank you,' I said again to Scott. 'Reece has obviously had a nice time.'

'Yeah,' Scott said. 'So have I.' I thought whatever the truth of the allegation in connection with Susie, Scott clearly had feelings for his son, and seemed far more level-headed than Tracey. I found Tracey's illogical aggression very difficult to deal with. What also struck me about Scott, now he was standing in the light of the lamp, was that Reece didn't look anything like him: he had inherited none of Scott's characteristics at all. Reece was short and stocky with pale skin, brown hair and eyes and the unusual front teeth, like the other siblings I had met, and like Tracey. Scott, on the other hand, was tall, very thin, with fair hair, blue eyes, high cheekbones and a sharp chiselled face, and perfectly normal front teeth. Had you asked me if they were father and son, I would have said no.

I fastened Reece's seatbelt while Scott stood to one side, and Tracey went over to have a go at the social workers.

'Say goodbye,' I said to Reece.

'Dad! Dad!' he yelled. Scott put his head into the car. 'Can I have a kiss?'

Scott kissed his cheek. 'Bye, son. See you Friday. I'll try and remember your Nintendo.' I assumed Tracey had forgotten it. Scott lightly cuffed Reece's shoulder. 'Be good,' he said, and stood back. I hesitated. Reece was ready to go now, but he hadn't said goodbye to his mother. I looked over to where Tracey was. She was still shouting at the social workers about Susie's care, or what she perceived as lack of it, so I closed the car door.

'Bye,' I said to Scott. 'See you Friday.' I got in and started the engine. I then drove from the car park with Reece waving to his mum who was oblivious and embroiled in her battle of words.

Although Reece wasn't as hysterical as he had been on Wednesday, he was still pretty hyped up. Some of it was from the excitement of seeing his dad, and some of it was just general hyperactivity, with him making lots of loud and unrelated noises.

But my thoughts were elsewhere as I drove; I was occupied with Tracey's accusation that I had hit Reece. I was really hurt that she could even begin to think that I would harm him when I was investing so much in looking after her son and trying to improve his future. And apart from my hurt feelings, her accusation could have far-reaching implications. The social workers would be noting it in their report and it was possible that Jamey Hogg, when he returned, or Mary, the team manager, might feel it needed further investigation. At least 40 per cent of foster carers have accusations made against them at some point in their career, and an investigation into such a claim is a lengthy and in-depth process. If it is felt there is cause for concern, then the foster child is removed from the carer until the investigation is complete. Very very rarely does the investigation find actual abuse by a foster carer towards the child, but the investigation has to run its course. And while I was aware that such an investigation was necessary to ensure the safety of the child, I was also aware that in the vast majority of cases, as tonight, there were no grounds for the accusation, which was that of a distraught mother trying to get her own back on the 'system' she felt was against her.

By the time we arrived home Reece was a little calmer, but it still took me a long while to get him ready for bed. As he changed into his pyjamas I stole a look at his legs and could see no sign of a bruise or anything that resembled one. Being light skinned, he had quite a few freckles but that was all.

Reece was finally asleep at 9.30. I went downstairs to the living room and wrote up my log notes, including details of Tracey's accusation, and that I had found no sign of any bruise. Presumably the supervising social workers hadn't either when Tracey had examined him.

* * *

As there was nothing I could do until the social worker returned from leave, we continued as we had been doing. The weekday routine I had started remained more or less the same, with Reece and I spending part of each day 'playing schools' and then going out to the park or shops, for a walk and occasionally for a special treat like the cinema and ice-skating.

We met up with Marie and Susie on the last Sunday in February, and the two children spent an hour, well wrapped up from the cold, playing in the park before we all adjourned to the park's café for hot drinks and a light lunch. Marie was lovely and very good company. She was younger than me and had been fostering for five years. She had no children of her own and told me that she had decided to foster because she herself had been in care as a teenager when her father had been killed in a road accident and her mother had suffered a nervous breakdown as a result. Like me, she was waiting for Jamey Hogg to return, for although Susie was attending school, there were a lot of other issues which Marie wanted to raise with Jamey as soon as possible, including what Susie was now telling her about her stepfather. Marie didn't go into the details; she knew, as I did, that such details were confidential and were not discussed even between foster carers.

However, we did mention contact, for like me she was having to contend with Tracey's endless complaints, aggression and accusations. Susie was seeing her mum with the other siblings – Sean, Brad and Sharon – on Monday and Thursday evenings, and Marie had felt so intimidated by Tracey that Marie's husband had started going with her to collect Susie at the end of contact. Marie also mentioned the likeness in all the siblings, and that unfortunately they all appeared to have learning difficulties, although Susie didn't have Reece's hyperactivity and behavioural problems. Jamey Hogg was due back in the office the following day, Monday, and Marie and I agreed we were looking forward to hearing from him asap. We said goodbye, with an arrangement to meet again in three weeks. The children waved through their car windows as Marie and I drove out of the park and then went in separate directions, home.

'I've had a nice time,' Reece said in the car, and his gleeful expression and endless chatter confirmed this.

'Good,' I said. 'I am pleased. I enjoyed chatting with Marie.'

'Thank you for taking me, Cathy,' he said. And my day was complete.

Chapter Nine:
Starting to Get Annoyed

If Marie and I had been looking forward to Jamey Hogg's phone call on Monday we were to be disappointed, for there wasn't a call, not to me at least. By Tuesday afternoon, when I still hadn't heard anything, I telephoned Jill and she said she'd phone the social services to find out if Jamey was back at work. She phoned back quarter of an hour later to say he was in the office and 'catching up'. He had told her he would be in contact with me as soon as was possible. Jill suggested I emailed him, so that he had something in writing, and gave me his email address. As with many organizations email had to some extent taken over from the telephone and mailed letters. So, with Reece sitting on the floor beside my desk and trying to do a big-piece jigsaw puzzle, I emailed his social worker.

I stated that I was Reece's carer and I was looking forward to meeting him, as was Reece. I also reminded him we were still waiting for a school for Reece and that Reece's first review was due. I wrote (diplomatically) that I looked forward to discussing all the other issues surrounding Reece when I met him. I clicked send. Later I checked my email inbox to see if there was a reply. There wasn't.

On Wednesday morning, when there was still nothing from Jamey, I emailed Jill with a copy of the email I had sent to him and asked her if I had his correct address, as I hadn't received a reply. She emailed straight back to me and said that the email address was correct and that she would also email him a reminder to contact me. On Thursday, still having not received a reply, I emailed Jamey again, tagging on my previous email. I wrote that I was very concerned that Reece was still out of school, as Tracey had been when I had seen her at the last contact.

In fact Tuesday's contact had been horrendous, the worst one yet. The security guard had had to break up a fight between Tracey and Scott; then, when Tracey turned her wrath on me, he'd had to distract her while Reece and I made a dash from the car park. We were both pretty shaken and it was ten o'clock before Reece was calm enough to go to bed.

Jamey emailed back an hour later to say he was very busy dealing with a priority case and he would get back to me when he had a chance. I considered Reece's case a priority and emailed him to that effect, adding that Reece hadn't been in school for nearly a term, and his LAC review was overdue. The LAC (Looked-After Children) review is a meeting of all parties to make sure everything that can be done is being done for the child, and to discuss the child's progress. A review should be held four weeks after the child is first brought into care, then every three months for the first year and then twice a year. My email was terse, but I hadn't liked the way Jamey had marginalized Reece. Someone has to speak up for foster children and if it's not the carer, then who else have they got?

An hour later the phone went. It wasn't Jamey but Mary, his team manager.

'Cathy,' she said. 'As from tomorrow an escort will collect Reece and take him to contact, and also return him to you afterwards. I am aware the situation hasn't improved and I'm not having it continue.'

'Thank you very much,' I said. 'I have tried to talk to Tracey but it's impossible.'

'I know. I've read the supervisors' reports. Don't take it personally. Tracey is very angry and she is taking it out on the carers as well as the social workers. I'm arranging escorts for all the siblings. I will not have our foster carers verbally abused and it's not doing the children any good to witness it either.'

The decision to use an escort wouldn't have been taken lightly, as they are expensive and costed on time and distance. The other children lived miles away from the council offices, which were still to be used for contact. Not only was it very efficient of Mary to put all this in place but it also showed how sensitive she was to the effect this type of verbal abuse has on foster carers when we are striving to do our best.

'Reece will be picked up at five thirty,' she said. 'The escort is called Sabrina.'

'Thanks,' I said again. I hesitated. 'Mary, is Jamey in the office?' The office was open plan and I guessed she would be able to see his desk from where she sat.

'Yes, he is,' she said.

'Is it possible to speak to him, please?'

'He's on the phone at present. I'll tell him to phone you as soon as he's finished.'

'Thank you, and thank you again for organizing the escort. It's much appreciated.'

We said goodbye and I hung up, feeling very relieved. Tracey's continual haranguing of me at the end of each contact had started to worry me more than I cared to admit; I was getting to the position of dreading Tuesdays and Fridays. Now I felt as though a huge weight had been lifted from my shoulders. All that I needed now was for Jamey to phone and things would really start to take off.

Jamey did phone, at the end of Thursday, but things didn't exactly take off. He didn't know what was happening about Reece's school and he didn't seem in any hurry to push it with the education department either. But he did say he would visit Reece and me the following day.

'Excellent,' I said. 'Is there a number at the education department I can phone, to find out what's going on?'

'Yes. I don't have it to hand. I'll try and find it for tomorrow.'

'Thanks,' I said, then wanting to get off to a good start I asked: 'Did you have a good holiday?'

'No. I had time off to sort out my divorce.'

'Oh dear,' I said. I wished I hadn't asked.

* * *

I explained to Reece about the escort and also that he would be meeting his social worker the following day. Neither of these facts prompted any comment from him, as he was up to his elbows in paint, glue and glitter from a compendium of activities I had bought the day before. Reece was gradually becoming more adept at sitting and doing activities and for longer and longer periods. I was very pleased. His behaviour generally was far calmer now, unless he became anxious or over-excited, when he would take off as he had done when he'd first arrived. But there was no aggression and I was far more relaxed looking after him.

He was making such good progress all round that I was looking forward to him starting school. I was convinced that, although Reece clearly had learning difficulties, he could learn, and that with the right support in school he would continue to improve dramatically. We had gone from a sight vocabulary of one word, 'a', to fifteen words in a few weeks. Reece knew these words and was reading them without prompt from a picture. Also his writing, while laborious and way behind what it should have been, was starting to show some improvement. When we went out shopping I continually gave him little sums to do in relation to what we were buying. He enjoyed this immensely, particularly when we went into a corner shop and I gave him the money to pay.

We hadn't had any more repeats of him biting or head-butting and neither had we had a repeat of overt sexualized behaviour as in the incident with Paula. However, I remained concerned that Reece did seem to view both my daughters in a sexual, rather than sisterly way. He often passed comments on their appearance and also tried to hug and kiss them (and me sometimes) with what could only be described as passion, rather than a little-boy hug.

All this I would be discussing with Jamey when he came the following day. I assumed that, as well as giving me some more background information, Jamey would bring me a copy of Reece's statement of special educational needs, which would give me some direction while I continued to help Reece until he started school.

The following morning I opened the door to a very distinguished-looking man in his late thirties with a ponytail, dressed casually but smartly in jeans and jumper. His round, open face smiled warmly.

'Hello, Cathy. I'm Jamey. Pleased to meet you.'

We shook hands as he came into the hall. I showed him through to the living room and offered him coffee.

'Thank you. That would be much appreciated,' he said. About 5 feet 10 inches tall, he had a very calm manner and a smooth, relaxing voice, which I thought would put anyone at ease. Reece was sitting on the floor in the living room with the Snakes and Ladders board game which I had been teaching him to play prior to Jamey's arrival.

'Hi, Reece,' Jamey said. 'I'm Jamey, your new social worker.' Jamey immediately squatted down on the floor beside Reece and asked him who was winning.

'Cathy,' Reece said, pulling a face.

I smiled. 'Jamey, mine is the red counter. Do you want to take over while I make coffee?'

He did, with great enthusiasm, and I left Jamey and Reece playing together and getting to know each other. In the kitchen while making coffee, I could hear Reece trying to explain to Jamey how you played the game, although quite clearly Jamey already knew. Reece was repeating the phrases and words I'd used when I had explained the game to him. They sounded very quaint and old-fashioned on the lips of a child.

When I carried the coffee and biscuits through, Jamey had the red counter on the top line and Reece was just disappearing down another snake.

'Oh shit!' Reece exclaimed.

'Reece,' I warned lightly. Jamey looked up and smiled.

'He seems a lot calmer than I'd been led to expect,' Jamey said.

'Yes, he's made huge progress, with only the odd relapse now and again. He really is a lovely boy.'

But while I was happy to say positive things about Reece in front of him, I knew that a lot of the discussion Jamey and I would be having, for example on Reece's background and his difficulties, wouldn't be suitable for Reece to hear.

'When you have finished that game,' I suggested to Jamey, 'shall I let Reece watch a DVD in his bedroom, to give us a chance to talk?'

Jamey nodded. Reece immediately stopped playing, unable to believe his good fortune, for I rarely let him watch television in the daytime unless I had to make an uninterrupted phone call.

'I want a DVD now,' Reece demanded.

'No, finish the game first,' I said.

'I'm losing. I want the DVD now.' For a moment I thought Reece was about to erupt and throw a tantrum and undermine all the positive things I was saying about his progress and good behaviour.

'OK,' Jamey said, coming to the rescue. 'We needn't finish the game but I would like to talk to you first before you rush off.'

Reece looked at him suspiciously, ''Bout what?' he asked.

'Nothing in particular. Just talk a bit so I get to know you.'

I passed Jamey his coffee and put the biscuits within reach. 'Shall I make myself scarce?' I asked Jamey. It is usual to leave the child alone with their social worker for a while when they visit, in case the child has an issue they don't feel comfortable about discussing in front of their carer.

'I'm happy for Cathy to stay. Are you?' Jamey said to Reece.

Reece nodded vigorously. I took my coffee from the tray and, resisting the chocolate biscuits, sat on the sofa, while Jamey, still on the floor next to Reece, asked him what he liked doing.

'Don't know,' Reece said.

'Well, I know you like television, don't you?' Jamey said. 'What about roller-skating? Do you like that?'

'Don't know,' Reece said.

'So what are your favourite programmes on television?' Jamey tried again in his softly spoken and gentle manner.

'Don't know,' Reece said.

'Favourite foods?' Jamey asked. 'What do you like to eat, Reece?'

'Don't know.' Then he added, 'Burgers, and what Cathy makes me.' Bless him, I thought. 'Can I watch me DVD now?'

Jamey smiled. 'Yes, and I'll come up and see your bedroom before I go, if that's all right with you?'

'Yeah,' Reece agreed. Jumping up, he shot over to the shelf, where he quickly chose the DVD of *The Lion King*.

I left Jamey making himself comfortable on the sofa while I went upstairs with Reece and settled him on the beanbag with the DVD. 'I'll be in the living room if you want me,' I said, but my words fell on deaf ears. The dramatic opening scene had begun, with the fiery orange sun rising over the plains of Africa as all the animals gathered.

'He could watch television all day,' I said to Jamey as I returned to the living room. 'And while I think of it, "Don't know" is Reece's response to most questions, particularly if they relate to him or home.'

Jamey nodded, sipped his coffee and took another biscuit.

'I'm pretty certain,' I continued, 'that he has been warned off saying anything. Actually I am certain of it, and that this child has secrets.' I looked at Jamey, hoping he might now give me the background information that would help me in my care of Reece. He didn't. He seemed happy to sit on a comfortable sofa, in a warm stress-free room, and enjoy the coffee and biscuits. I had quickly formed the impression that Jamey was a caring, amiable, warm-hearted person who related easily to children but who was also very 'laid back'. So laid back, I thought, that if he relaxed any further he might nod off.

I took the file, which I had already brought from my desk and opened it on my lap. 'I don't have much background information,' I said. 'Can you tell me anything more about Reece that might help me to look after him?'

Jamey drained the last of his coffee and set the mug on the table. 'To be honest, Cathy, I don't know much more than you do. I was assigned the case immediately before I took leave. The files are huge, and at many different locations. I'm trying to bring them all together and put them on the system so that I can get a clearer picture. I'm fairly new to this area and I'm still learning this council's procedure. I know Tracey's other children have been in care a long time, and I'm not sure why Susie and Reece were left at home for so long. Certainly Reece's behaviour at school, and with his previous carers, suggested a pretty disturbed child. What Susie is now saying about her stepfather increases my concerns. I understand there have been on-going issues for years and that there were concerns about Tracey's father behaving inappropriately to Sharon, her eldest daughter, fifteen years ago. That's when Sharon came into care. But I'm still trying to bring all the information together to get a clear picture.'

I nodded, and while I could have hoped for more, I understood what Jamey was saying and the problems he was facing. 'There's another half-sister, isn't there?' I said, glancing at the placement forms in my open folder. 'Lisa. She is twelve now. Tracey mentioned her once at contact.'

'Yes, but again, I don't know the details. I shall be visiting Lisa as well as all the other siblings. My understanding is that Lisa was placed with the aunt, Tracey's sister, voluntarily, when Lisa was a baby.'

'Why was that? Do you know?' I asked, more from interest, because I couldn't imagine Tracey doing anything voluntarily, and certainly not giving up a baby.

'No idea,' Jamey said, 'but apparently Lisa has escaped the learning difficulties which plague the rest of the family.' I wondered if she had also escaped having the same features, including the unusual front teeth, but it seemed insensitive to ask.

'All the other siblings look identical, don't they?' I said.

'So I hear, although, I have only met Brad and Sean so far. I'm going to see Sharon and Susie next week, and Lisa the week after. It's very time consuming with the children living so far away: it's virtually a whole day out of the office.'

I nodded sympathetically and thought that as I didn't want to be responsible for keeping Jamey out of the office I'd better get a move on. 'I haven't taken Reece to the optician or dentist yet,' I said. 'I didn't know if this was done with his previous carers.'

'I shouldn't think so. He wasn't there long enough. Take him for a check-up, please, and let me know the results.'

'Yes. And what about a medical?'

'I'll arrange to have the forms sent.'

'Thanks. Shall I register him with my GP? I haven't done so yet. I was waiting for you to return in case you wanted him to stay where he was. He's still in the catchment area of his last doctor.'

'No. Register him with yours. Tracey uses the other one and I understand she spends a lot of time there.'

I looked at Jamey. 'Were you aware just how close his mum lives?'

'Not until I looked at the file, and I guess the placement team wasn't either. Let's hope it doesn't cause a problem. Tracey won't be told your address.' I wondered again what the chances were of us bumping into each other in the high street, although it hadn't happened yet.

'Reece's school?' I asked hopefully. 'Any chance of Reece starting school in the foreseeable future?'

'I'll chase the education department when I get back to the office,' Jamey said.

'Can I chase them as well?'

'Yes, by all means. Sorry, I forgot to bring their number with me but it will be in the directory.'

'Do you know who is dealing with it?'

'No, but just mention Reece's name and I should think they'll find the right person.'

'Do you have a copy of Reece's statement of education needs?' I asked, ever the optimist, and recognizing that although Jamey had come with a briefcase, he hadn't opened it or taken anything out.

'I haven't seen one yet,' he said. 'Could you ask the education department to send you one when you speak to them? I must have a copy on a file somewhere, but goodness knows which file or where.'

Aware that Jamey had just joined this council, had just taken on this (complicated) case, and that the files were exhaustive and not all in one place, I had to accept what Jamey was saying, almost.

'I understood there was a requirement to have all fostered children in school within twenty-eight days of being placed,' I said.

He nodded thoughtfully, running his hand over his ponytail. 'Yes. It's twenty-four days actually.'

'And from what I understand Reece has been out of school for a term or longer. Do you know he could only write his first name without help?'

'That's dreadful,' Jamey sympathized and tutted. He was one of those people who I felt like hugging before giving them a good kick up the backside to get them moving. 'I'll phone education and see what I can do,' he added.

'Thank you. It's not fair on Reece to be out of school. Apart from his education, he needs the social interaction. I can only do so much.'

He nodded again, and then sighed. 'I'm in court next week on this case.'

'Again?' I asked surprise. 'I thought Mary was there the other week, while you were away?'

'She was. Apparently Tracey makes a habit of going to court. This time she is asking for another half an hour of contact time, so that it would be two hours twice a week. She won't get it: it's not in the children's interests. They couldn't cope with two hours. But we have to go through the motions, and each time she takes us to court it costs the social services £15,000 – money that could be better spent on other things like the kids who are in care. Add up all Tracey's spurious court actions over the years and I bet you could afford to take every foster kid in the county to Disneyland in Florida for two weeks.'

It was the most Jamey had said since arriving and I agreed with him. Tracey's legal actions were a huge drain on the social services' already overstretched budget and the money could be better spent on other things. But if Tracey was hell bent on pursuing her court actions, then she had a legal (and some would argue moral) right to do so, and there was precious little the social services could do, other than defend their actions.

'When is the final court hearing?' I asked.

'The fourteenth of September. The court has set aside six days to hear the case. When I've got all the files together I shall be compiling my report. If it helps, Cathy, you can come into the office to read it.'

'Yes, thank you. I'd appreciate that. It would give me a better insight into Reece's early years.'

Jamey was being helpful, but he seemed over-whelmed with work, and I suspected his divorce wasn't helping with his work commitments. However, he had that very relaxed casual air which suggested he took everything in his stride and remained unfazed. I couldn't help but like him, despite my wanting to put some skates under him to get him going on Reece's case.

I told Jamey of Reece's sexualized behaviour and Jamey said that he wasn't surprised because from what he had learnt so far, there'd been a lot of inappropriate sexual behaviour at home, much of which was documented in the files he had yet to recover. What he did know was that while Scott had been in prison for a drink-related assault he had made friends with a paedophile who had visited them at the flat, which of course meant he'd had access to Reece and Susie.

'Do you think Reece has been sexually abused?' I asked.

'I don't know. He's been in that environment, so it's possible. Do you think he has?'

'I really don't know. He is more sexually aware than he should be for a child of his age, but that could be from inappropriate television viewing. He's happy here but he is still closed about his home life, as you saw. I don't think he will say anything for a very long time.'

Jamey nodded. 'Mum is quite a formidable character. I had to have security remove her from the offices again yesterday. It took two security guards and she headbutted one. It's quite possible Reece is frightened of her and has been frightened into silence.'

'Yes,' I agreed. 'He seems to have a better relationship with his dad, for all Scott's faults.'

'Does he? That's interesting, particularly in the light of what Susie is saying.' Jamey considered this thoughtfully but didn't add anything.

Before he left he spent some time with Reece in his bedroom, admiring and playing with his toys. When Jamey came into the hall he renewed his promises that he would send me additional information as he found it and also chase up the education department immediately on his return to the office. As I was seeing him out I suddenly remembered Reece's review.

'I don't think Reece has had his first review,' I said.

'No,' he agreed, 'he probably hasn't. Well, let's call this meeting a review then.'

I looked at him. 'OK,' I said hesitantly. It wasn't for me to query it, but I'd never heard of a home visit replacing a review before. A review is usually quite formal, with a chairperson and recorded minutes, but it was Jamey's decision.

After Jamey had gone, and while Reece was watching the last fifteen minutes of *The Lion King* DVD, I made appointments at the optician and dentist for Reece for the following week, and our routine continued.

In fact our routine continued for the whole of March. We did some schoolwork each morning, and Reece's sight vocabulary went up to thirty-five words, and he could write all the letters of the alphabet, and count to a hundred. We went out for part of each day and Reece watched children's programmes for an hour in the evening. I met Marie and Susie again at the same park. Lucy and Paula taught Reece draughts and Four-in-a-Row, and he even beat Lucy once. I got to know Sabrina, who took Reece to and from contact. When I asked Reece how his mum and dad were and if he had had a nice time, he said: 'Don't know.'

When I took Reece to the dentist, the dentist wasn't unduly worried by the unusual arrangement of Reece's front teeth. He said that such a configuration was often inherited and that Reece might need orthodontic treatment when he was older. The optician said Reece's eyesight was fine.

Also during March I emailed and telephoned the education department, who said they were in the process of identifying a school for Reece; Jamey, who was still collating the files; and Jill, whom I regularly updated. Foster carers are supposed to attend training, and the expectation is that we attend one or two courses each month to keep abreast of change. The courses are very helpful and include topics like hyperactivity, first aid, attachment, challenging behaviour, and sexual abuse. But with Reece not being in school it was impossible for me to attend this training, which Jill appreciated and reassured me wouldn't count against me when the time came for my annual review.

Easter was fast approaching and, aware that there was still no sign of a school on the horizon, and feeling increasingly frustrated and incensed on Reece's behalf, I upped my telephone calls and emails to the education department and Jamey.

'I'm sorry, Cathy,' Jamey said in his usual unflustered mellow voice. 'I'm doing all I can. I don't really understand what the hold-up is.'

'Well, can you find out, please? This is ridiculous. The kid hasn't been in school for nearly six months now. Also the education department won't give me a copy of his statement. They say it has to come from you.'

'I've found the statement,' Jamey said, 'but I haven't had a chance to read it. Shall I fax it over?'

'I don't have a fax,' I said bluntly.

'OK, no problem. I'll put it in the post then.' But he didn't and another week passed. I was starting to get annoyed.

Ironically, in the end, it was Tracey who finally got Reece into school. She employed her usual method and, armed with a barrister and solicitor, took the social services to court (at the taxpayers' expense). The judge directed that Reece had to be in school within five days, although I didn't know this until I received a telephone call on Monday – the last Monday in March. But it wasn't the social worker who phoned me, or the education department, but the head of a local school, at 7 p.m.!

Chapter Ten:
Summoned to the Head

'I am not at all happy with this,' the headmaster began. 'I am being forced into taking this child. We are not equipped to deal with him. He needs a special school.' I knew the head's name was Tom Fitzgerald; he had at least introduced himself before beginning his negative discourse. 'I have already told the director of education that my school isn't suitable. In fact I wasted a lot of time compiling a report to this effect, but he has chosen to ignore it. I understand a judge has said that Reece must be in school immediately, so that I have no choice but to take him.'

'Really?' I said. I was taken completely off guard and my initial surprised delight at receiving a phone call from a head quickly turned to shock. We had waited so long for this call, this new start for Reece, and now the head was phoning to say he didn't want him but was being forced to take him. I'd never experienced anything like it before; all the heads I'd dealt with previously had been exceptionally welcoming, going out of their way to accommodate a foster child. 'Why has Reece been sent to your school then?' I asked, at last collecting my thoughts and sitting on the chair in the hall by the telephone.

'Because you are in the catchment area of this school and we have a vacancy.' As if I was to blame for living where I did! Although we were in the school's catchment area it was not a school I had previously had children at. It was about a mile away, on the other side of town, and I didn't know the school or the head. 'We really can't cater for his needs,' he said again. 'Why isn't he in a special school?'

'I don't know.' I said. 'I thought children with learning difficulties were catered for in mainstream schools now, with support from teaching assistants.'

'They are usually,' he said bluntly. 'But not when they have Reece's level of behavioural problems as well. He has been excluded from two previous schools, and I will have no hesitation in doing the same here.'

I was annoyed, not to mention disappointed, and really struggling to keep my emotions and tongue under control. It sounded as though Reece was being set up for failure even before he had begun. 'His behaviour isn't that bad,' I said lamely. 'In fact he has settled down really well with me.'

'Have you seen his statement of special educational needs?' he demanded.

'No,' I had to admit.

'Right. I will have a copy ready for you in the morning. I want to see you before he starts on Wednesday.'

'He's starting on Wednesday?' I asked.

'Yes. I was told he had to start tomorrow, Tuesday, but I've made it clear to the director of education that that isn't possible. I need to see you first.' I felt like a child summoned to the head's office.

'All right,' I agreed. Without a copy of Reece's statement of special educational needs, I really was impotent to argue with him about Reece's behaviour or confirm how much he had improved. I was annoyed that Jamey hadn't found the time to send me a copy so that I could have defended Reece. With no details before me I had to accept what the head was saying, although I thought he must be exaggerating and was possibly overreacting – probably annoyed by being forced into accepting a child who didn't fit the 'norm' and would require extra time and effort. However, the head would be receiving an extra payment for his school budget in respect of supplying the extra help Reece would need. 'Reece has settled down incredibly well,' I said again. 'He really does want to learn. Now his home life is stable, I'm sure his behaviour at school will reflect this.'

'That's what the director of education said,' he said, unimpressed. 'But I will reserve my judgement. I would like you to come to the school tomorrow at ten o'clock. Somehow I've got to put together an education plan by Wednesday morning. I want you to stay the first morning in case he becomes a problem.' The implication was that if Reece did 'become a problem' I would be taking him straight home again, excluded on his first day!

'Yes,' I agreed. 'I'll do all I can to settle Reece into school.'

'Right. I'll see you at ten o'clock then. Goodbye.'

I set down the phone and sat for a moment. I was fuming. All the weeks of looking forward to Reece starting school, and my hopes for him making real progress, and friends, had been dashed. From what I had just heard not only was the poor kid going to be spending the greater part of each week in an environment where he was not wanted but at the first sign of any trouble he would be excluded and sent home in disgrace. I wondered if there was anything I could do about finding him another school, but quickly came to the conclusion there wasn't. The system for allotting children places in schools had changed in recent years, and Reece's situation was complicated by him being a 'looked-after' child. If he had been my own child it would have been different: I would have found a suitable school with a vacancy and applied for a place. Now I was confined (as was the head, Mr Fitzgerald) by the education department's decision based on the directive of the judge.

Reece had had his bath and was in his pyjamas and dressing gown, being read to by Lucy in the living room before I took him up to bed. I knew I couldn't let Reece see my disappointment and concern when I told him he was going to school. I would have to make it sound positive, although I knew this wasn't going to be easy. The other thing I needed to do immediately was to find someone to look after Reece the following morning while I went to see the head. Fortunately I have a number of good friends who also foster and are therefore approved by the social services to look after another fostered child for a short while. I could hear Lucy still reading to Reece in the living room so I quickly phoned my friend Nicola and, resisting the temptation to offload my anger and worries about Mr Fitzgerald and his attitude, explained that the head of Reece's new school wanted to meet me alone the following morning, and asked if she could look after Reece for a couple of hours. Nicola had already briefly met Reece when we had been out shopping in the high street.

'Of course,' she said. 'Happy to. Bring him as soon as you like.'

'Thanks,' I said. 'I owe you one.'

'No, you don't,' she said. We often helped each other out, and Nicola fostered very young, pre-school children, so if she had a dental appointment or wanted to go to the hairdresser I would look after her toddler. I was happy to help her out, as she was happy to help me.

'Thanks,' I said again. 'Can I drop Reece off at nine thirty? That will give me plenty of time to get to the school for ten o'clock.'

'Sure. No problem. Tell Reece I'm looking forward to meeting him again. And I've lots of toys for him to play with.'

We said goodbye and I hung up. Then I went through to the living room. I waited until Lucy had come to the end of the story and they both looked up at me expectantly, aware it was time for Reece to go to bed.

'Reece,' I said, squatting just in front of him, 'I have some good news.'

''Ave you, Cathy?' he asked, his eyes growing wide with anticipation.

'Yes. Now listen carefully.' Lucy was listening carefully too. 'You know how we have been waiting for a school for you to go to?' He nodded. 'Well, they have found one. The headmaster has just telephoned me and you will be able to start on Wednesday.'

'Wow!' he yelled. 'A new school!'

'Yes, that's right. I know you will be a good boy when you start, because you know how to behave now, don't you?' He nodded vigorously. 'So, today is Monday.'

'I know that,' he put in quickly.

'So tomorrow is?'

'Tuesday.'

'And the next day is …?'

'Wednesday!' he shouted.

'That's right, good, but don't shout.' I smiled. 'Tomorrow morning, Tuesday, I have to go to your school and meet the headmaster. I shall be talking to him and telling him how well you are doing, and what a good boy you are. While I am there you will be going to my friend Nicola for two hours.'

'Who's Nicola?' he asked.

'She is a very good friend of mine and we met her once in the high street, but I don't suppose you remember?' He shook his head. 'Nicola is very good at looking after children, and she said to tell you that she has lots of toys for you to play with.' It might sound as though I was labouring the point, but when children have been moved around as much as Reece had, they can easily become insecure.

Reece pulled a face. 'I want to go to school with you.'

'We will both go to school on Wednesday, but tomorrow, just for a couple of hours, I need you to stay with Nicola. You can play, and she will give you a drink and a biscuit, and then it will be time for me to come and collect you.'

The drink and the biscuit seemed to seal it and Reece said: 'Yeah. I'll go to Nicola's for a drink and a biscuit and you will go to my school.'

'That's right, love. Well done.'

'Will we go in the car?'

'Yes. I'll take you to Nicola's, and then I will go on to school. OK?'

He nodded again, and my heart went out to him, so naïve and vulnerable, and so looking forward to starting his new school. I hoped that by the time I had finished talking to the head he would have decided to give Reece a fair chance. I would tell Mr Fitzgerald how much Reece's behaviour had improved, and how well he was doing generally. Perhaps, I consoled myself, he'd been put out by being forced into taking him and having his view overruled. I hoped Reece would prove himself.

Reece was still chatting about his new school as I took him up to bed and said goodnight. 'Do they have a uniform?' he asked.

'Yes. I think it's navy, but I'll find out tomorrow.'

'Good. I like navy. Do they have a playground?'

'Yes, they will have.'

'Good. I like playgrounds. What's my teacher's name?'

'I don't know yet, but I'm sure I will be told tomorrow.'

'Maybe it's Miss Smith,' he said. 'Same as my last one.'

I smiled. 'Maybe. Now, come on, off to sleep. We have both got a busy day tomorrow.'

'Yes, Cathy. I'm asleep,' he said screwing his eyes tightly shut. 'I like my school, and I like my home. I'm very 'appy 'ere, Cathy. I like you.'

'Good, darling. I'm pleased to hear that. I like you too, very much.' I kissed his forehead and then came out and closed his bedroom door.

I didn't sleep well that Monday night, as the head's words were buzzing round in my head, and I was also pretty anxious about meeting him the following morning. My brain kept trying to formulate the words and sentences I would need to win him over, and persuade him that Reece wasn't the 'bad lot' he thought he was. With his learning difficulties Reece would need support in the classroom from a teaching assistant (TA), but his behaviour was not only manageable but also quite sweet. 'Clear and consistent boundaries' is a cliché among foster carers looking after children with behavioural difficulties, but it is a strategy that works. Once the child knows what behaviour is expected and is acceptable, and the boundaries for good behaviour are consistent, then the child adjusts accordingly and, hey presto, you have an angel, or almost. The same 'clear and consistent' expectations of behaviour would apply at the school, which obviously the staff would know and already have in place as a matter of course. Assuming the teacher and TAs were proficient in their jobs, I couldn't see Reece was going to cause them any more of a problem than the average seven-year-old.

Reece was in good spirits as we arrived at Nicola's the following morning and the first thing he said to Nicola was that he was starting school the next day.

'I know,' she said. 'Aren't you lucky?' I thought if you did but know! I saw Reece into her living room, kissed him goodbye, then thanked Nicola again and drove to the school. I parked in the road outside at 9.50 and got out. I straightened my skirt and jacket and then went up to the security gates and pressed the intercom buzzer. My stomach was churning at the thought of meeting the head, but I was ready to do battle with him if necessary on Reece's behalf. He deserved a proper chance at school.

'Hello?' A female voice said from the intercom grid.

'It's Cathy Glass. I have an appointment to see the head at ten o'clock, about Reece Williams.'

'Yes. Push the gate. I'll open it now.'

Hearing the security lock click its release, I pushed open the massive iron gate and went into the playground. The gate clanged shut behind me and I crossed the playground and went up the two steps to the main entrance. I tried the door but it was still locked, so I pressed the buzzer on the intercom grid to my right, and the door immediately opened.

The small reception was empty but seemed quite welcoming, with children's work displayed on two of the walls and a large pinboard with photographs of all the staff, and their names printed beneath. The word

'welcome' in as many languages as you could imagine
was printed on coloured card and pinned to the door
opposite me. This door now opened and a man in his
late fifties dressed in a grey, slightly creased suit came
in.

'Mrs Glass?'

'Yes.'

'I'm Tom Fitzgerald, the head teacher. I'm sorry our
receptionist is off ill.' I nodded and we shook hands.
Although he didn't smile, he wasn't the ogre I had
imagined. In fact, short, with a worried expression, he
seemed more anxious than intimidating. 'Do come
through to my office. Can I get you a coffee?'

'No, I'm fine, thanks.'

I followed him through the door with all the
'welcome' signs, and along a short corridor, where we
turned right, and into his office. This was warm and
pleasantly furnished with a bright blue carpet, light
blue emulsion walls and a huge desk with a computer,
and four armchairs dotted in front of it.

'Do sit down,' he said. 'I'm going to have to leave you
for five minutes while I sort out a problem with another
child. I have a copy of Reece's statement of special
education needs here. Perhaps you could read it while
I'm away.'

'Yes, thank you.' I sat in an armchair and Mr Fitzgerald took a wad of papers, stapled at one corner, from his
desk, and passed it to me.

'I shouldn't be too long,' he said.

I nodded and smiled, and he left the room. Undoing
my jacket, I looked at the top page of Reece's statement,

which contained his full name, age, date of birth, religion and language spoken. The statement, like most educational documents now, was computer generated, so it was printed. Beneath his details were family details; the names of his parents with their address had been crossed out and my details written beside them in ink. I made a mental note to remind the head that my address was strictly confidential and mustn't be divulged under any circumstances, just in case his mother found out which school Reece was attending and approached it.

All statements of special educational needs follow the same format and I began to read the first section which was about behaviour. To my horror I read that Reece was reported as being impulsive and aggressive, rude and violent, and that he often hit other children and adults, causing them real harm. It said he was unable to play or cooperate with his peers and refused to take part in any organized activity, becoming rude and violent, that he was disruptive, emotionally very immature and that he often banged tables, shouted, screamed and threw things when angry which was very frightening for other children and staff. It said he would only complete a task if someone was sitting beside him, and that he often spoke in a very loud voice or shouted to gain attention.

I stopped and looked up. I couldn't believe what I was reading! It was far, far worse than I could have ever imagined. Of all the statements about all the children I had ever fostered, this was the worst by a long way. I sat staring around me, trying to equate the child whose details I was now reading with the one I had left at Nicola's playing with her toddler. The only clause I could relate to was the last one about Reece's loud voice. No wonder Mr Fitzgerald had reacted as he had. With only the statement to go on it appeared Reece was violent, aggressive and completely uncontrollable. If I'd been the head in charge of this large town school, I wouldn't have wanted Reece in my school either. I noticed there was no mention of the head-butting and biting which I'd had to deal with in the early weeks, so I assumed that behaviour had been reserved for home, and I was grateful for small mercies.

I drew my eyes downward again, and to the second section, which was entitled 'ACADEMIC SKILLS'. It began by saying that Reece had global delay and then continued with what I already knew – that he couldn't read or write; but it included the statement 'Reece has a poor short-term working memory, and is reluctant to improve on his skills.' Reluctant in education terms means he refused point blank to do whatever was suggested. I had found Reece anything but 'reluctant' in his wish to learn. The statement didn't say that he was capable of learning, given the right encouragement. I turned back to the first page to see the date, wondering if it was a very old statement that omitted any recent improvement, but found it had been amended only eight months previously, presumably just prior to him being excluded from his second primary school, and a couple of months before coming into care.

I returned to the assessment page and started to read the next section, which was entitled 'LANGUAGE

SKILLS'. It began with 'Reece has severe difficulties with receptive and expressive language skills'; and continued by stating that when asked a question he responded with one or two words; that his speech was 'generally unintelligible', and he was 'unable to identify complex concepts'. 'He is unwilling to reflect on his progress, will not discuss his views sensibly, and cannot follow simple instructions.' Again I could not believe it was the same child.

I turned the page to the 'SKILLS' section and read that Reece had a short attention span, couldn't function in a class or group situation and was 'easily distracted'. I had just started the next section, which dealt with his 'SOCIAL SKILLS', where I was reading that Reece could 'not successfully interact with his peer group at any level', when the door opened and the head returned.

'I can't believe what I'm reading,' I said before he'd even sat down. 'This child is so unlike the one I know that I could believe it was the wrong statement.'

'It's the right one, and it's recent,' he said bluntly.

'I know.'

Mr Fitzgerald was sitting in the armchair opposite me, waiting for my further response. I had read the sections that detailed Reece's needs; the rest outlined what provision had been put in place at the previous school to meet those needs.

I looked at him. 'All I can say is that Reece has made huge progress in the last three months, since he has been with me. I can only assume his behaviour was because he was so unsettled at home. His mother is very aggressive, so I think that Reece was copying her while he was at home.'

'That's what the director of education said, but it is true he was moved from a number of carers before he came to you.'

'Well, yes, but since he's been with me we have seen nothing like the behaviour reported here.' I tapped the papers on my lap. 'Reece was a bit aggressive when he first arrived,' I added, reluctant to remember the head-butting and biting, 'but he soon settled down. He wants to do the right thing, and he seeks approval, which makes a huge difference. I have fostered children before who have not wanted adult approval, and their behaviour is very difficult to modify, but that has never been so with Reece. He wants to do the right thing and he wants to learn as well.'

Mr Fitzgerald was looking at me carefully, apparently slightly tempted to believe what I was saying but not convinced. I wondered if his hostile and brusque manner on the phone the evening before had been a knee-jerk reaction to Reece's statement – the portrayal of a truly horrendous and uncontrollable child.

'So you haven't seen any of Reece's aggression replicated at home?' he asked presently.

'Not since he first came to me, no, and then it was very short-lived. He does have special needs, but it is his learning that requires attention now, not his behaviour. And he can learn. When he came to me he had a sight vocabulary of one word; now he's up to forty-five. He has problems writing: his fine motor skills are poor, though improving. He can sit still for quite long periods, and yes, I am by his side, but he will have a teaching assistant in school, won't he?'

He nodded. 'There is provision for a full-time TA, including playground supervision.'

'Is there? Good,' I said. But the level of provision was a double-edged sword, for it suggested a child who couldn't be left alone for a minute. With full TA support, Reece would have adult supervision and support for the whole day, including when he was having his lunch and in the playground.

'All right,' he said thoughtfully after a moment. 'We'll just have to see how it goes. Now I want you to meet his TA, and I would also like you to be in school tomorrow morning, but not with him.'

'That's fine with me,' I said.

'If you'd like to wait here, I'll find Mrs Morrison, his TA, and you can perhaps allay some of her worries as well. I haven't decided which class Reece will go in yet. We are a two-form entry, and unfortunately both the teachers for Reece's year are in their first year of teaching. They are very enthusiastic but lack experience in dealing with this type of child. However, from what you are saying, that shouldn't be a problem.'

'No.' I gave a small nervous laugh, for having read the statement and felt the head's concerns, I was beginning to have doubts. Then I caught myself. 'Reece will be fine,' I said.

'Good.' Smiling for the first time, Mr Fitzgerald went in search of the TA, while my thoughts ran to Reece. When we got home I was going to have a long chat with Reece and explain how this was a fresh start for him, and that he must forget all his previous bad behaviour at the other schools and behave now at school as he did at home. But my next thought was that it wasn't a good idea to remind Reece of how he used to behave, and that I must have faith in him, and in his ability to behave well at school as he did with me.

When the head returned with Mrs Morrison, a well-rounded, motherly figure in her mid-fifties, the three of us spent some time talking. I continued to emphasize how much improvement Reece had made, and that he was a delightful child. Mrs Morrison listened very carefully and seemed relieved. After about fifteen minutes the head suggested I go with Mrs Morrison to sort out Reece's school uniform, explaining that normally the school secretary-cum-receptionist would have taken care of it but she was off sick. I thanked Mr Fitzgerald for all he was doing for Reece and then left his office with the TA.

We went back along the corridor to a large walk-in cupboard, which was the stockroom and contained shelves of school uniforms in plastic bags. I had been right about the colour of the uniform – it was navy – and Mrs Morrison helped me to sort through the packages, looking for Reece's size. I knew from holding up the garments what would fit him, and as we worked side by side, collecting together the navy trousers, navy sweatshirt, white T-shirt and PE kit, we chatted.

'You'll be fine with Reece,' I reassured her. 'He's a good boy really. He's just had some bad examples in his past. I expect you've had a lot of experience as a TA.'

She smiled nervously. 'Actually this is a bit new for me. Before this term I was helping children with some extra reading in the library. I used to be a dinner lady, you know.'

'I see,' I said. 'Well, I'm sure Reece will like you a lot.' She was a lovely lady, warm and friendly, and very approachable, but I wondered at the wisdom of putting her in charge of Reece as her first experience as a TA, given his previous history in school. If I'd have been the head, I would have opted for a specialist TA to begin with, someone with loads of experience in working with children with challenging behaviour, and then once Reece had settled into school again, gradually introduced Mrs Morrison. But it was the head's decision, and also the cheaper option, for anything left over from the allowance he would be receiving for a specialist TA for Reece could be used in another area of his doubtless tight budget. But then I'm a bit cynical about these things.

Thanking Mrs Morrison for all her help, I came away with the uniform, having arranged to meet her in reception at 8.30 the following morning. The head had suggested Reece and I come in early on his first morning so that he could look round the school before the bell went at 8.50, and the other children came in, which I thought was a good idea.

I had been gone nearly three hours by the time I arrived at Nicola's at 12.20. 'Sorry,' I said as she answered the door. 'It took longer than I expected.'

'No problem,' she smiled. 'Reece has been keeping Maisie amused. I hope it's OK: I've given him some lunch. He's having it now.'

'Thank you. That is sweet of you.' I followed Nicola through to the kitchen, where Reece was perched on a breakfast stool, tucking into a sandwich and a bag of crisps. Beside him in a high chair sat Maisie, nearly ten months old, and making a good attempt to eat a banana.

'Hi!' I said to them both.

Reece grinned with his mouth full. 'I'm looking after Maisie,' he said proudly.

'Well done. Good boy.' Smiling, I went over and kissed the top of his head.

'He's been helping me all morning, haven't you, Reece?' Nicola said.

Reece nodded, and then turning to Maisie said: 'Come on, eat up, and you will grow big like me.' Maisie giggled.

'Time for a coffee?' Nicola asked.

'I'd love one,' I said.

I hovered in the kitchen, keeping an eye on Maisie as Nicola made some coffee. 'Was he really OK?' I asked her quietly as we leant against the kitchen cabinets and sipped our coffee. We were at the far end of the kitchen and out of earshot of Reece.

'Yes. Why?' Nicola said. 'You sound as though you were expecting something different.'

'No. It's just that I have seen his education statement and it's horrendous. Apparently he was quite aggressive at his other schools. I must admit I was shocked by what I read.'

Nicola shrugged. 'He's been great with me.' We both looked down the length of the kitchen and at the children. 'It was probably learned behaviour,' she added.

'Yes, that's what I told the head. I hope Reece proves me right.'

'He will do. You worry too much. Look at him: he's fine.'

I nodded. 'Yes, he is, isn't he?'

We stayed for about half an hour, Nicola and I finishing our coffee and chatting, while Reece and Maisie finished their lunch. Then Nicola lifted Maisie out of the high chair and Reece and Maisie played with her push-along toys. Thanking Nicola again, we said our goodbyes and left.

'Can I play with Maisie again?' Reece asked in the car.

'Maybe. But tomorrow you will be playing with children your own age at school.'

'Yippee!' he yelled from the back.

'I've bought your school uniform and guess what colour it is?'

'Navy!' he yelled.

'That's right, but Reece, try not to shout. You'll be in school tomorrow and you can't shout there.'

'Why not? I did before.'

'I know, and it got you into trouble. You will need to speak more quietly at your new school. And do as you are told.'

'OK, Cathy. I will.'

'Good boy. I know you'll do just fine.'

Chapter Eleven:
An Uncertain start

I took a photograph of Reece the next morning before we left for school. He stood in the living room, grinning proudly and posing in his new school uniform with his PE bag over his shoulder. Because we were going into school early we were leaving before the girls. They stood behind me as I took the photograph, telling Reece how smart he looked and wishing him luck on his first day. It was a real family occasion for all of us, and Reece knew that we would all be thinking about him and rooting for him as he completed this milestone.

I was also looking pretty smart in my suit, as I too would be in school for the morning and presumably meeting some of the staff. With Reece chatting about all the things he anticipated doing – PE, eating lunch, making new friends and even some work – we said goodbye to the girls and got into my car, parked on the driveway. Lucy and Paula waved us off, and I drove up the road, and then took a number of 'back-doubles' to avoid the traffic in the high street. Reece was now

telling me what he thought he would be having for his
school dinner – beef burgers and tinned spaghetti
hoops, for while reducing the number of times he ate
these, I hadn't eliminated them from his diet. He ate
healthily the rest of the time, so processed was all right
once a week, and it was still his favourite meal.

I parked in the road a little way from the school and
held Reece's hand as we walked along the pavement
and up to the main gate. It wasn't security locked, as
the children would be arriving shortly to wait in the
playground until the bell rang at the start of school. I
heaved open the massive iron gate and we crossed the
playground. Reece was holding my hand very tightly
now and was uncharacteristically quiet. I could feel his
nervous anticipation, as indeed I could feel mine. It was
a big day for us both.

True to her word, Mrs Morrison was waiting for us in
reception. 'Hello,' she said, smiling first at Reece and
then at me. 'Lovely to meet you, Reece.'

'Hello,' I said. 'Reece, this is Mrs Morrison, the lady
who will be looking after you in school.'

Reece smiled sheepishly but didn't say anything. I was
reminded again of how much progress he had made,
for had this meeting taken place three months previously he would have pulled his hand from mine and
run off, making lots of loud and silly noises.

Mrs Morrison bent forward so that she was at eye
level with Reece. 'I'm going to show you round the
school first,' she said. 'Then we will join your class.
Your teacher is called Miss Broom. She is new to the
school like you.'

Reece nodded, while I thought of the maxim of new brooms sweeping clean. I also thought that Mrs Morrison, despite her inexperience as a TA, was pitching her introduction exactly right. She clearly had a natural rapport with children. Reece was happy to take her hand and the three of us exited through the door with all the 'welcome' signs and into the corridor.

'We are going to take your mum to the staff room first,' Mrs Morrison said. 'Then I'll show you the rest of the school.'

Reece looked at me questioningly and I knew why. 'Actually Reece calls me Cathy,' I said to Mrs Morrison. 'It's not so confusing for him then.' She nodded. It was a mistake made by a lot of people, calling the foster carer 'mum'. But we are always called by our first names, acknowledging that the child already has a mother, unless the child has been with the carer for years and isn't seeing his or her natural mother, in which case it is left to the child to use whatever name he or she feels comfortable with.

I followed as Mrs Morrison and Reece went up a flight of stairs and to a door on the left labelled 'staff room'. She opened the door for me and then stood aside with Reece. 'Help yourself to tea or coffee,' she said. 'Some of the staff will be in shortly. Betty, our secretary, wants to see you with some forms to sign, and also about dinner money. Betty was off sick yesterday when you visited.'

'Thank you.' I said to Mrs Morrison; then, before going into the staff room, I gave Reece a big hug and kissed his forehead. 'You have a lovely day and I'll see you at three twenty.' The head had asked that I didn't see Reece in the building, only that I was present as a precautionary measure in case there was a problem.

He returned my hug and then asked quite sensibly, 'What do I do with my coat and PE bag?'

'We will do that first,' Mrs Morrison said. 'I'll show you where your peg is in the cloakroom.'

I hugged him again; then as they turned and headed back towards the stairs, I went into the empty staff room. I didn't want a drink – I'd just had breakfast – so I sat in one of the armchairs and looked around. Carpeted in dark beige, with magnolia walls, the room was similar in its furnishings to other primary school staff rooms I'd been in. A dozen or more chairs of various shapes and sizes surrounded two long low coffee tables. There were two higher tables with computers, and lots of cupboards and work areas which were littered with piles of books and papers. There was a stainless-steel sink at one end, and beside that was a kettle with a jar of coffee and a box of tea bags. On the wall above hung a dozen or more mugs on a wooden rack. The room was light and airy, and patterned curtains hung at the windows. Staff meetings would presumably take place here, and the staff would seek respite from the school at break and lunchtimes here. I now realized that I should have brought a book with me to read, for as I understood it I would be remaining here until the end of the morning. I looked around for something to read, but there was nothing beyond piles of exercise books and paperwork that clearly belonged to individual members of staff.

The door opened and a young woman in black trousers and a light grey blouse came in.

'Mrs Glass? I'm Annette Broom, Reece's teacher. Nice to meet you.'

'And you.' We shook hands. She was in her mid-twenties, tall, with long shiny black hair, and seemed very pleasant and efficient.

'I have just met Reece briefly,' she said sitting in the chair next to mine. 'I will see him again when he comes into the class. Mrs Morrison is showing him around now. He's hung his coat on his peg. He seems fine. I've read his statement of special educational needs. We haven't heard from his social worker yet, but from what the head has told me Reece has settled with you and all the behaviour described in the statement is behind him.'

'Absolutely,' I confirmed. 'It's Reece's learning I'm more concerned with now. I've been trying to teach him a bit at home, but he is way behind.'

'Yes, I can see from his statement. I'll probably test him when he's settled in to see exactly what stage he is at. I have another child in the class, Troy, who is special needs. He hasn't had Reece's behavioural problems, but I would think that they are about the same stage academically. I have put a place next to Troy for Reece, at the same table in the classroom, so they will be company for each other.'

'Oh, that's lovely,' I said. 'Thank you so much. Reece hasn't got many friends.'

She smiled. 'It will be good for Troy too. He has difficulty making friends. Their work will be differentiated from that of the rest of the class, allowing for their needs, while still following the national curriculum.' I was really impressed for, despite the short notice of Reece's arrival, Annette Broom had clearly put a lot of thought and effort in integrating Reece back into school and making him feel welcome.

'Do tell me what I can do to help him with his learning at home,' I said. 'I'm sure he can make real improvement now. He wants to learn, and was looking forward to coming to school.'

She nodded. 'Yes, the head said. I'll be starting him on a basic reading scheme. We use the Oxford Reading Tree scheme. Are you familiar with it?' I nodded. 'I'll start Reece at level one to give him confidence and then he can go at his own pace.'

'Terrific,' I said. 'Thank you so much for all you are doing.'

'You're welcome.' She smiled. 'I need to go now, as I'm on playground duty this morning, but I'll catch up with you later. Help yourself to tea or coffee.'

'Thanks. I'm fine for now.'

As Annette Broom left the staff room another woman came in.

'I'm Betty Smith, the school secretary and general dogsbody,' she said, smiling and coming over. 'I've got some paperwork for you.'

She sat in the chair that Miss Broom had just vacated and began working through the papers on her lap. The first was Reece's school registration form, which needed all his details and the signature of his parent, together with consent forms that would allow him to do PE and go on any school outing.

'I'm going to have to get Reece's social worker to sign these,' I said. 'As his carer, I'm not allowed to, as I don't have legal parental responsibility for him.' This was the case with most forms that required the parent's signature: the local authority acting *in loco parentis* – in place of the parent – had to give the necessary permission, which in practice meant the child's social worker. 'Can I take these with me? Then I can get him to sign them while I wait.'

'Sure,' she said. I held these forms on my lap as Betty passed me the next two sheets of paper. 'Here is a copy of our term's dates,' she said, 'and also the school's policy.'

'Thank you.' I glanced at the top sheet. 'So you break up next Wednesday for Easter?'

'Yes, Easter is early this year, so it's been a short term for us.'

'That will be nice for Reece. He'll have a chance to settle in, and then have a break before the long summer term.'

She nodded, and handed me another form. 'I take it Reece is having school dinners?'

'Yes, please.'

'Can you fill in that tear-off slip for me now, please? The dinner money is £2.00 a day, which to the end of term is £14.00.' This was a form I could fill in so, taking the pen she offered me, I filled in Reece's name, and then signed the slip that said I agreed to pay in advance for his school dinner. I handed it back to the secretary, and then delved into my handbag for my purse and gave her the £14.00.

'Thank you,' she said. Then she passed me yet another form. 'This is for his dinner money for next term. You can pay weekly, half-termly or termly. It is up to you.' I looked at the list of amounts payable. It was a long term and therefore expensive. 'I'll pay half-termly,' I said. 'Would you like a cheque now?'

'That would be helpful, yes, please.'

I delved into my bag again and pulled out my cheque-book. I wrote a cheque for £70.00, tore it off and passed it to her.

'Thanks. And this is a copy of the school's prospectus,' she said, passing me the last document. 'I don't suppose the head remembered to give you one yesterday.'

'No. Thank you very much.'

'You're welcome.' She stood. 'Well, let's hope Reece settles in, for all our sakes.'

I looked at her and smiled. 'He will,' I said, and I thought that clearly Reece's reputation had preceded him, for even the school secretary who had been off sick yesterday seemed to be aware of his past.

As Betty left the staff room, a procession of teachers began entering, all saying hello and introducing themselves before leaving with a mug of coffee each. At 8.50 the bell sounded and I was alone again in the staff room. Now I had some reading material, and I began looking through the prospectus to gain a better idea of the school. In fact I read it from cover to cover before the staff room door opened again at 9.45 and the headmaster, Mr Fitzgerald, came in.

'Everything is all right so far,' he said, remaining by the door. 'Reece is with Mrs Morrison in his class-room now. If he is still all right by lunch, then you can go.'

'Fine,' I said. Although I had warmed somewhat to Mr Fitzgerald, having appreciated that his initial reaction was based on seeing Reece's statement and not knowing of his subsequent improvement, I still found his manner over-formal and cool. 'Help yourself to coffee,' he said stiffly before leaving. I did this time. Then I returned to my chair and began filling in Reece's registration forms, apart from the one that would require Jamey Hogg's signature.

I thought that, assuming I was dismissed at twelve noon, I could phone Jamey as soon as I got home and arrange to take the forms to him for signing. I also wanted to discuss with him the possibility of taking Reece on a week's holiday at Easter. I hadn't booked anything yet, but I thought it would be nice for the girls, Reece and me to have a short break at the coast. My son, Adrian, had already said he wouldn't be coming home from university for Easter – he had decided to spend two weeks with his mates in Spain. It was the first time he hadn't come home for the holidays, but I recognized that at twenty he had his own life to lead, although I still missed him.

At 10.45 the bell rang for morning break and the staff room filled again with teachers making coffee and generally chatting. Annette Broom took the opportunity to update me on what Reece had been doing so far – some number work and science, where he had had the same work sheet as Troy. Mrs Morrison had sat between them, helping them both.

'No problems?' I asked.

'No, although we have to keep reminding him to talk more quietly. It's a long time since he's been in a classroom and he's obviously excited. We're doing PE later. Has he got his PE kit?'

'Yes. He had it with him this morning.'

'Mrs Morrison will have put it on his coat peg. So I'll see you at the end of morning lessons then.' Annette Broom smiled and left to talk to a colleague. Ten minutes later the bell sounded and the staff room cleared again. It was now eleven o'clock and I flicked through the papers Mrs Morrison had given me and found that the morning finished at twelve noon. I took my mobile, which I had left on silent, from my bag, and checked the messages. There was a text from Nicola saying, 'Good luck. He'll be fine!', which was very sweet of her. I texted back: 'Thanks. He is!'

With the staff room empty, and warm, I rested my head back in the armchair and could easily have dozed off. As much as Reece had been excited about his first day at his new school, I had been excited for him and also apprehensive. Now he was here and settling in, I could relax. I felt my eyes begin to close, but then caught myself and sat upright. I could hardly be found asleep in the staff room if anyone came in. I made myself another coffee, found the staff toilet, and then wandered around the staff room looking at the notice boards, and out of the window to the playground.

A class was in the playground for PE, running around and throwing small beanbags to each other. As I looked I saw Annette Broom, and then further over Mrs Morrison with Reece. They were standing completely separately from the rest of the class, throwing a plastic football back and forth. Reece was dropping it more times than he was catching it, and I saw from his clumsy attempts just how uncoordinated he was. The reason he was doing this activity separately from the rest of the class was obvious: he could never have coordinated his movements enough to have thrown and caught the hand-sized beanbags while running at the same time. I was taken aback by seeing him now compared to his peer group. It was a stark comparison, emphasizing how much catching up Reece had to do in all things before he came anywhere near the level he should be at. I was sad for him, for I would have loved to see him completely integrated in his class. I vowed to continue to do everything possible to help him to fulfil his potential.

At midday the bell went and the staff room filled again. Mr Fitzgerald appeared and sat in the chair next to me.

'I expect you want to go now,' he said.

'Well, yes, if Reece's OK.'

He hesitated. 'He is, but he became a bit overexcited after PE. I understand from Annette Broom that he has settled down again now.' I didn't think that overexcitement was too big a crime and I hoped the head wasn't going to view any excitement on Reece's part as a sign of impending trouble. 'You go then,' he added. 'We have your mobile number if we need you.'

Clearly Mr Fitzgerald was still expecting problems, but I supposed that was natural, given Reece's school history.

'Is he having lunch now?' I asked.

'Yes. Mrs Morrison is with him.'

'All right,' I said. 'I will return at three twenty then. Do I wait in the playground?'

He thought for a moment. 'No, come into reception and I'll tell Mrs Morrison to bring Reece to you there. She can also tell you how he has been. I think Annette was hoping to see you, but she is tied up at present.'

'Thank you.' I said goodbye and made my way down the flight of stairs, along the corridor and into reception, where I let myself out. The playground was empty; presumably all the children were having their dinner in the canteen, wherever that was. And I thought that at some point I would like to be shown around the building so that I would have a better understanding of what Reece was telling me when he described his day at school.

I arrived home at 12.30, had a sandwich lunch and then phoned the social worker. He wasn't at his desk, so I left a message with a colleague, asking for him to phone back. He didn't. So at 2.30 I phoned again and Jamey answered.

'Hello, Jamey, it's Cathy, Reece's carer.'

'Hi, Cathy,' he said in his soft tranquil voice.

'I left a message earlier. Did you get it?'

'Yes. Is everything all right?'

'Reece started school today.'

'Good. Is he enjoying it?'

'Yes, I think so. Have you read his education statement?' I asked.

'No. I haven't had a chance. I've been so busy with another case.' Which seemed to be Jamey's refrain and I wondered now, as I had before, what exactly this 'other case' was that merited so much time and distracted him from the time he should be putting into Reece's case.

'His education statement is pretty horrendous,' I said, 'but I have reassured the school that Reece's behaviour is fine now. They were very apprehensive and I had to stay all morning to make sure he settled.'

'That's good,' he said leisurely.

'There are a couple of things I need to talk to you about, Jamey. First, I have a set of consent forms from the school that you need to sign. And second, I was thinking of taking Reece away for a week's holiday at Easter, possibly to Brighton. Is that OK?'

'It is with me, although I'll have to run it past mum. Will he miss contact?'

'Well, yes,' – obviously, I thought – 'on the Tuesday and Friday we are away. I can hardly bring him back from Brighton to attend contact. It's a return journey of four hundred miles.'

'No, quite.'

'So can I come into the office tomorrow morning for you to sign these forms?' I asked.

'Yes.'

'Thank you, Jamey.' Again I felt the need to give him a good kick up the backside to get him moving.

* * *

When I collected Reece from school, Mrs Morrison and Miss Broom were waiting with him in reception. All three of them were smiling, so I guessed he'd had a good afternoon. Almost.

'Can I have a quick word?' Annette Broom said, taking me to one side.

I felt that little surge of anxiety that always follows a teacher's 'Can I have a word' because invariably it means the day has been flawed by some misdemeanour. Mrs Morrison and Reece were standing together, talking about the children's work that adorned the walls in reception. Miss Broom spoke quietly and had her back to Reece, so he couldn't pick up what she was saying.

'He's been a good boy,' she said, 'apart from one small incident which I think you should be aware of. He became a bit overexcited and loud while in music, so to give him a break, Mrs Morrison took him out of the classroom and to the quiet room. As they sat down and she began reading him a story, Reece suddenly grabbed her breast.' She stopped, and looked at me, clearly embarrassed both at having to report something negative on Reece's first day and also, I suspected, by the nature of the incident. And who could blame her?

'I'm sorry you've had to deal with that,' I said. 'Is Mrs Morrison all right?'

Annette Broom nodded. 'Yes, it was a shock more than anything. She told him firmly that it wasn't acceptable behaviour and that you never touch a woman there. Then they returned to the classroom.

Mrs Morrison didn't feel comfortable with just the two of them alone in the quiet room.'

'No. I appreciate that.' I paused, choosing the right words that would allow me to give Miss Broom enough information so that she could take the necessary measures and reduce the likelihood of it happening again, while not breaking confidentiality. In an ideal world the social worker would have given background information to the school. 'We had a similar incident at home with my teenage daughter,' I said, 'when Reece first came to me. But I dealt with it and it hasn't been repeated, although Reece does still sometimes try to hug us inappropriately. From what I understand he witnessed a lot of inappropriate sexual behaviour while at home. I'm still waiting for the social worker to give me some more background information. I think Reece is testing the boundaries here and Mrs Morrison was right in making him immediately aware that it wasn't acceptable behaviour. I will speak to him as soon as we get home. Can I also suggest Mrs Morrison continues to make sure she isn't completely alone with Reece, and puts a bit of distance between them, until he has settled in?'

Annette Broom nodded. 'It would mean not using the quiet room. It's where we take children if they need time out to calm down.'

'For the time being I think that would be a good idea, until Reece understands that what he has learned at home with us applies to school as well.' She nodded. 'I will speak to him firmly,' I added. 'He should know it's not acceptable behaviour.'

'Thank you,' she said. 'Apart from that he's had a good afternoon.'

'Excellent,' I said. 'I won't say anything to Reece now in front of Mrs Morrison because it could be embarrassing for her. But please explain to her and give her my apologies.'

'I will do.'

I returned to Reece and thanked Mrs Morrison for all she was doing. Reece said goodbye to her and Miss Broom.

'See you tomorrow,' Mrs Morrison said as we went to the door. 'It's normal start time, eight fifty, but will you bring Reece into reception again? Mr Fitzgerald thinks it a good idea for now.'

'Yes, will do, and thanks again.' Taking a special needs child directly into school rather than leaving them in the playground was something I was used to. It gave the carer and TA a chance to pass on any relevant information that might affect the child, and also gave the child a safe and calm passage in and out of school. Special needs children can be very vulnerable, particularly in a big playground.

Once we were home I sat Reece down in the living room and went through the rules relating to our bodies and what we called our private parts again. I let him know I was aware of how he had touched Mrs Morrison, for he needed to understand that appropriate behaviour was needed everywhere, not just with us at home. He said he couldn't remember the incident, and I wasn't going to resurrect it and labour the point, so I finished by saying: 'Remember, Reece, you don't touch anyone else's private parts – not at home, or school, or anywhere. Not on a child or adult.'

He nodded, and the evening continued happily, with Reece recounting over and over again what had gone well for him at school.

He settled easily that night, exhausted from the day, and before I knew it, it was morning again and Reece and I were in the car in our new school routine.

When we arrived, the playground was full of children playing before the bell rang, when they would line up. We entered reception and Mrs Morrison was already there, spot on 8.50, to welcome us.

'Morning, Reece,' she said brightly.

'Morning.' Reece grinned.

I felt I had to say something to Mrs Morrison in addition to whatever Annette Broom had said yesterday, just to let her know that I had taken the matter seriously and had spoken to Reece. 'We have spoken,' I said pointedly. 'I'm sure it won't happen again.'

She smiled and nodded. 'Thank you. Annette had a chat with me yesterday.'

'Good. And thanks for all you are doing for Reece. It's much appreciated.' I said goodbye to her and Reece and, leaving the building, returned to my car. I drove straight to the social services with the school forms for signing in my handbag.

At the council offices I gave my name, showed my ID to the receptionist and said that Jamey Hogg was expecting me. 'Go on up,' she said. I climbed the two flights of stairs to the floor occupied by the social services and entered the open-plan office. Jamey was at his desk with his back to me. As I approached, unseen from behind, I had to resist the temptation to tweak his ponytail.

'Oh, hi,' he said looking up as I came into view, and vaguely surprised. 'What are you doing here?'

'Reece's registration and consent forms for school,' I said.

'Oh yes. Have a seat.' He pulled up a colleague's chair that was empty. The office was slowly filling as social workers came in and turned on their computers.

I took the forms from my bag and, unfolding them, quickly explained what each one was for. He signed and dated them, crossing out the word 'parent' in the printed 'parent's signature' and writing 'social worker' underneath. It took only a couple of minutes and once he had finished I refolded them and tucked them back into my bag.

'Have you had a chance to speak to Tracey yet?' I asked. He looked at me questioningly. 'About my taking Reece on holiday at Easter?'

'Oh, yes,' he said with a jolt of memory. 'Good and bad news, I'm afraid. Mum is OK, sort of, about you taking him away, but won't have him missing contact.'

'That makes it difficult,' I said. 'Can't she be persuaded to change her mind? It is her son who is benefiting, after all. Reece doesn't know what a holiday is, apart from the sort his dad takes when he disappears after being found guilty in the magistrate's court.'

Jamey smiled. 'Unfortunately not. Tracey is very angry, and to be honest I don't want to upset her further at present. Can you go away for a few days between contacts, instead of a week? I don't want Reece to lose out.'

'Neither do I,' I said, 'and it seems that might be the only option. It will mean leaving very early on a Wednesday morning and having him back by 6.00 p.m. on Friday.' It hardly seemed worth it, but I was determined to give Reece a holiday of some sort, and even if I waited until summer, it was quite likely that the same restraints of contact would apply. 'So I have your permission to go ahead and book something then?' I clarified.

'Yes.' Jamey leant back nonchalantly in his chair. 'Will you email me the details so I have them on file?'

'Yes. And I'll also send you a copy of my log notes. There was an incident of sexualized behaviour at school yesterday – nothing major, but you need to be aware of it.'

'OK, fine. I'm going to a meeting soon, so we will have to discuss it another time.'

'Sure,' I said. I stood to leave.

'And by the way,' he added, swivelling round in his chair, 'there's a child protection case conference on Friday morning. You will be able to attend?'

I looked at him. 'Tomorrow?'

'Yes. It's to deregister Reece and take his name off the child protection register now that he's in care.'

I nodded. I had known there would be a child protection case conference, because once a child is in care the concerns surrounding the child when he or she was at home no longer apply, so the child is removed from the child protection register (CPR). However, I didn't know when it would be and I could have done with a bit more notice. I wondered how long Jamey had known of the date and when he would have told me had I not come into the office.

'What time?' I asked.

He swivelled his chair towards his desk and drew himself forward to his computer. I looked away from the screen as he clicked the mouse, for quite obviously there would be a lot of confidential files on his computer, unrelated to Reece's case, and which were no business of mine.

'Ten o'clock,' he said at last. Thank goodness, I thought, because if it had been in the afternoon I would have had to make arrangements to have Reece collected from school, at very short notice. 'It's here,' he added, 'in the conference room.'

'OK,' I said. 'I'll see you tomorrow then.'

'Yes, and thanks for bringing in the forms.'

'You're welcome.' It was no use getting annoyed with Jamey, not yet anyway; it was just his laid-back nature.

I put the rest of the day to good use. I caught up on the housework, made a cottage pie for dinner that evening and read a chapter of the novel I'd started before Reece had arrived in January. I left in good time to collect him for the end of school at 3.20. When I arrived, the playground was starting to fill with parents and carers waiting for the bell to ring, when the children would stream out. I went up the steps and into reception, where I waited until bell sounded. A couple of minutes later Reece appeared, grinning broadly. Mrs Morrison, his TA, was with him and also the head, Mr Fitzgerald.

'Hello, Cathy,' Reece cried, happy to see me again. He rushed into my arms.

'Have you had a good day?' I asked, hugging him.

'Yeah.' He looked up at me and grinned.

Mr Fitzgerald hovered. 'Can I have a word, please, Mrs Glass?' he said. My heart sank. We stood to one side in reception while Mrs Morrison and Reece once again looked at the children's artwork. 'You're aware of the incident yesterday involving Mrs Morrison?' The head began, speaking quietly and dispassionately.

'Yes,' I said, nodding. 'I spoke to Reece.'

He looked at me carefully. 'We've had another incident today. At lunchtime in the canteen. Reece was sitting at a table with a few others, Mrs Morrison was close by supervising him, and he put his hand under the table and tried to interfere with the girl sitting next to him.'

'What do you mean by "interfere"?' I asked. It was no use resorting to euphemisms: I needed the details so that I could speak to Reece, and also to record in my log and inform the social worker.

'He put his hand up the girl's tunic,' Mr Fitzgerald said.

'And did what? Tickled her knees?'

'No, it was worse than that. He pushed his hand straight up to her pants and said, "Can I feel your fanny?" The girl was very shocked, as you can imagine. So were we.'

'Yes,' I said. I was shocked and dismayed. Hadn't Reece listened to anything I'd said to him the evening before? And why did he feel he could do this at school, when he knew very well it was completely unacceptable behaviour with us at home?

'I'll speak to him,' I said. 'Very firmly. I did talk to him last night at some length, but clearly it was not enough. I am so sorry. Is the girl all right?'

'She is now. Obviously I will need to speak to her mother. Annette Broom is in the playground now, trying to find her. Mrs Glass, will you please make it clear to Reece that this behaviour is completely unacceptable? We will not tolerate it in school.'

'Yes, of course. I thought I had made it clear last night, but obviously the message hasn't sunk in.'

'And I will need to speak to his social worker,' Mr Fitzgerald added. 'He needs to be informed and I want more details from him about Reece. We are going to have to be very careful when it comes to changing for PE. Our school is a safe place and has to remain so for all our children.' I totally agreed with him.

'I'm sorry,' I said again. 'I will speak to Reece. Has he apologized to the girl involved?'

'No. She doesn't want to see him, understandably.'

I nodded. 'When you see her mother, will you pass on my apologies, please?'

'Yes. And if I don't speak to the social worker before, I will see him about this at the child protection case conference tomorrow.'

'You're going?'

'Yes, I've been invited, although my input will be minimal as Reece has only just started here. Now I need to see the girl's mother. Please make sure you speak to Reece.'

'Yes, I intend to, and severely.'

I was quiet in the car as I drove Reece home. When he began chatting about his day at school, clearly unaware there was any fallout from what he had done, I stopped him.

'Reece,' I said, glancing at him in the rear-view mirror. 'I am not happy. I will hear about your day later. First I need to talk to you about something very serious that happened today. Can you think what it could be?'

'No,' he said. 'I had a good day. I did lots of work and …' He was off again talking about what he had done at school, minus the incident.

Once home, I sat him down in the living room and, being direct, I told him exactly what he had done, and why it was very wrong. Again, he claimed not to remember; then he agreed with everything I said about our private parts being private. I went over the areas of the body that we didn't touch on other people, and he nodded and said 'Yes, Cathy' to every statement.

I looked at him. I wasn't convinced that even now he fully appreciated what I was saying. Seven years of living in an environment where it was possibly considered acceptable to grab and feel another person's private parts would take some undoing. But what I didn't understand was why Reece had stopped behaving like this at home with us but felt it was acceptable at school.

Unless it was my influence, in which case the school would have to invest a lot of time in building up the same guidelines and respect for the people there as those Reece now had for Lucy, Paula and me. It was true that he did still try to kiss us on the lips sometimes, rather than the cheek, and that his cuddles were a bit lingering towards me and I had to gently finish them and ease him away. But he hadn't repeated the overt sexual touching since he had first arrived, and he never spoke about sex in the crude terms he had when he had talked about 'giving the girls one'.

'All right, Reece,' I said at last. 'Just remember what I have told you. It's probably best if you don't touch anyone at school. There is no need to, and then you can't possibly get into trouble for touching in the wrong way.'

He nodded, and I let him watch children's television, while I put the cottage pie in the oven to heat. While it heated I went to my computer and searched online to see about booking up a few days' holiday at Easter. We ate and the evening passed happily. In the morning I would be taking Reece into reception at 8.50, and then going straight to the child protection case conference. If it followed the format of the previous ones I had attended, then, apart from taking Reece's name off the child's protection register, it should also enable me to learn more about Reece's background and the reasons for him being taken into care.

Chapter Twelve:

The Wider Family Picture

The oblong oak table in the conference room was laid out formally, with a set of case conference notes and a glass of water for each person. Places had been set for nine people, which was about the number I would have expected to attend. As I sat in one of the leather chairs I smiled at the two women seated opposite. I didn't know who they were, but they knew each other, and they were talking quietly between themselves as the room slowly filled. I slipped off my coat and draped it over the back of my chair. Then I took the opportunity to read the CP (child protection) case conference notes that were on the table. It was quite a thick bundle, stapled at one corner.

The top sheet gave the date and reasons for the meeting, and listed those who would be attending, together with those who had sent apologies for absence. The next page was the minutes of the previous CP meeting, which I quickly read. Behind these were three reports – from the police, social worker and Reece's previous doctor. There was no report from the school, which was hardly surprising as Reece had only been there a few days, and no report from me, which there should have been, had I been sent the relevant forms.

I began reading the police report. Then Jill arrived. I'd emailed to say the conference was taking place but she hadn't been sure she could attend. I was pleased to see her.

'How are you?' she said, sitting on my right.

'Good.' I smiled. 'Thanks for coming.'

'I thought I'd give you a bit of moral support. Hopefully we'll learn something.' She began reading her set of notes as the door opened again and another woman entered, whom I didn't know. She sat on my left and we exchanged a 'good morning'. Then she too looked at her notes. A couple of minutes later the head, Mr Fitzgerald, appeared, and took a seat at the table opposite me. I guessed I was the only familiar face, for it was to me he directed his 'hello'. Two more women came in and sat together at one end of the table. The last to arrive was Jamey. As he entered and looked down the length of the table, I was surprised to see that his usual calm demeanour had been ruffled and he appeared flustered.

'Morning,' he said, out of breath and taking the vacant chair next to the head. The rest of us murmured, 'Good morning,' while Mr Fitzgerald took the opportunity to introduce himself and they shook hands.

I hadn't finished reading the notes when one of the two women at the end of the table opened the meeting.

'I'm Kim Stacey,' the woman said. 'I shall be chairing this case conference, which is in respect of Reece

Williams. The purpose of this meeting is to review the health, development and safety of the child, and to decide if his name needs to remain on the Child Protection Register. Apologies for absence have been received from the GP, the designated CP nurse, the education welfare officer, the family worker, the principal solicitor and the team manager.' There was no need for these people to attend, as either their input would be covered by someone else present or their involvement had finished when Reece had been taken into care. They had been asked to attend as a formality, having attended previous CP conferences.

The chairperson then said she wanted to draw attention to the fact that Reece's parents had been excluded from attending the conference because of their 'abusive and threatening behaviour towards professionals and others in the past'. For the parents to be excluded from the meeting was unusual but not unexpected, I thought.

Jamey, who still had a high colour and was uncharacteristically on edge, then addressed the chair. 'Could I add that I have just been speaking to Tracey, Reece's mother. She is outside the building now, although she was informed by her solicitor that she wasn't allowed to attend. She is very angry and we have two security guards with her to stop her from entering the building. I have tried talking to her but it is impossible. I am assuming she will be gone by the end of this meeting, but I suggest that those of you whom she knows by sight should take particular care when leaving the building. She has been known to lie in wait and assault staff. The security guards will remain there until the meeting has finished, but they only have jurisdiction in the building, not the car park.'

Eyes met across the table as we exchanged sober glances.

'I take it she doesn't know me? ' Mr Fitzgerald said dryly.

'No,' Jamey said; then, looking round the table: 'She knows Cathy, Kirsty and the county nurse.'

'Don't worry. I'll see you out,' Jill whispered to me.

'Thanks,' I returned. I saw the minute-taker noting what Jamey had just said.

'Thank you, Jamey,' the chairperson said. 'Now, we seem to have got a bit ahead of ourselves because of this, so can we continue with the introductions. I'm Kim Stacey, the chairperson and conference organizer. Next to me is our minute-taker, Hannah Giles.' Hannah looked up from writing and smiled. We then went round the table introducing ourselves. Apart from the chairperson and the minute-taker there were Jamey, Jill and Tom Fitzgerald, whom I knew, and three people I didn't know – Kirsty (the police liaison officer), and two nurses, one the county nurse and the other the school nurse for the area.

Introductions over, the chairperson looked at me. 'Cathy, would you like to start by telling us how Reece is doing? He came to you in January after a number of moves.'

'Yes, that's correct,' I said. I sat upright and looked at those present. I still felt a bit nervous addressing meetings, even after the hundreds I'd had to attend in the twenty-plus years I had been fostering. I knew I had to remember to speak slowly, because sometimes when I'm nervous I speed up and gabble. 'Reece has settled in very well indeed,' I said, 'and his behaviour has improved dramatically. He still needs reminding some-times about what is acceptable but he wants to do the right thing, and accepts the guidelines I have set. He eats well and sleeps well, and joins in all family activi-ties. He likes going to the cinema, ice-skating and play-ing in the park. When Reece first came to me he appeared to have been given no responsibility for himself and could do very little. Now he takes care of his own hygiene and can dress himself. He is a special needs child but he is willing to learn, and can learn slowly. He often needs reassurance for quite small tasks. At present we are working towards him tying his own shoelaces. I always hold his hand when we are out in the street, as he has no sense of danger. He is a long way behind with his learning and has only just been found a new school.' I glanced at Mr Fitzgerald and he nodded. 'We have had some incidents of sexualized behaviour and I have made his social worker aware of these. Reece is a loving boy but he can become hyperac-tive, so I make sure he has some form of exercise every day. I'm also careful with his diet.' The chairperson nodded and smiled. 'Reece has some understanding of why he is in care, and obviously I will be talking to him more about this as time goes on. However, for Reece, "being in care" seems quite normal, as all his half-siblings are. Reece and I meet up with his half-sister Susie and her carer every three weeks, and although

Reece enjoys this outing he never mentions his sister in between meetings.'

'Does he ever mention his parents?' the chairperson asked.

'No. Never. If I ask him anything about his home, like "Did you have a garden?" he says, "Don't know."'

Jamey nodded. 'I have witnessed this. When I visited Reece at Cathy's home and tried to talk to him he repeatedly resorted to "Don't know" as a means of evasion. My feeling is he has been sworn to secrecy, possibly even threatened by his mother.'

'Yes,' the chairperson agreed, 'without a doubt. I have met her and she can be very frightening when angry. Why she keeps having all these children when there is no hope of her looking after them I will never know.' Good question, I thought, as no doubt many of the others present were also thinking, but it was a personal view and not part of the proceedings. 'Do you think Reece is frightened of his mother?' she asked me.

I paused. 'It's difficult to say. When I used to take and collect Reece for contact he appeared to have a much better relationship with his father than with his mother.'

'You don't see him with his parents now?'

'No. An escort takes Reece and brings him home.'

'It wasn't felt safe for Cathy to continue,' Jamey put in. 'Tracey refused to say goodbye to Reece in the building and subjected Cathy to a lot of intimidation and verbal abuse in the car park.'

'I see,' the chairperson said. I saw Mr Fitzgerald look-ing at me, and looking very concerned. He was clearly worried by what he was hearing, and with good reason. 'Thank you, Cathy,' the chairperson said. 'And thank you for taking such good care of Reece.'

I smiled and relaxed, for although I would be contributing to the discussion later, the spotlight was off me. All eyes were now going towards Jamey as the chairperson said: 'Would you like to tell us about Reece and his family now, James, please?'

Jamey had now calmed down from his earlier run-in with Tracey and had resumed his usual pallor and relaxed demeanour. 'Reece was brought into care on an Interim Care Order,' he said languidly, 'and I was assigned the case at the beginning of the year. I was on annual leave until the end of February, so I am still getting to grips with the case. I am also the social worker for all the other siblings. The family has a long history, and has been known to the social services for over fifteen years. I am in the process of gathering together all the files for this case, which I have so far located in five different buildings. The family has moved around a lot, in this county and others. This partly explains why there has been no continuity, or any overall picture. Had there been, I believe Reece and Susie would have been taken into care years ago. The family has a history of violence, both in the home and outside. Scott, Reece's father, has served a number of prison sentences for drink-related assault, and at least one paedophile has been visiting the house. For what purpose no one knows. Tracey is aggressive and volatile, and in the past has assaulted social workers, teachers, carers, police officers, other adults and even children. Although she has been arrested on many occasions she has never been sentenced.'

'Why not?' the chairperson asked, amazed.

'I don't know. Perhaps the police liaison officer can help. My guess is that Tracey makes such a commotion and shouts so loudly that the police and others are just pleased to get her out of the building, as we are here. I have come across over a hundred incidents on file where the police were called to affrays where she was involved.'

Kirsty, the police liaison officer, nodded. 'I think you're probably right about wanting to get her out of the police station,' she said. 'There is always at least one investigation pending where Tracey has accused a police officer of assaulting her. Over the years we have received hundreds of these formal complaints. We know they are rubbish but we still have to go through the whole lengthy and costly process of investigating them. In some instances the police officer involved has had to be suspended pending the investigation. The woman knows her rights and knows how to work the system. She has made a full-time career out of threatening and accusing the police. We think she likes the attention. And the elder children are turning out the same, particularly Sharon.'

The chairperson nodded sadly, and there was a pause as we considered what Kirsty had said. What a dreadfully sad state of affairs, I thought, particularly if the children were following in Tracey's footsteps, despite being taken into care and having the benefit of a fresh start. After a moment the chairperson looked to Jamey to continue.

'I have found a psychologist's report that was written ten years ago,' he said. 'It says, even then, that Tracey has a poor grasp of reality, and an IQ equivalent to that of an eight-year-old child. She and the children – Sharon, Brad, Sean, Reece and Susie – all have learning difficulties. The only child who doesn't is Lisa, who lives with an aunt.'

'Does Lisa have a different father?' the chairperson asked, wondering, as I had, if a different set of genes could provide the answer.

'Yes,' Jamey said. 'But so do all the children.'

'And who are the fathers of the other siblings? Do we know?' the chairperson asked.

'No, the fathers' names were never registered on the birth certificates, apart from Reece's,' Jamey said.

'And why was that?' the chairperson asked.

'Apparently Scott insisted he was on Reece's birth certificate. I don't know why the other fathers weren't shown. Perhaps the fathers weren't aware of the births. Tracey wasn't in a relationship with any of them, and as far as I can see we don't even have their names.'

'I see. Thank you,' the chairperson said. 'Please continue, James.'

'I have not visited the family home but I have read a number of reports of colleagues who have. The house was always very dirty, and Susie and Reece were uncared for, and sometimes unfed. There was never any food in the cupboards or fridge. There were no carpets and very little furniture, apart from a wide-screen television, which Reece watched endlessly. Susie spent most of her waking hours sucking her thumb and rocking on the mattress where she slept. Reece slept on the same mattress or on some blankets. The heating was rarely on in winter, and concerns were expressed about gross neglect since the time Reece was born. Susie and Reece were finally removed following Tracey's assault on Susie, and also because the paedophile was still visiting, despite Tracey having been warned about this.'

'I take it Tracey won't know which school Reece is attending,' Mr Fitzgerald put in.

'No,' Jamey said. 'Although it's possible she may find out.'

'How?' The head asked, almost demanded.

'Reece could tell her at contact, or she might hear it through the grapevine,' Jamey said. 'She is well known round the estate, which is only a mile from the school and Cathy.'

'Is it wise to have Reece living so close to his mother?' Mr Fitzgerald asked, clearly very concerned. I looked at Jamey and the chair.

'No,' Jamey said. 'But the placement team were running out of options of where to put Reece. He needed a carer with a lot of experience, and Cathy was the only one who was free and suitable in the whole of the county.'

'And what happens if his mother should come to the school?' Mr Fitzgerald continued.

'You could try talking to her at the gate,' Jamey said. 'But don't let her into the building. She is not allowed to see Reece, apart from at the supervised contact. If she won't go quietly, then call the police.' The police liaison officer raised her eyes to heaven, as though imploring help.

Tom Fitzgerald was visibly shaken by all he'd heard and I sympathized. Most childcare cases weren't this fraught, and sometimes the natural mothers liaised with the school, and accompanied the carers to school functions and parents' evenings.

'Can you make sure Reece doesn't know the name of the school?' he asked me.

'I'll do my best,' I said, but I silently acknowledged that it was going to be difficult, for what was I to say when Reece asked me the name of his school, which he was bound to do eventually? Make up a name or say that I didn't know? Apart from which, Tracey knew the area and would know that there were only three primary schools in the vicinity to choose from. It wouldn't take her long to find which one Reece attended if she positioned herself outside each school gate in turn at 3.20 p.m.

'I'll have to alert the school staff,' the head said; then, as though reading my thoughts, 'and perhaps, Mrs Glass, you could start collecting Reece a bit earlier? Say three o'clock?'

'Yes,' I said. 'If you wish.' But here would be yet another occasion when Reece would be standing out as different from his peers, as he was in PE by having a TA at his side continually, and when I took him in and collected him from reception instead of the playground.

'From today, please,' he added to me; then, addressing the chair, 'Could I give my report now, as I really should be getting back to school?'

Kim nodded.

'I haven't much to say, as this is only Reece's third day with us,' the head began, 'but what I would say is that the manner in which I was forced to accept Reece into my school amounted to bullying.' All those present, apart from Jamey and me, looked at him questioningly, unaware of what he was referring to. 'The judge in this case gave a directive to the education department that Reece had to be in school immediately,' he clarified. 'My school was chosen for no other reason than that it had a vacancy and is local to where Reece now lives. I was forced to accept him.'

No one commented: it was outside the remit of the conference to pass an opinion on this, although his comments were noted by the minute-taker.

'However,' Mr Fitzgerald continued, 'while I do not believe it is the most suitable school for a child with Reece's schooling history, we are doing our best. And I have his carer's reassurance that his behaviour has improved. Reece is at the level one would normally expect to see in a reception class – about the age of four and a half. He is still working towards Key Stage 1, and has a full TA support, including lunch and playtime.' The head continued by quoting the results of some tests which had been done at Reece's previous school, and which underlined the level of his needs. He said it was his history of behavioural difficulties that gave him the greatest concern, particularly as he had already been involved in two incidents of a sexual nature.

The chairperson stopped him to ask what these were, and Mr Fitzgerald described what had happened. Then the chairperson looked to Jamey and me for further comment. Jamey explained that Reece had been exposed to inappropriate sexual behaviour at home, and that the social services knew for certain he had watched X-rated adult videos, but added that no one really knew the full extent of what had been happening.

'Do you think Reece has been sexually abused?' the chairperson asked him.

'It's impossible to say at present,' Jamey said. 'There is an investigation going on at present into Scott, Reece's father, in respect of allegations Susie, his stepdaughter, has made against him. There is nothing to suggest that Reece was also sexually abused by Scott, although it is possible.'

'Not by his own father, surely?' the head asked, disgusted.

'We can't rule it out,' Jamey said. Mr Fitzgerald looked absolutely appalled, but I knew, as Jamey did, that such horrendous abuse did happen in families, even by fathers of their sons. 'And there was a paedophile visiting the house,' Jamey added.

'Do you think Reece has been sexually abused?' the chairperson asked me.

I could only agree with what Jamey had said. 'I don't know. It's possible. Reece can touch inappropriately, but we haven't seen any overtly sexualized behaviour since he first arrived. I think it will be a long time before Reece tells anyone, as Tracey appears to have quite a hold over him.'

The chairperson nodded. 'Thank you, Cathy.' The minute-taker wrote. Mr Fitzgerald finished his contribution as he had begun by saying that in view of Reece being in his school for only a few days, it was too early to comment on his progress, but that everything was being done to accommodate him.

The chairperson thanked the head for coming and Mr Fitzgerald left the conference. The two nurses were then asked to give their reports, which were brief. The community nurse confirmed Reece's immunizations were up to date, and his weight and height were within the normal range. She said she had known the family for a year, and had expressed concerns about Reece (and Susie) when she'd first visited the home. She was pleased the children were now in care and being well looked after. The school nurse followed, and said that she hadn't met Reece yet but would be seeing him after Easter when she was scheduled to visit the school. She said she would be testing his eyesight and hearing, as she would that of the other children in his year.

All that remained now was to hear from Kirsty, the police liaison officer, who had already spoken briefly when she had outlined recent police involvement. She started by drawing our attention to her report in the case notes, and we all turned to the relevant document. Her report had a list of dates on the left-hand side of each page, and a corresponding paragraph on the right, which set out the incident to which the police had been called.

Kirsty summarized as we read, and her report was a shocking indication of the high level of involvement the police had had with this family. Twenty-four separate incidents were listed, and that was only in the last three

months, since the last CP conference at the beginning
of the year. Sharon, Tracey's eldest child, who lived in a
teenager residential care home in the county, featured
strongly, as did Tracey. Sharon had been picked up on
the streets by the police for being drunk and under the
influence of drugs, and for assaulting a member of the
public. On each occasion she had been given a cooling-
off period at the police station before being returned to
the care home. On two occasions when she had been
taken to the police station Sharon had hit an officer and
then accused him of assaulting her, threatening him
with her mother's solicitor. On another occasion Sharon
had been found in a locked children's playground at
midnight, crying hysterically, and having tried to cut
her wrists. The police had taken her to hospital and she
had later been discharged with the wound sutured.
Sharon had been offered counselling but had refused it.
'All the older children have been offered counselling,'
Kirsty said, 'but none of them has attended.'

The next list of incidents were assaults by Tracey – on
a doctor, a social worker, members of the public, a
shopkeeper, an ex-teacher of Reece's, neighbours, Scott
and finally Susie. Each time the police had been called
they'd had to physically restrain Tracey, which had
resulted in her accusing them of assault. Tracey had
been taken to the police station six times during this
three-month period, but after a verbal warning had
been released. Tracey and Sharon had been picked up
together on two occasions in the high street, late at
night and both drunk. The second of these incidents
had occurred in early February, a couple of weeks after

Reece had come to me. When the police had asked Tracey and Sharon what they were doing they had said they were going to see 'Reece's new foster carer'. Kirsty said she didn't know if they had my address or if it was bluff.

Kim, the chairperson, sighed and looked at me. 'If any of the family does come to your house you must call the police immediately.'

'Yes,' I said. 'I will.' And I meant it.

'And I should be careful in the high street,' Kirsty added. 'Tracey and Sharon are often there during the day as well as at night.'

'Yes,' I said, wondering where exactly it was safe for me to go.

'Isn't Sharon supposed to be back in the care home by nine thirty?' the chairperson asked.

'Yes,' Kirsty replied. 'But she never is, and there is nothing they can do about it. It's not a secure unit: they can't lock her in.'

The next two incidents detailed when the police had been called to the care home after Sharon had been fighting another resident. Although this case conference wasn't about Sharon, Kirsty's report was important to the conference as it set Reece in the wider family picture.

The last five dates detailed incidents when the police had been called to the council offices when Tracey had been ejected by the security guards but had refused to leave the car park. She seemed to make a habit of standing in the car park and accosting staff and members of the public as they walked in and out of the building.

Kirsty came to the end of her report and stopped. The room was quiet.

'Good heavens!' Jill whispered under her breath to me.

'I know,' I said. 'Just as well the head isn't present to hear this lot.'

'Absolutely,'

'It's dreadful,' the chairperson said. Then, looking at Jamey: 'What are the long-term plans for Reece?'

'Assuming we are granted a full-care order at the final hearing in September, we will be looking for a long-term carer, as far away from this area as possible. We hope Reece and Susie will be the ones we can save in all this.'

The chairperson nodded in agreement. 'Does anyone want to add anything?'

'It's a pity Sharon can't be moved out of the area too,' Kirsty said, 'right away from Tracey's influence, but I guess it's too late.'

Jamey agreed. 'Sharon is eighteen now. She will be leaving care soon. I understand she wants to go back to her mother. There's nothing we can do to stop her.'

'Is the paedophile still visiting the family home?' the chairperson asked, obviously concerned.

'Yes,' Jamey said. 'That's one of the reasons why Sharon wants to go back home. She says she fancies him and he fancies her. ' My stomach lurched and I heard Jill sigh. The case just got worse and worse. 'There have also been suggestions,' Jamey continued, 'that Scott has been having a sexual relationship with Sharon as well, but there is no proof.'

'That's correct,' Kirsty said. 'Sharon made an allegation against Scott nearly a year ago, but withdrew it under pressure from Tracey. The latest I have heard is that Sharon is claiming to be pregnant.'

Jamey nodded. 'But it could just be fantasy – she has made similar claims before. Let's hope it is.'

We were all quiet again. Clearly there was no end to the abuse that was being perpetrated in one form or another in this family. I would like to say that I had never heard anything like it before but sadly I had. Not too often, fortunately, but there are families who seem to flaunt all the laws of morality and exist at a basic, almost feral level.

All that remained now was for the conference to go through the formality of deregistering Reece by taking his name off the child protection register, now that he was no longer living at home and in need of the monitoring and protection that being on the register allowed. The chairperson asked us each in turn if we agreed to the deregistration, and we all said yes. This was minuted. Then the chairperson thanked us all for coming, and said again what a sad case it was. She thanked me for all I was doing for Reece, and we stood to leave.

'Who is leaving the building apart from me?' the chairperson asked.

'I am,' I said. So too were Kirsty, Jill and the nurses. So the five of us left the conference room together and went downstairs and into reception. The two security guards were at the main entrance and Kay, who had been chairing, asked them if Tracey was in the area.

'We don't think so,' one of them said.

We left the building in a vigilant little crowd, and then went our separate ways to our cars. Jill came with me to mine, and waited until I had driven away.

It was with a sad and heavy heart that I drove the twenty-minute drive home, my thoughts entirely occupied by Reece and his life before he came into care. It didn't make it any easier having heard of similar families before: each child is an individual with their own personal suffering. In some ways it made it worse, as all the work seemed a bit pointless, like a small drop in a very large ocean. Social services had been trying to help Tracey's family for years, yet from what I'd heard today, their efforts had come to nothing. And while Reece and Susie, being younger, might have a chance to escape the cycle of abuse, I wondered about the damage that had already been done to them, and the wounds that were now festering. Certainly Reece (and Susie) must have suffered dreadfully and for a long time. Reece must now be starting to see that the life he led with his mum was not normal, compared to the life he now led in care. But unless he lost some of his fear, and started to talk, his wounds could continue to fester for years to come.

My thoughts were still sombre as I pulled onto my driveway at nearly one o'clock. It had been a long meeting and apart from a glass of water, I had not had anything since breakfast at 7.00 a.m. I opened the front door and was looking forward to lunch, and sitting quietly for a few minutes, but it wasn't to be. The light on the answerphone was flashing, signalling a message. As I played it back my spirits sunk even lower.

It was Betty, the school secretary. 'Please come to the school as soon as you get this message. Reece has stabbed a member of staff with a pencil. He is now excluded.'

Chapter Thirteen:

A 'Done Bad' Day

The message from the school secretary was timed at 11.37, over an hour before. Having just closed the front door, I opened it again and returned to my car. I drove fast, my thoughts reeling. I felt hot and slightly nauseous. The head had left the meeting at 11.15, so I presumed the incident had happened while he'd been at the child protection case conference, and he had dealt with it by issuing this exclusion on his return to school.

It was the end of the lunchtime play when I arrived at the school, and the children were lining up in the playground, ready to go in for the afternoon lessons. I pressed the security buzzer and the gate clicked open without my having to give my name. Likewise as I went up the steps to the main door it opened from inside.

'The head wants to see you straightaway,' Betty, the secretary, said. I guessed she'd been watching for my arrival from her office, which overlooked the main entrance. 'He's in his office. You know where it is – down the corridor, and then left.'

'Thank you,' I said. I opened the door with all the 'welcome' signs and then went along the corridor to Mr Fitzgerald's office. The door was closed, so I knocked.

'Come in,' he called brusquely.

Mr Fitzgerald was seated behind his massive desk and speaking on the phone. He gestured to the armchair in front of his desk and I sat down. I noticed he didn't make eye contact as he wound up the phone conversation. Only when he'd replaced the receiver did he look at me, and there wasn't an ounce of warmth.

'Mrs Glass, while we were at the case conference there was a very serious incident here. My deputy dealt with it as best she could but it has shocked everyone.'

I met his gaze and waited for the details.

'Mrs Morrison was helping Reece in the classroom during a science lesson when it happened. Reece had been annoying Troy, whom he sits next to, on and off for the whole of the lesson. I understand he kept poking Troy in the ribs, and going up close to him and making loud noises in his ear. Mrs Morrison asked Reece to stop many times and eventually she sat between them. At that point Reece shouted to her, "Get the fuck out of here." Then he stabbed the back of her hand with his sharp pencil. It pierced the skin and I have sent her to the hospital for a tetanus injection.'

The head paused, but continued to look at me. I hadn't got a clue what to say, but my expression said it all – I was mortified.

'Everyone is shocked,' he continued. 'The children in the class are very upset at seeing a beloved member of staff attacked in this way, and also by Reece's shouting.

He was completely out of control. It took his class teacher ten minutes to persuade him to leave the room.'

'Where is he now?' I asked, sombrely.

'In the quiet room, with my other two TAs. They have had to leave the children they were working with, but I wasn't having one TA alone with Reece. It isn't safe. That child is dangerous. He's an animal.'

Upon hearing Reece being described and segregated in this way, my first instinct was to protect and defend him, but what could I say? Clearly it was a vicious attack and on a lovely lady who was kindness itself, and had gone to a lot of trouble to look after Reece and help him. 'I'm so sorry,' I said at last. 'I really don't know what else to say. Is Mrs Morrison all right now?'

'I shall phone her later. I have told her to go home after she has been to the hospital. Apart from the shock of the physical injury she was very upset that Reece should attack her. She's taken it personally.' The head was looking at me intently now, awaiting an explanation, which I didn't have. 'Has there been an incident like this with you or when he was with his previous carers?' he asked. 'I still haven't received anything from his social worker, although he promised me this morning that he would fax something over.'

Although I wanted to defend Reece as much as I could, I had to be honest. 'When Reece first came to me he was very confused and angry. Right at the beginning we had some incidents of aggression, but he responded very quickly, and we have had nothing since.' Mr Fitzgerald continued to look at me carefully and I knew he doubted what I was saying. 'As I told the meeting this morning, Reece has settled down remarkably well,' I said, 'although I can see where this type of behaviour has come from. Without doubt he has resorted to learned behaviour from his past with his mother.'

'I appreciate that,' he said, 'but I can't have it in school. I have spoken to the director of education, and I shall be excluding Reece for the rest of the day. Normally I would issue a formal exclusion for three days following an incident of this nature. However, the director of education has advised me not to. I am therefore making allowances for Reece's appalling past, the fact that he has only just joined us and that there are only three days next week before we break up for Easter. I shall make this an unofficial exclusion. He will be allowed back into school on Monday, but I shall be monitoring him very closely.'

'Thank you,' I said. 'Thank you very much.' I was truly grateful: an unofficial exclusion meant that it wouldn't appear on Reece's school record. The last thing he needed was another exclusion.

'You must make it very clear to Reece,' the head continued, 'that I will not tolerate this type of behaviour in school. It is vicious and very upsetting for everyone. When I spoke to him he seemed oblivious to the fact that he had hurt Mrs Morrison, let alone his anger and foul language. I assume that is how his mother behaves.'

'Yes,' I agreed, 'she does. I will be speaking to Reece very firmly when we get home.'

'I appreciate he has had a very bad start in life,' he said, 'but if Reece is to make anything of his future, then he is going to have to learn what is right, and change. When he is out of control, as he was in the classroom, it is very frightening for those around. Miss Broom said she feared for everyone's safety and some of the girls were in tears.'

I could say nothing but apologize again. 'Will you please say how sorry I am to Miss Broom, and to Mrs Morrison when you speak to her? I will make it very clear to Reece that this type of behaviour is wrong, and must never happen again. I don't know why it has happened now.'

The head looked at me and seemed to still doubt that I really couldn't throw any light on Reece's behaviour; it was as if he thought that I must be concealing something, which I wasn't. 'All right,' he said at last. 'I will take you to him. I have already spoken to him about the incident and why he is going home early, but I don't know how much he has understood.'

'I'll explain,' I said.

Mr Fitzgerald stood behind his desk and came round. I followed him out of his office and down the corridor where the children were now working in the classrooms. I glanced in as we passed and looked enviously at the small groups of children seated at their tables working together, with the teachers walking between the tables, offering help and advice. How I would have loved to see Reece in there working happily alongside others, but that certainly wasn't going to happen this afternoon, and part of me now wondered if it ever would.

Mr Fitzgerald opened the door to the quiet room and I followed him in. Reece was seated at a small table between the two TAs and he was painting. He looked up as I entered and grinned, pleased to see me and apparently oblivious to the reason for my being there.

'Hi, Cathy,' he said, waving his paintbrush in the air. 'Look, I've painted a big spider, and 'ere are the 'airy legs.'

My first thought was why had he been allowed to indulge in one of his favourite activities, painting, when he was supposed to have been reprimanded and in disgrace? By letting him paint, the school had effectively rewarded his bad behaviour and sent him the message that if he stabbed a TA with a pencil then he would be taken from the classroom and be allowed to enjoy himself by painting! The school should have known that.

'Yes, I can see,' I said to Reece, with no enthusiasm for his painting. I purposely didn't show my usual delight for his work, as I was about to tell him off. 'Reece, do you know why I am here? It's not the end of school, is it?'

'No,' he said, dipping his brush into the paint again. 'Why you 'ere, Cathy?'

The head was hovering to one side and the two TAs were looking expectantly from me to Reece and back again. I hoped that Reece had been told off at the time of the incident and that they hadn't simply left it to me, for too much time had elapsed for anything I could say to have a real impact. Cause and effect has to be immediate with children, particularly those with behaviour problems, so that a bad act is sanctioned with the loss of a treat or privilege at the time, and the reason for the withdrawal of the privilege explained. Absolutely no way would I have allowed Reece to paint.

'Reece, put that paintbrush down now, please,' I said firmly. 'We are going home early because of what you did and said to Mrs Morrison.'

He didn't put his paintbrush down but looked up at me, amazed. 'Why we going 'ome, Cathy?'

'Because you hurt Mrs Morrison with a pencil and shouted something very rude at her.'

Reece continued to look at me and I could see he was trying to retrieve the incident from his memory. But of course it had happened over two hours before, and for a child with learning difficulties that is a very long time, and since then he had been playing happily.

'Did I?' he said, grinning self-consciously.

The head and the TAs looked at me, waiting for my response.

'It's not funny,' I said sharply. 'You have hurt Mrs Morrison and she has had to go to hospital. Now put down that paintbrush straightaway. We are going to get your coat and go home. I will need to talk to you.'

Reece put the paintbrush in the paint pot, stood up and silently came to my side.

'I'm not pleased, Reece,' I reinforced. 'I have heard bad things about what you did. You will say you are sorry to Mr Fitzgerald now, and on Monday you will say you are sorry to Mrs Morrison and Miss Broom.'

'Sorry,' Reece said to the head.

Some of the fear in the head's eyes went, as it did in the TA's. For it was fear I'd seen on their faces when

I'd first walked into the quiet room, with the head keeping his distance from Reece, and the TA's indulging him and keeping him amused. And if I'd seen their fear so too had Reece, for he'd had the example of his mother, who instilled fear through her aggression and shouting. I'd little doubt that Reece had been in control of the situation in the classroom, and also here in the quiet room before I'd arrived. I also knew that he would continue to push and challenge the boundaries in school until someone stood up to him.

Mr Fitzgerald took us to the cloakroom, where Reece put on his coat. Then he saw us out of the school.

I was silent in the car driving home, allowing Reece time to reflect and feel my disapproval. When we arrived home, I first made myself a cup of tea before sitting Reece in the living room and going over what had happened and why it was so very wrong. Intentionally harming someone is obviously wrong to anyone from a 'normal' background, where the rules of good and kind behaviour have been put in place from the start, but not so with Reece. He had spent his life in a highly dysfunctional family and, from what I'd heard at the case conference, one where violence was an acceptable part of every day. It was therefore nothing to him to lash out at someone as he'd doubtless seen his mother do countless times before. Reece listened as I spoke, and agreed it was wrong, as he had done when I'd previously told him about the sexual incidents. But I inwardly sighed as I spoke, for three incidents in three days had hardly got us off to a good start. I knew the head was doubting my claims that Reece's behaviour had improved at home, as I would have done in his position.

'Reece,' I finished by saying, 'I have told everyone at school what a good boy you are. Please don't let me down.'

'No, Cathy, I won't let you down. I'm trying to be a good boy, really I am.' He gave me a big hug.

I didn't impose any additional sanction as a punishment for Reece's behaviour; being sent home early from school was sufficient. Reece liked school and was sad that he hadn't been allowed to stay for the remainder of the afternoon. When Lucy and Paula arrived home he told them that he was sad because he had been sent home early from school, while omitting the reason. When they asked him why he just went very quiet and looked sheepish and I viewed this as a positive sign. I hoped that Reece understood his behaviour was wrong and knew that the girls would have disapproved, which suggested that, unlike his mother, he did have some moral conscience. Out of Reece's earshot, I explained to the girls what had happened and they were as shocked as I had been. I told them not to say anything more about it to Reece unless he mentioned it first, for I had dealt with it and we had to move on.

That evening, after Reece had been collected by Sabrina to take him to contact to see his parents, I made an online booking for the four of us to spend two nights (three days) at a very nice four-star hotel in Norfolk for the Easter break. I would not normally have booked us in such splendour, but I had anticipated going away for a full week, so the money I had saved on the week covered the two rooms for two nights. The girls would share one room, and Reece and I another with single beds. I emailed Jamey with the name and the address of the hotel, and then replied to an email from a Mrs Wendy Payne, who introduced herself as the Guardian ad Litem for Reece.

The Guardian ad Litem is appointed by the court for the duration of a childcare case and she (or he) reports directly to the judge. She visits all parties in the case and her report is based on her findings. She advises the judge what is in the child's best interest. The Guardian ad Litem's report is probably the most influential of all of the reports before the judge and he will normally follow its recommendations. Jamey must have given Wendy Payne my email address, as it was the first communication I'd received from her. In her email she asked if she could visit us the following Thursday, when Reece would have broken up from school. I replied that that would be fine.

When Reece was returned home from contact that evening I asked him, as I always did, if he'd had a nice time, and he answered as he always did: 'Don't know.' I no longer asked him anything about his life before he came into care. My initial questions about his bedroom etc. had been designed to help him settle in and were no longer needed. I knew that if and when Reece felt ready to talk in more depth, he would do so, for he was beginning to trust me. He had quickly formed a bond with my daughters and me – too quickly, considering he had been with his mother for seven years. And with no attachment to his natural family I wondered yet again what had been going on at home to produce a child who after three months appeared to love us more than he did his own family. Reece had started telling us that he loved us at the end of his second month. He also added how much he liked the house, and his bedroom, Paula, Lucy and me. Often when he returned home from seeing his parents, he would rush in the door, and the first thing he would exclaim was 'Home sweet home!'

On Saturday we had a relaxing day at home, with Reece playing in the conservatory that acts as a play-room. Then we ordered a Chinese take-away in the evening. On Sunday I took Reece for one of our rendez-vous with his half-sister Susie and her carer, Marie. For the first time that year the sun had some real warmth in it, announcing that spring had truly arrived and summer was just around the corner. We spent a lovely three hours in the park that had become our regular meeting place. We had lunch in the park's café, where the owner of the café was starting to recognize us and ask us how we were.

All too soon it was Monday morning, and I was laying out Reece's school uniform and telling him it was time to get dressed. I won't pretend I wasn't apprehensive at the start of another school day, after the previous week, but having had a really relaxing and pleasant weekend I was also very optimistic, and so was Reece.

'I like school,' he said over breakfast. 'I like my teacher, and I like Mrs Morrison, and I like Troy.'

'Excellent,' I said. 'So let's make sure they know that you like them by being kind to them. Mrs Morrison and Miss Broom are there to help you. And Troy wants to be your friend.' Although after Friday's incident this was more hopeful speculation on my part than hard fact.

'I like them,' he said, 'and I love you.'

'We love you too, sweet,' I said. It wasn't an exaggeration. Reece was so vulnerable and could be so kind and loving that in the relatively short time he had been with us he'd easily found a place in our hearts.

In the car, driving Reece to school, I reminded him of the rules for good behaviour. 'There is no need to touch anyone,' I said. 'Then you won't touch them in the wrong way. Listen to what Mrs Morrison and Miss Broom tell you. If you're not sure about anything, ask. They will help you – that's their job.' For I wondered if some of the problem on Friday had been because Reece had become confused and anxious. His learning difficulties required that quite simple instructions had to be repeated, and although Mrs Morrison was very kind, she didn't have a lot of experience, and I wondered if perhaps she hadn't fully appreciated the extent of Reece's difficulties. Not that I was making excuses for Reece's behaviour on Friday – it was wholly unacceptable – but if he had felt very frustrated by a task, it was possible he had expressed his frustration in the way he had in the past: through anger and lashing out.

'Now, the first thing we are going to do is apologize to Mrs Morrison,' I said as we got out of the car. 'You need to say you are sorry, and promise never to do anything like that again. Do you understand, Reece?'

'Yes, Cathy, I will.'

'Good boy.'

And he did. Mrs Morrison was waiting for us in reception and the first thing Reece said when he saw her was: 'Sorry, Mrs Morrison, it won't happen again.' She was truly a lovely lady and had clearly put the incident behind her.

'That's a very good boy,' she smiled. 'Have you had a good weekend?'

'Yes, thank you,' Reece said. 'I have.'

I smiled at Mrs Morrison. 'I'm so sorry,' I said, lowering my voice. 'Is your hand all right?' I noticed she still had a small plaster on the back of it.

She nodded. 'The tetanus injection hurt more. I still can't sit down.' She patted her rump and laughed.

I said goodbye to Reece, and wished them both a nice day. Then I watched them disappear through the 'welcome' door before returning to my car.

With Reece now at school I was free to attend training, and I had signed up for a four-hour refresher first-aid course. Foster carers, like most professionals who work with children, are required to have a current first-aid certificate, which is renewed every three years. Mine was still current but the council was offering a short refresher course, so having seen Reece into school I drove straight to the church hall that was being used for the training. Inside I saw a couple of familiar faces and, helping myself to coffee and biscuits, I spent some time chatting and catching up before the course began at ten o'clock.

It was run by a nurse who was very bubbly and easy to listen to. As the course was a refresher, she assumed we had a basic knowledge, and she spent the morning session going over the essentials for the treatment of cuts, burns, scalds, poisoning, epileptic fits and CPR (cardiopulmonary resuscitation) – i.e. mouth-to-mouth resuscitation and heart compressions. We had a thirty-minute break for lunch, in which I chatted to the other carers and thoroughly enjoyed the sandwiches with really tasty though not always identifiable fillings. They made a lovely change from the ham and cheese I usually dragged from the fridge for my lunch at home.

The afternoon session was spent practising what we had learnt in the morning on life-size dummies. We bandaged them, put their arms in slings, tended to their cuts, reassured them and then on our knees gave them mouth-to-mouth resuscitation. While we had a bit of a laugh trying to breathe air into the lifeless dummies, who stared up at us accusingly but fortunately couldn't complain, I knew how important this technique was. About ten years previously I'd been in the high street when a man had collapsed in front of a shop. He had stopped breathing, and another lady and I had given him mouth-to-mouth resuscitation until the ambulance had arrived. The paramedic said that without doubt we had saved his life. A year later I saw the man with his wife, out shopping. Although he obviously didn't recognize me – he had been unconscious – it was quite emotional for me to see him. I knew that without this life-saving technique he wouldn't have been out shopping with his wife.

When the course finished at two o'clock, and I was outside, I switched on my mobile. With great relief I saw that there weren't any messages from the school. I had checked my mobile at lunchtime and taken heart that Reece must have had a good morning; now I was elated that all was well in the afternoon as well. I stopped by briefly at home to take something out of the freezer for dinner and the answerphone was silent too. Then I continued to school for three o'clock.

Parking a little way from the school in what had become my usual spot, I went up to the main gate and pressed the security buzzer. I gave my name and the gate released. I continued across the empty playground (the rest of the school wouldn't come out for another twenty minutes); then I pressed the buzzer at the main door, and it was opened too. I waited for about five minutes in reception before Mrs Morrison and Reece appeared through the 'welcome' door. They were both smiling broadly.

'He has done so well,' Mrs Morrison said, 'I have given him a good work sticker.'

'I've done well,' Reece repeated, proudly showing me the good work sticker on his sweatshirt.

'Excellent,' I said to them both, then to Mrs Morrison, 'Thank you very much. I am so pleased Reece has settled.'

'We had a minor incident in the playground,' she continued. 'When Reece got a bit overexcited in his play. But it was dealt with by the dinner ladies, and Reece understands now that he has to be more careful.'

I smiled. 'Good.' I was sure most boys had to be reminded to be careful at one time or another.

I praised Reece immensely as we said goodbye to Mrs Morrison and then left the school. I continued to praise him in the car as I drove home and Reece talked endlessly about his 'done well day at school'.

'There are only two more days in this term,' I said, 'and then it is the Easter holidays. We're going away to the seaside for a few days.'

'What seaside?' he said.

'One in Norfolk, which is on the east coast of England. We will go in the car with Lucy and Paula, and stay in a hotel.'

'What seaside?' he said again. I glanced in the rear-view mirror.

'A seaside town in Norfolk,' I said.

'No, what seaside?' he said louder and more insistent. Then it dawned on me that what Reece was really asking was 'What is a seaside?' presumably having no idea, having never been on holiday or seen the sea.

'Do you mean what is a seaside?' I asked.

'Yeah.' He nodded vigorously, so I explained. He wasn't the first child I'd looked after who had never been on holiday to the seaside. We live on an island, surrounded by sea, yet it's incredible the number of deprived children who have never even made a day trip to the coast.

When Lucy and Paula came home Reece told them over and over again that he had 'done well' and we 'was going to the seaside'. The girls praised Reece for having 'done well' at school, but eventually tired of having the description of the seaside I had given him repeated over and over again.

'Can't you buy him a toy seagull to keep him quiet?' Lucy said at last. 'All that squawking is doing my head in.' I had told Reece that he would see birds called seagulls at the seaside, and he remembered seeing them on a *Blue Peter* television programme, and also the noise they had made, imitations of which he honed to perfection during the course of the evening.

I had high hopes when I said goodbye to Reece at school on Tuesday morning. He was still talking about his 'done well' day on Monday, and was looking forward to another 'done well' day today, as I was. I believed that the setback of the week before was about Reece reverting to learned behaviour when he'd had to cope with a new school, after so long out of school. Starting a new school is pretty stressful for the most able of children. I remember having to move house (and school) as a child myself and feeling very unsettled. How much worse was it for a child like Reece, who had been out of school for six months, moved homes five times and had a pretty traumatic start to life, so had nothing to build on?

At a little after 11.00 a.m. I was in the supermarket, pushing the trolley up and down the aisles to restock the cupboards at home, which seemed to empty faster than I could fill them, when my mobile went off, the 'Blue Danube' waltz ringing from my coat pocket. As I took out my mobile and pressed to accept the call, I saw that it was Reece's school number that came up.

'Hello?' I said.

'Mrs Glass, it's Betty Smith, the school secretary. We need you here now.'

My heart started to pound. 'Why? What's the matter? I'm in the supermarket.'

'It's Reece. He's attacked another child and is now running round the school completely out of control. The head and the year head are trying to contain him now. Mr Fitzgerald says you must come straightaway. How long will you be?'

'About twenty minutes,' I said. I could hear the urgency in her voice.

'I'll tell him.' She hung up.

I pushed the half-full trolley to one side of the aisle, hurriedly left the supermarket and ran to my car. Five minutes into the journey my mobile rang again.

I touched the button to put it on handsfree. 'Yes?'

'Are you on your way?' It was the secretary again. I could hear panic now. 'The head wants to know if you will be here soon. If not we will have to call the police. It's not safe for the other children or staff.'

'I'm driving now,' I said. 'I should be there in ten, fifteen minutes at the most. What's happening? Where is Reece now?'

'Somewhere in the school, out of control. We are clearing the building and taking all the other children on to the playing field for their own protection. You need to be quick. Come as soon as you can.'

'I am,' I said, nearly shouted. 'Tell Reece I will be there soon.' But she had hung up.

* * *

When I arrived, ten minutes later, the gate was
unlocked and I could hear the children on the playing
fields at the rear of the school. I ran in, hot and nearly
faint with fear. The head was waiting for me in reception, his face stern and severe.

'I've been in touch with Education,' he said, immediately turning and leading the way through the
'welcome' door. 'This can't go on. The child is
disturbed. It's not safe for the other children, or the
staff. I shall be writing a full report and I will send
you a copy. I can't discuss it all now, as I need to get
the children back inside the school.' He was walking
quickly, a little way in front of me, talking as he went.
The corridors were deserted. As we passed the classrooms I saw they were all deserted too. We stopped
outside the quiet room and Mr Fitzgerald hesitated
before going in.

'He's in here,' he said, as though some dangerous
animal had been contained within. 'The head of year
finally cornered him in the cloakroom and persuaded
him in here.'

He pushed open the door and stood aside to let me go
in first. Mrs Morrison, another TA, and his teacher,
Miss Broom, their faces tight and anxious, stood in a
semi-circle around Reece, who was seated at the small
table in the centre of them, painting!

'Why is he painting if he's in trouble?' I asked, unable
to hide my annoyance. 'I've only been ten minutes. The
last time the secretary phoned he was running riot.'

'I can't go into all that now,' the head snapped. 'I'll
phone you later. Please get his coat and take him home.

He is formally excluded for the rest of the term. What happens next term, I don't know. I will need to speak to the director of education. But this can't be allowed to happen again.'

With no detail about what Reece had done I couldn't start to tell him off because I didn't know where to begin, apart from which, it was obvious the head just wanted us out, and as quickly as possible. 'I'll phone you later,' he said again. 'And I'll send you a copy of my report.'

'Come on, Reece,' I said. 'We're going home.'

'I want to finish me picture,' he said looking at me. The three staff members and the head looked at me too. I sensed they were watching me to see how I dealt with his refusal.

'No. We need to go home straightaway. You've had a bad morning.' It would have helped if I had known what the bad was, for clearly Reece had either forgotten or had no idea in the first place.

'Have I, Cathy?' he suddenly asked, very sad, and putting down his paintbrush. 'Have I had a bad morning?' He stood and, coming to my side, took hold of my hand. 'I done well yesterday, didn't I, Cathy, but done bad today?' My heart went out to him. I wanted to hold him close and kiss him, despite whatever it was he had done.

The head took us straight to the cloakroom and stood waiting pointedly while Reece put on his coat. He then took us to the main gate and saw us out. I felt as though we were being escorted off the premises, which in a way we were.

As Reece and I walked towards the car I heard the whistle blow on the rear playing field, so I assumed the children would be going back into school to resume their lessons, which had been interrupted by whatever atrocity Reece had committed.

'Reece, what happened?' I asked in despair as soon as we were in the car. I hadn't started the engine but had turned in my seat and was looking at him. 'What did you do? What went wrong? You had a good day yesterday.'

'I done well yesterday, Cathy,' he said sadly.

'I know, love, so what went wrong today?'

'Somefing 'appened. I've had a bad day, but Monday I done well.'

'Reece, look at me, sweet.' For his eyes were darting all over the place, as they used to when he had first come to me. 'Reece, can you remember what happened this morning to make it a bad day?'

He thought for a moment. 'No, Cathy, but it was bad. Monday I done well.'

I turned to the front and, with tears in my eyes, started the engine, and began the drive home. Reece sat in the back, quiet and subdued. Every so often I glanced at him in the rear-view mirror. I really didn't know if he remembered what he had done or not, but he looked so very sad. I desperately wanted to make it all OK for him, but how?

* * *

It was a very different Reece from the one who had greeted Lucy and Paula at four o'clock the day before. 'It's not a done well day,' he said quietly as they came in. 'I can't go to school tomorrow. I am bad.'

I took the girls to one side and told them what I knew and they were as shocked and puzzled as I was.

'Do you really think he was that bad,' Lucy asked, 'or is the head overreacting?'

'I don't know. He cleared the school and was going to call the police, so it must have been pretty bad.'

'Perhaps Reece is like Jekyll and Hyde,' Paula said. 'When he gets to school, he changes.'

'That wasn't a very helpful comment, was it, love?' I said.

She shrugged. 'Well, something's happening to him, because he's not like that here.'

'I know, but what?'

The head phoned at nearly six o'clock and I was even more at a loss to understand what was happening to Reece at school. I'd asked the girls to keep Reece occupied in the living room so that I could talk without being overheard or interrupted and I took the call on the extension in my bedroom.

'I'm afraid I can't give you long, Mrs Glass,' Mr Fitzgerald began. 'I'm due at a board of governors' social in an hour. I have spoken to the director of education this afternoon. He has said Reece must return to school on Tuesday 18 April, which is the first day of next term, after a reintegration meeting. I have been advised that I will need to bring in the educational psychologist to reassess Reece. Then I will have to call a meeting to review his statement. Both of which I will set in motion on my return from the Easter break. That is the only way to have him permanently removed from this school. I shall send you a copy of my report detailing the incidents in school to date.

'Oh, I …'

'This morning's incident was by far the worst,' he continued without breath. 'Reece pinned a child against a wall and when the head of year went to intervene, Reece punched him. Then he ran berserk around the school, kicking and punching everyone and everything he came into contact with. At least ten children received a thump as a result. We also have a broken door and a smashed window. I have spent all afternoon phoning parents, apologizing and trying to explain. That child is disturbed, Mrs Glass, and looking at the reports from his previous schools, his behaviour is exactly as it was then.'

He stopped. I didn't know what to say. I heard his challenge to my claim that Reece was good at home, and I could understand it, for clearly the child he was describing was completely at odds with the one we saw at home.

'Was there a trigger to Reece's behaviour?' I asked lamely. I wondered if something had sparked his behaviour – not that it would have mitigated what he'd done, but it might have offered a clue in helping me understand it, and thereby help Reece.

'No. None,' he said flatly. 'Reece was walking down the corridor with Mrs Morrison when he leapt at a boy who was passing and pinned him against the wall. The boy is in the year above Reece and big for his age, so you can tell the strength Reece had in him. Reece said the boy was laughing at him but the boy denied it. As I said, Reece then took off round the school, out of control.'

Supposing the boy had provoked Reece by laughing at him? I thought but didn't say, for really that was no excuse. I could only repeat what I knew. 'I'm sorry. He doesn't behave like that here.'

'No. Well, count yourself lucky. It was extremely frightening for us all.'

And in the 'us all' I felt the school closing ranks and shutting out this demon intruder – us and him.

'Although Reece has to return to school next term, following the reintegration meeting,' the head continued, 'I shall not be allowing him in the classroom for some considerable time, if ever. He will be taught separately from his class by his TA. The other children are frightened of him now, and the parents of the children he harmed have expressed concerns about their children's future safety. I have reassured them that Reece will not come into contact with their children, not in the classroom, not in the corridor and not in the playground.'

'You're not letting him in the playground?' I asked in disbelief.

'Not while the other children are there, no. He will be able to have some fresh air after they have come in. I'm sorry, Mrs Glass, but you didn't witness what we did. If you had, you wouldn't be so sympathetic to Reece's case.

Now, I have to go. I'll email you a copy of my report.' I couldn't bring myself to say thank you. 'And would you explain to Reece the new arrangements, please? I don't want a scene on the first day back. Goodbye, Mrs Glass.'

'Goodbye,' I said. The line went dead and part of me felt dead too.

Chapter Fourteen:

Seaside Escape

The following day, Wednesday, which should have been a school day, I reverted to the routine I had used before Reece had started school. I got out the work sheets that I had only just packed away, we did some reading, writing and number work, and then we went for a walk by our local lake. I had tried to talk to Reece about what had happened at school, using the details the head had given me, but Reece just kept saying, 'I'm sorry, I done a bad day,' followed by: 'I will say sorry, won't I, Cathy?' I nodded, but thought, to whom? From what the head had told me, it wasn't just the boy he had pinned against the wall who needed the apology, nor the head of year whom Reece had punched, but also ten other children whom Reece had come across and attacked at random. Again I struggled to equate the child who was now feeding the ducks on the lake with the one who had run riot in school.

The head's emailed report arrived in my inbox on Thursday morning and I printed it out and read it straightaway, even before Reece was up. My concerns grew with each paragraph, for the head had described in great detail all the incidents, including the quite minor ones when Reece had become overexcited in music and in the playground, both of which I thought had been dealt with, and more or less forgotten. His grabbing Mrs Morrison's breast and putting his hand up the girl's skirt in the canteen were, he said, further evidence of why Reece shouldn't be in a mainstream school. His report culminated with Reece's attack on the boy in the corridor. In graphic detail he described how he had 'viciously pinned the boy to the wall in a completely unprovoked attack' before 'running berserk' through the school. Set down like this, it certainly did appear that the child he described was so disturbed and such a danger to other children and adults that he should be removed not only from his class and that school but also from society at large.

I was mortified by the time I came to the end of the head's report, and at a complete loss to know what to do or say to Reece. I was also aware that any chance Reece had been given to prove himself as a reformed character at school had now been dashed. He had fulfilled all the head's expectations based on the previous schools' reports, and if he did permanently exclude him part of me felt it would be a good thing. For it would be virtually impossible for Reece to lose the tag of a disturbed and dangerous child, as the head and the rest of the school now perceived him to be.

When Wendy Payne, the Guardian ad Litem, arrived, as arranged, at eleven o'clock that morning, I handed her the head's report to read while I made her coffee. It was a lovely warm April day and I had the French windows open in the living room. Reece was playing on the swings in the garden. Wendy Payne, casually but smartly dressed in trousers and a white open-neck shirt, seemed approachable as well as efficient. She sat in the living room and read the head's report, keeping an eye on Reece in the garden, while I made coffee. When I carried the tray of coffee and biscuits through she was just finishing the last of the report's six pages.

'Absolutely dreadful!' she exclaimed, not looking up from the page, as I entered. By that I thought she meant Reece was absolutely dreadful. I was about to defend him by explaining that he wasn't like that at home, when she continued, 'Clearly the head didn't want him there in the first place. Unfortunately Reece has played right into his hands.'

I passed her the coffee and sat on the sofa, relieved, and surprised to find this sudden ally. 'But why is he behaving like this at school?' I asked in desperation. 'It is pretty atrocious stuff. He's never like that at home.'

'You've seen his family,' Wendy said. 'I don't doubt Reece has seen his mother act like that – pinning people up against walls, punching them, and screaming and shouting. One report I have read details an attack by Tracey on a teacher in front of Reece at his previous school. Reece is copying his mother. It is learned behaviour, and let's face it, three months here isn't going to blot out all that.' Her words were like a

breath of fresh air to me. I passed her the plate of chocolate biscuits and could have kissed her feet.

'But why isn't he behaving like that with us then? If
he is reverting to learned behaviour?'

'Because he trusts you, Cathy. You have invested a lot
of time and effort in building up that trust, and managing his behaviour. What strategies have the school put
in place for managing Reece's behaviour? They had all
the previous school reports and his statement of special
educational needs. Have they drawn up a behavioural
management plan?'

'I don't think so. I'm not aware of it.'

'Exactly. The head made it quite clear at the start he
didn't want a child with Reece's high level of needs in
his school. He was forced into taking him, so he palmed
him off on a TA, who is doubtless very nice and is
probably an ex-dinner lady who is used to giving extra
help with reading.'

I smiled, and the relief I felt was enormous. 'Yes, that's
exactly Mrs Morrison.'

'The head must put something in place to manage
Reece's behaviour or else he is on a hiding to nothing.
And what about his IEP?' She was referring to the
individual education plan that all special needs children have. 'Have you seen that yet?'

'No.'

'Ask to see a copy. Because one thing is for certain: the
head won't be excluding Reece permanently very easily.
He is a looked-after child, and he must be in school. It's
policy to have all looked-after children in school
quickly. Bearing in mind it took over three months to

find Reece this school place, the education department won't be looking for another in a hurry, which is what Mr Fitzgerald will have been told.'

'I wondered why Reece was being allowed back into school next term,' I said. 'That explains it.'

Wendy nodded. 'It is possible that in the end we decide that Reece's needs would best be met in a special school, but that's for the special needs panel to decide once the educational psychologist has reassessed him, not the head. In the meantime the head needs to invest a bit more in managing Reece's behaviour instead of demonizing him.' I couldn't have put it better myself! 'When you have a date for the meeting to review his education statement, let me know and I will attend,' Wendy said. 'Actually I'll make contact with the head myself. I need to be included in the loop. He can email his reports direct to me.'

'Thank you,' I said. 'That would be terrific. I've been feeling as if I have been fighting a lone battle here.'

'I take it that Jamey Hogg hasn't been too proactive in this?' she said.

Again I was surprised by her directness. 'Well, no, I keep him informed but he seems very busy with other cases.'

'Busy with his divorce,' she said. 'I've left him three telephone messages to call me, and emailed him twice. I haven't had a reply to any of them. Jamey will need to pull his finger out, and pretty smartly. I know it's a complicated case but we're in court for the final hearing in September, and all the reports need to be in by the end of July – which isn't that far away.'

Reece bounded in from the garden, ready for a drink and a snack. He was in such good form that I felt it reinforced what I was saying about him – not that Wendy needed any convincing. She was excellent, and had hit the nail on the head in her appraisal of the school and what was happening to Reece there. She spent some time talking to Reece and then played a high-spirited game of Snap.

When he returned to play in the garden Wendy continued to discuss the case. She said there was no chance of Reece (or Susie) being returned to their parents' care, but that the aunt who was looking after his half-sister Lisa was considering offering to look after Reece too. Wendy said she would be visiting the aunt in due course, and that if the aunt did feel she could look after Reece then she would be assessed as to her suitability. I was sad to think that Reece might eventually be leaving us, but as a foster carer I have to accept this, difficult though it is.

Wendy had been with us for nearly two hours by the time she stood to leave. I was very impressed both by the knowledge she had of the case and by her astute and sympathetic understanding of Reece. She went down the garden to say goodbye to him, and then left with the promise to see me again at the statement review meeting.

'Have a good holiday,' she said as she left.

'Thanks. We will.'

* * *

I was determined we would have a good holiday. Feeling considerably relieved now that I had an ally in the Guardian, the following week we packed a suitcase, and early on Wednesday morning – very early, at 5.00 a.m. – climbed into the car and headed south. The early start was a huge adventure for Reece, but considerably less so for the girls. Teenagers seem to need more sleep, not less, as they grow older, and the girls were worried the impact the lack of it would have on their beauty.

'I've got dark rings under my eyes,' Lucy moaned, peering into her compact mirror, which had become a permanent appendage. 'And eye bags!'

'Gross,' Paula said, when Reece wanted us to stop for fried egg and bacon. 'Not at five o'clock!'

We did stop for breakfast at seven o'clock, when Reece had his fry-up, and the girls had the benefit of the well-lit mirror in the ladies, in order to apply the make-up that they said was necessary to counteract the damage of sleep deprivation. We arrived at our hotel at just gone twelve noon, and it was superb. The two rooms were next to each other, as I had requested. They were more like suites, with a large 'living room' area, Sky television, music centre, sofa and armchair, two four-foot single beds and generous en suites.

I had clarified with the hotel when I had booked that at least one of the rooms would have single beds rather than a double, as it wouldn't be appropriate for a seven-year-old boy to share a bed with his carer. Lucy and Paula were impressed with their room, particularly the generous mirror allocation in the en suite. The hotel

had once been a grand manor house and enjoyed pano-
ramic views over the surrounding countryside and
coast. From our first-floor bedroom windows we could
see the bay, and further up a small harbour with half a
dozen fishing boats. Reece had spotted seagulls from
the car when we had taken the coast road, and now
with them circling just outside the hotel window he set
up a loud squawk.

'No, darling,' I said after a while. 'You will need to be
quiet as we leave the room. There are other guests in
the hotel and they may not appreciate your seagull
impersonations as much as we do.'

With a final squawk we left the room, collected the
girls from next door and went to explore the coastline.
Although there was a strong breeze it was relatively
warm. We went down the steps at the front of the hotel
and along a narrow lane that took us straight on to the
beach. Reece was in his element on the beach, as we all
were, for there is something about walking barefoot
over the sand that brings out the children in us all.

Lucy and Paula, having overcome their initial
concerns about wind damage to their hairstyles, helped
Reece to collect a variety of shells and different pieces of
seaweed. Then we all held hands in a line facing the
sea and, with our trouser legs rolled to our knees,
jumped over the small cold waves that broke steadily
on to the shore. There was a beach café further along
that had made its first opening of the season for the
Easter holidays. We sat behind the windbreak they had
erected and, looking out to sea, enjoyed toasted cheese
sandwiches and hot chocolate. When we'd finished I

bought a bucket and spade from the café's little shop, and we spent a couple of hours making sandcastles, digging moats and watching the whole lot disappear with the incoming tide.

By 4.30 the sun was starting to lose its warmth and I suggested we head back to the hotel to get washed and changed for dinner. I had booked us dinner at the hotel for that evening, as I thought it would be easier than trying to find a restaurant after the long drive, but I now wondered if Reece would be able to sustain the time he would have to sit at the table waiting for the courses to arrive. When we'd passed the dining room as we'd left the hotel I'd noticed it had been laid out quite formally with silver service and a white linen tablecloth and napkins.

As it turned out I needn't have worried, for when we went down to the dining room at seven o'clock the hotel staff were excellent. Although Reece was the youngest child there, the atmosphere was child friendly and the waitresses went out of their way to talk to him. I had taken the precaution of bringing crayons and a small colouring book to the table, as I did when we ate at restaurants at home. Reece was happy to sit and colour, with Lucy and Paula helping him, and when the courses arrived he was happy to eat. We had home-made vegetable soup, followed by roast chicken with all the trimmings and finally something from the all-too-tempting sweet trolley.

By the time we had finished, tired from the early start, being on the beach and eating ourselves to a standstill, it was nearly nine o'clock. We went up to our rooms and, leaving Paula and Lucy to watch television in bed, Reece and I said goodnight and went to our bedroom. I helped him with his wash, for he was so tired he could hardly keep his eyes open. When I tucked him in and kissed him goodnight, he let out a final squawk, and one very tired seagull closed his eyes and was asleep in seconds. I had a quick shower, changed into my night-dress and was asleep by ten o'clock.

When I woke with the early-morning light I was on my side, facing Reece's bed. As my eyes opened I saw that his bed was empty. The adrenaline immediately kicked in and I sat bolt upright. Then I saw with great relief that he was standing in the bay window, looking out, probably watching for seagulls. He didn't know I was awake, and I relaxed my head back on to the pillow and watched him for a few minutes. His little profile was completely entranced by the view outside. I could hear seagulls in the distance, fishing for their early-morning breakfast. Reece was very still and quiet, enthralled, and seemed to be deep in thought. He wasn't a child who usually stood and pondered; like many young boys, once awake he was on the move. I watched him for some minutes; then he must have sensed I was awake, for he turned to look at me and grinned.

I was expecting a very large seagull squawk, in reply to those outside, but instead, his face still calm, he said quietly, 'I like it here. There aren't any secrets.'

I looked at him carefully. The word 'secret' can be loaded with connotations for an abused child and is often very different from the surprises that come with a birthday present or Christmas. Secrets for an abused child can be a threat from an adult: 'This is our secret and if you dare tell anyone you will be ...'

'We don't have secrets at home either, do we?' I said.

'No,' he agreed. 'I like it there too.'

I had a feeling, that sixth sense that comes from years of fostering and seeing children start to try to disclose, that Reece was trying to find the strength, the words, to tell me something; possibly he felt empowered by being right out of the catchment area of life with his mother.

'Have you got secrets that you don't like?' I asked gently, staying where I was, propped on the pillow and not wanting to disturb the rapport.

He gave a small nod.

'Can you tell me about them? Sometimes it helps to tell people you trust.' He didn't say anything but turned again to look through the window.

I slowly got out of bed and, slipping on my dressing gown, went to join him at the window. We both looked at the view. It was truly magnificent, and the morning sun, which was rising over the sea, made the water shimmer like highly polished glass.

'I like it with you,' he said. 'You don't have secrets.'

'No, that's right. We have nice surprises like this holiday. This was a nice surprise, wasn't it, but no bad secrets.' He was quiet again, watching the seagulls circling above. I felt he was so close to saying something. I could feel the tension; his trying to tell was almost palpable. So I took a chance. 'Reece, the secrets you don't like, are they from when you were living at home?'

'Don't know,' he said quick as a flash, and I knew the moment had gone.

'OK, no problem. I just wondered,' I said. 'Reece, if you ever remember and want to talk, I'm good at listening.'

'I know,' he said. Then with a loud squawk he headed for the bathroom to get dressed.

We made the most of our one full day at the coast, for we had to return the following day by 5.15 for Friday's contact. I used the car so that we could explore more of the coastline and surrounding area. In three separate stops we took in a small museum with dinosaur fossils, which Reece needed some convincing were real; the ruin of a medieval castle; and a ride on a steam train, which was part of an on-going restoration project to reinstate a local service made obsolete fifty years before. At a little after six o'clock I found a pub in a beautiful picture-postcard village with a family room, and we ordered our evening meal. The girls had a game of pool after we'd eaten while Reece played with another lad of a similar age who was on holiday with his family. We left at eight o'clock and, after nearly an hour's drive back to the hotel, we were all in bed and asleep by ten o'clock. Although it was a pity we couldn't have stayed a few more days, I felt we had made the most of the time, and had also showed Reece what a holiday was.

The following morning, after a magnificent cooked breakfast, we took in a walk on the beach, said goodbye to the seagulls and began the journey home. It being a Friday, the traffic was already building up in the afternoon as we left the A14 and joined the M6. Once on the motorway we stopped for the toilet at a service station, where I also bought sandwiches and packets of juice for Reece and the girls. They ate as I drove, and we arrived home at 4.30. The girls unpacked the car while I sat with a mug of tea and recovered from the drive. Reece had disappeared straight up to his bedroom, pleased to be surrounded by his possessions once again.

When Sabrina arrived to collect Reece for contact, I called up to him to come downstairs and put on his coat and shoes. I called him a second and then a third time, before he finally appeared.

Coming slowly down, he said: 'I don't want to go.'

It was the first time Reece had said he didn't want to go to contact. While a child would never be forced to see their parents, contact was something that was encouraged at this stage in a placement. If there were good reasons why a child did not want to go, then contact could be stopped, but only after discussion with the social worker, who would have to apply to the court to have the judge's order changed.

'You want to go to see your mum and dad, don't you?' I asked him.

'No,' he said firmly.

'Why not, Reece?' I glanced at Sabrina, who was waiting in the hall.

'Don't know,' he said.

I knew that 'Don't know' wasn't going to satisfy the judge, let alone Tracey, Scott and his social worker. 'Reece,' I said, bending forward to make eye contact, 'if you really don't want to go, you don't have to. But I will need a reason to tell your social worker. Why don't you want to go?'

'Don't know,' he said again. Then, perhaps realizing the wider implications of not going, i.e. having to find a reason and possibly even tell a secret, he changed his mind: 'OK, I'll go.'

After I'd seen him out I set the washing machine going – I was surprised at how much washing the four of us had generated in only three days away – and then I wrote up my log notes for the time away, including Reece's comment about secrets. Having finished the log notes I closed the diary and ignored the unpalatable fact that Tuesday 18 April, the start of the school term, was only four days away.

As if to underline that date, lest I should forget, in the mail was a letter from the head stating the arrangements for Tuesday morning. I was to bring Reece into school at 9.30 a.m., when Mrs Morrison would look after him while I attended the reintegration meeting, scheduled for 9.45. The head, Reece's social worker, the head of year and I would be present, and the meeting was scheduled to last an hour.

When Reece returned from contact he seemed fine, although he did come in with a message from his mother: 'Mum says you 'ad better 'ave me in school next week or else.'

I smiled sweetly. 'You will be, darling. Don't worry.'

Chapter Fifteen:

Set Apart

'Have you had a nice Easter?' Mrs Morrison said to us in reception. 'Did you have lots of Easter eggs, Reece?'

Reece nodded. 'And I saw seagulls at the seaside, and I stayed in a 'otel.'

'We've had a lovely Easter, thank you,' I confirmed. 'Did you?'

'Yes, thank you. The meeting is in the head's room,' Mrs Morrison said. 'Reece and I will get on with some work. I know we're going to have a really good term. We are going to use a table at one end of the canteen. Come with me, Reece, and I'll show you.'

Good, kind Mrs Morrison was starting the new term afresh. I sincerely hoped her enthusiasm would rub off on Reece and ensure he did the same. I kissed Reece goodbye. Then I went along the corridor to the head's office, where I knocked. He called, 'Come in.'

There was just the head present, seated behind his desk and talking on the phone, talking to – I subsequently realized – Jamey Hogg.

'Right, I'll tell her,' he tersely said, and replaced the receiver. 'The social worker won't be coming,' he said to me. 'He has been called to an emergency.' He tutted. 'I don't suppose it matters too much. This meeting is more a formality than anything.'

'Yes,' I agreed. I had attended reintegration meetings before, although not for some time, as all my recent foster children had been successfully in school.

'The head of year can't make it either,' Mr Fitzgerald added. 'He's covering another class, where a member of staff is off sick. So it will just be the two of us.' I nodded and waited. 'I'll start by going over the reasons for Reece's exclusion, and the arrangements I have now put in place until he can be reassessed by the educational psychologist.'

I sat and listened as Mr Fitzgerald went over the contents of the report he had emailed to me, incident by incident, and then finished by saying that the ed psych (educational psychologist) would be observing Reece in school, retesting him, and once her report was available, a statement review meeting would be called. He added that he sincerely hoped the 'arrangements' he had put in place for Reece would minimize the chances of a similar incident taking place.

'So will Reece be having any contact with the other children?' I asked.

'Not to begin with. If he settles down we will think about reintroducing him to the class, starting with a PE lesson.'

'You don't think he will become frustrated working one-to-one all day with Mrs Morrison? It's very inten- sive, and not just for Reece.'

'I have arranged for Mrs Morrison to have her lunch hour and for another TA to sit with Reece.'

There wasn't really much I could say, apart from what the Guardian had advised me to ask for. 'Could I have a copy of Reece's IEP, please? It would be useful so that I can help him at home.'

Mr Fitzgerald looked slightly taken aback. 'I haven't got it to hand,' he said. 'In fact I'm not sure I've seen one yet.'

What! I thought. The school should be working from one, and also drawing up a new one, given the time that had elapsed since Reece had left his last school. The IEP is what it says: an individual education plan, detailed and tailored to the child's educational needs i.e. what the child is working on now and what he or she will be progressing to in the future.

'Reece should really have a current IEP,' I said, aware I was probably making myself even more unpopular but determined to get Reece what he should be having in school: an education.

'I'll ask our SENCO,' the head said, referring to the special educational needs coordinator. 'But she works part time, so it will have to be tomorrow.'

'Thank you,' I said, and continued with the next Guardian-inspired question, which was probably going to reduce my popularity even further: 'Is there a behavioural management plan for Reece?'

The head looked at me completely nonplussed, as though he'd never heard of one.

'It might be useful to have one,' I continued, 'in the light of what has happened. Then all the staff will be working with the same strategies in managing Reece's behaviour.'

'I'll look into it,' he said, dourly, and made a note on a piece of paper on his desk. 'Well, I think that's all. Let's hope the new arrangements improve Reece's disposition, and that the ed psych comes up with something. How long do you think Reece will be staying with you?'

I had been waiting for this question, the 'get-out clause'. 'It's difficult to say. The final court hearing is in September, so a decision on Reece's future will be made then.'

'Is it possible he could come back here in the autumn term then?' the head asked, trying to hide his dismay.

'Oh yes. I would imagine he will be with us until Christmas, whatever happens in court.' Which wasn't what he wanted to hear – not at all.

The head's 'new arrangements', as he called Reece's segregation, far from helping Reece made his behaviour worse. It was obvious from the end of day one that Reece was very unhappy about his exile. He had grumbled to Mrs Morrison that he wanted to be with the other children, refused to do any work and hardly eaten any lunch – which for Reece was unheard of. When I met him at the end of the second day, Mrs Morrison took me to one side and said Reece had been miserable all day, and despite her best efforts, all she had succeeded in doing was keeping him occupied; she hadn't been able to teach him anything. I could see that she was as unhappy as Reece was with the new 'arrangement', but while she expressed her concerns to me, as a (new) TA she didn't feel able to take her worries to the head (although I doubted it would have done much good).

'Hopefully tomorrow will be better,' Mrs Morrison said. 'It's still all a bit new for Reece, and the canteen is noisy with the preparation for lunch. I can't do anything about the noise but at least Reece will be a bit more used to his surroundings. Another problem I have is that we can't leave our work out, as the table is used for dinner. I have to pack everything away for lunchtime and then get it all out again for the afternoon.' Mrs Morrison kept touching her head nervously as she spoke and looked absolutely exhausted; the arrangement was obviously putting pressure on her too.

'Are you all right?' I asked, feeling responsible.

'I've got a bit of a headache,' she said. 'It's nothing much. But I do feel this is unfair to Reece. He really needs to be with children his own age.'

I agreed, but there was little I could do, for I knew as she did that this new arrangement would have to fail before the head looked at any alternatives. 'I'll have a chat with Reece tonight,' I said, 'and try to get some cooperation.' Though goodness knows what I was going to say. That it was for his own good? I doubted even he would have swallowed that.

What I did say to Reece later was that the head felt it was better he was taught separately for now, until he could be certain he would do as he was told and not get angry or hurt anyone. I thought it might give him some incentive if he knew there was an achievable goal. 'If you show Mrs Morrison what a good boy you are, then I'm sure it won't be long before you are in the classroom again.'

How wrong could I be!

When I collected Reece at three o'clock the following day, Thursday, Mrs Morrison told me that an hour into the morning Reece had overturned the table on which he was 'working' in the canteen, then picked it up and was about to throw it when she had called for assistance from the kitchen staff. Between them they'd stopped him and calmed him down, but everyone had been shaken by Reece's burst of anger.

The next day was even worse, and Reece was excluded for the afternoon, but informally, so there was no paperwork or reintegration meeting. I was called to the school at 12.15. Mrs Morrison was nearly in tears, blaming herself for the incident that had led to his informal exclusion.

'I should have taken him from the canteen earlier,' she said. 'It was having to leave the canteen, when all the other children were going in for their lunch, that made him upset.' It appeared that Reece had wanted to stay in the canteen to eat lunch with the others, instead of having it brought on a tray to the quiet room. When Mrs Morrison had said it wasn't possible, Reece hit the boy leading the queue to come into the canteen. Obviously Reece shouldn't have hit anyone, but Mrs Morrison saw, as I did, the frustration that had led to it.

That first week the incidents escalated, leading to exclusion; and the pattern repeated itself in the second week, when Reece was informally excluded on

Thursday for the rest of the week. In the third week he was informally excluded on Wednesday for the rest of the week; the same happened in the fourth week.

When it happened in the fifth week I'd had enough. I received the usual phone call from the school secretary telling me that Reece had hit/broken/sworn and that the head said I must come at once to collect him, as he was informally excluded for the rest of the week. The head was never around when I collected Reece; he left Mrs Morrison to bring Reece to me and explain what had happened.

However, now as they arrived in reception through the 'welcome' door, I said to Mrs Morrison: 'I'm sorry, I'm not taking Reece home without a formal exclusion. Would you be kind enough to tell the head? I'll wait here with Reece.' For it had occurred to me that while all these 'informal' exclusions were keeping Reece's school records cleaner than they would have been otherwise, they had become an easy option for the head. They removed Reece without having to do much about addressing the underlying problem: the management of Reece's behaviour.

Mrs Morrison looked at me very anxiously and a little upset. I was sorry but I wanted this problem out in the open. A formal exclusion with the consequent reintegration meeting would give everyone a chance to have their say and, I hoped, discuss a way forward.

'All right,' she said, nervously, and she disappeared through the 'welcome' door.

It took her twenty minutes to find the head and when they returned, the head was clearly on the offensive.

'He can't stay,' he said, even before he was fully through the 'welcome' door. 'He has been running riot, shrieking in and out of the classrooms.'

'No, I'll take him home, but I want a formal exclusion,' I said.

'I can't do it now,' the head said. 'The secretary is too busy.'

'OK, I'll wait.' And I did. Fifteen minutes later the head reappeared with the formal exclusion letter, which is a standard letter printed off the computer, with a date for the reintegration meeting: the following Monday at 9.00 a.m.

'I want his social worker there,' the head said.

'So do I,' I said. It was probably the only thing we agreed on. 'You need to notify him formally,' I added. 'I will email him the date and time as well. And I think it would be useful to have the ed psych present if possible,' although I knew this was an option and not a criterion.

Mr Fitzgerald nodded. I sensed I had gone up slightly in his estimation, perhaps even forcing a grudging respect.

When I got home with Reece, I did as I had done following all the previous incidents: I told him off, told him what he had done wrong and stopped his television time. I'm not sure it did any good, for when he could remember what had happened he was always remorseful and willing to apologize.

'I know you've seen your mother punch, scream and swear at people, but it's not right, Reece,' I said in desperation, trying to seize on anything that might help him change. 'You must forget all that behaviour. You don't see me swear at or hit people, do you?'

'No, Cathy,' he said. 'You don't punch, scream or swear. You are nice, Cathy. I love you. I must say sorry.'

My eyes immediately filled. I was at a loss to know what to do or say to help Reece change his behaviour at school, and I wanted advice from the educational psychologist.

The ed psych couldn't make the reintegration meeting but sent a letter saying she was in the process of reassessing Reece and would make her report available for the review of Reece's statement of educational needs, which the head was in the process of organizing.

'I'm calling all the professionals to the statement review,' the head said to Jamey and me at the reintegration meeting. 'The child is out of control and must be in a special school as soon as possible.'

It was the first time I had seen Jamey since I'd taken the school consent forms into his office for signing, although I had kept him regularly updated by email.

He turned and looked at me. 'Reece isn't out of control at home, is he?'

'No,' I said. 'He is continuing to make very good progress.'

'Which is further evidence of the need for having him in a special school,' the head said. 'It's clear that this is the wrong type of school.'

'Possibly,' Jamey said, in his laid-back way. 'But most children with special needs are accommodated in mainstream schools now. What provision have you put in place to manage his behaviour?'

'I am in the process of drawing up a behavioural management plan now,' he said. 'Mrs Glass knows this. I will send her a copy as soon as it's ready.'

Jamey nodded. 'And one to me, please.'

I wondered how long the behavioural management plan was going to be because I had requested it over a month before and it still appeared to be at the stage of 'work in progress'. However, the head's next comment gave an indication as to why it was really taking so long to produce the behaviour management plan and the IEP: he was hoping it wouldn't be needed.

'I understand Reece will be moving on after the final court hearing in September,' he said to Jamey.

Jamey looked at me questioningly and I shrugged, for I hadn't told the head that.

'Well,' Jamey said, 'nothing is definite. It will depend on what the judge decides.'

'But it is likely?' the head persisted.

'Yes, but how long it will take I don't know. And I don't think Reece can afford to tread water with his education for the rest of the year, do you?' He said this so casually and politely that it took the head a moment to realize the underlying accusation, as in fact it did me.

'I can assure you we are not treading water, Mr Hogg,' he said forcefully. 'I have a TA with Reece full time.'

'Good.' Jamey smiled. 'Reece is back in school today, and I hope there will be no more exclusions. He's a good lad and if Cathy can manage him at home then I'm sure this school, with all its resources and funding, can. I look forward to meeting you again at the statement review, Mr Fitzgerald.' And with that Jamey rose and the meeting ended.

'Thanks,' I said to him outside.

Chapter Sixteen:
Heated Debate

When the head had said he wanted all the professionals present at the meeting to review Reece's statement of special educational needs, he had certainly meant it. Two weeks and two exclusions later, fourteen of us sat in the staff room at the school, and after the introductions we looked towards the educational psychologist, who had been asked to speak first. Her assessment of Reece was the most important document before us, her conclusion critical in any decision that would be made about Reece's education and which type of school he should attend. We turned to the copy of her report in the pile of paperwork before us. The top page showed graphs, numbers and percentages, which at first glance seemed incomprehensible.

'Don't worry about the results of the tests for now,' the educational psychologist said. 'I'll explain them shortly. I'd like to start by saying a bit about my observation and assessment of Reece in school, and also suggest some strategies that may help. Reece appears to be quite damaged by his early years experience. In the school setting he can become frustrated and aggressive, which has resulted in a number of incidents, some of which have led to him being temporarily excluded. This is a pattern of behaviour that has been evident at his two previous schools, from which he was eventually permanently excluded. However, unlike before, Reece now has a stable home life and I understand from his social worker that Reece has settled well with his carer, Cathy.'

Both Jamey and I nodded.

'When Reece is under pressure,' she continued, 'or anxious, he reverts to verbal abuse and occasionally physical aggression. I have witnessed this in school, and it would appear he is reverting to actions and language he has previously seen or had done to him at home. It may take some time for the impact of his early years experience to disappear. The school needs to be aware of this in their management of him. Reece's loss of control is usually very short lived, and afterwards he is very remorseful, and can continue as though it has never happened. Situations that are likely to cause Reece frustration should be kept to a minimum, particularly with his learning and peer-group pressure. Reece will be aware that he is at a level well below his peers, both academically and socially. Situations that highlight this need to be avoided. Reece finds change and new situations difficult, and changes should be kept to a minimum too, and handled with care.'

She paused and glanced up, and I thought her assessment so far had been absolutely spot on. How perfectly and succinctly she had summed up Reece in the school setting. I also thought that so far there'd been nothing to suggest that Reece should be in a special school, though of course we hadn't looked at the test results yet.

'Now to the results of the test,' the educational psychologist said, continuing. 'I won't analyse every result but I will give you the overall findings. These include cognitive ability tests, which show Reece's verbal and non-verbal reasoning. All the results are lower than one would expect for a child of his age.'

Glancing down I could see this on the graphs, where Reece's results were compared to the average child of his age.

'As you can see,' she said, 'Reece is slightly better at non-verbal reasoning and this is probably because of his delayed speech development. While Reece's results are lower than average they are not low enough to put him in a special school. A child would have to be consistently scoring below 80, and Reece has shown he can learn. I believe his word recognition has improved since he has been with Cathy. I understand from his social worker that Reece has gone from being able to read one word to forty-five words.' I nodded, and was pleasantly surprised to hear the educational psychologist quoting this, for it showed that while Jamey hadn't responded to my emails, he had noted the contents and put them on file.

'I'm hoping that the progress Reece has made at home,' she continued, 'will soon be reflected at school. Now that's all I want to say at present, but I'm happy to discuss strategies for helping Reece in school.'

She stopped and there was quiet as each of us silently acknowledged what she had said: that Reece wouldn't be going to a special school but would be staying put. Eventually the deputy head, who was chairing the meeting, thanked the educational psychologist and asked if anyone wanted to comment.

'Yes,' Mr Fitzgerald said, looking directly at the educational psychologist. 'It is not Reece's learning difficulties that suggest he should be in a special school but his behavioural difficulties. That is the reason why he can't be taught here.'

John, who was from the education department, replied: 'The special school we have in the county is for severe learning difficulties. At one time there were also EBD schools' – for those with education and behavioural difficulties – 'but in line with government policy they have been phased out. It has been policy for many years now that children with mild to moderate learning difficulties are taught within mainstream school.'

'What about his behavioural difficulties?' the head said again.

'The same applies,' John said. 'Mainstream school with TA support.'

'So what you are saying,' the SENCO said, 'is that there isn't a school now open which is suitable for a child like Reece?'

John met her gaze. 'No. What I am saying is that there are no EBD schools left in the county and children like Reece are accommodated with TA support in mainstream schools. It is not just in this county: most others have phased out the EBD units and schools. There are only a handful left, and the one nearest to us is forty miles away. We certainly wouldn't consider sending a child on a return school journey of eighty miles, even if he did need an EBD school, which Reece doesn't.'

From there on the meeting got very heated, with everyone trying to speak at once.

'What Reece needs seems to be a matter of opinion,' the head said, tartly.

'It's ridiculous there are no EBD schools,' the head of year added.

'He doesn't need one,' the educational psychologist returned. I felt the debate on EBD schools was a bit futile, as the educational psychologist wasn't recommending one, and even if she had been it would have been highly doubtful Reece would go forty miles and out of county. I exchanged glances with Mrs Morrison and also the new TA, Mrs Curtis, who was looking after Reece at lunchtime. They, like me, were not contributing to the discussion but listening.

'So what are we supposed to do?' the head eventually asked the meeting in general. 'Clearly Reece can't function in mainstream school. We have tried but it hasn't worked.'

Mr Parks, who advised schools on behavioural management, took up the question, and said he would make himself available to come into the school for a morning or afternoon each week to advise the staff and TAs on strategies that would help. The head looked sceptical that these would work, and said so. The educational psychologist then commented that keeping Reece segregated both for his lessons and at playtime was fuelling his frustration and feelings of rejection.

'He is dangerous!' the head snapped. 'What are we supposed to do? You are forgetting he has attacked staff and pupils, and damaged property. I can't have him running riot!'

'He's not like that at home,' I said, feeling the head was exaggerating and it was time I had my say. All eyes turned to me. 'I should like to confirm that Reece's behaviour stabilized very quickly, and we have had no incidents since the first few weeks he came to me.'

'Perhaps some of your strategies could be applied to school,' John from the education department suggested. 'What have you done that has made Reece behave?'

'Just firm and consistent boundaries,' I said. 'I rewarded his good behaviour and sanctioned his bad. Reece wanted to do the right thing; he just didn't know what the right thing was. He responds very well to praise and encouragement because he doubts himself. I find that because of his learning difficulties I often have to repeat quite simple instructions, but in terms of his behaviour there hasn't been a problem.' I stopped and everyone looked at the head, who was clearly itching to say something.

'Home is very different from the school setting,' he barked.

'Yes,' the educational psychologist agreed, 'but that Reece has responded well at home is very promising, and an indication of what he is capable of in school. If Cathy was saying that Reece's behaviour was out of control at home I would be very worried. However, I am optimistic that the changes Reece has made at home can be successfully applied at school.'

The educational psychologist and Mr Parks then gave some advice to Mrs Morrison and Miss Broom on handling situations where Reece was likely to become frustrated and possibly angry, while the rest of us looked on.

'We will need extra funding to do all that,' the head put in quickly.

'You have the maximum,' John returned. 'You have funding for full-time TA support, including lunch and playtime. Do you know that Reece receives more funding than any other child in the county?' Which the head couldn't disagree with. I thought it was therefore more a matter of how the funding was being used, and possibly using it differently, if the present arrangements weren't working, which clearly they weren't.

Jamey picked this up too, and suggested that perhaps using more than one TA might help. 'So that Mrs Morrison doesn't bear all the responsibility and become exhausted,' he said, which was very similar to what the Guardian had said to me. I wondered, as I had when the meeting had opened, where the Guardian was, for she had said she had wanted to be present at this meeting.

I nodded in agreement and then I added: 'I know that looking after Reece can be very exhausting in view of his special needs, particularly working one to one and having to repeat instructions.' The ed psych agreed. 'Wendy Payne, the Guardian ad Litem, is aware of the level of Reece's needs,' I continued. 'She is very proactive and is concerned about Reece's schooling. Actually I had expected to see her here.' Everyone looked towards the head as the school secretary would have been responsible for sending out the invitations to this meeting.

'We weren't aware she wanted to be included,' the head said. 'In fact I don't think we even have her contact details.' The head should have known that a Guardian Ad Litem should have been included as a matter of course, and the secretary could have rung the social worker to find out her contact details. Jamey opened his mobile and read out the guardian's phone number and email address, which was written down by the deputy.

'Perhaps the minutes of this meeting could be sent to her?' I suggested, and this was also noted.

We then went round in circles for the best part of twenty minutes, with the head in one corner saying that it hadn't worked having Reece in mainstream school and he couldn't see how it was going to improve in the future, and John from education restating that there was no alternative.

'I understand Reece might return here in the autumn term,' the head eventually said.

Jamey nodded and repeated to the meeting what he had previous told him: that any decision on Reece's future would be made by the judge at the final court hearing on 14 September, and then it would take some months to implement the judge's decision, so yes, Reece would certainly be in school in the autumn term. I thought that as we were not yet halfway through the summer term, the head could no longer just 'tread water' with Reece, and I think he finally realized that.

'Right,' he said, tersely. 'I'll call a meeting with my staff and try to put in place some new strategies for managing Reece's behaviour. Mr Parks, we will need your input.'

Mr Parks nodded. 'We'll arrange dates after the meeting.'

There was then a silence before the deputy head said, 'Is there anything else?' She glanced at the wall clock as I did. We had been here for nearly two hours. Some of those present hadn't spoken, including the TAs – Mrs Morrison and Mrs Curtis – and the school nurse. The deputy head now asked them if there was anything they wanted to add. There wasn't, but they both said the meeting had been helpful.

Before the deputy closed the meeting the head had a final say: 'We will do our best to implement new strategies with the resources that are available but the bottom line is that if Reece's behaviour doesn't improve I will need to exclude him permanently.'

'I'm sure that won't be necessary,' Jamey put in quickly. 'Not with the behavioural management team's input. But if it is the case that Reece is permanently excluded, then I know the judge will want to know the reason; and obviously you, Mr Fitzgerald, will be the best person to tell him.' Which warning the head clearly understood and certainly didn't appreciate, for he went crimson. I almost felt sorry for him, and would have done so had he not been so against Reece right from the beginning.

The meeting closed and I left with mixed feelings. On the one hand Reece had been vindicated by the educational psychologist, but on the other hand, he was now sentenced to attend a school where he clearly wasn't wanted. Although I had my doubts that much would change for Reece at school at least he now had another chance to prove himself.

Chapter Seventeen:

A Dark Cloud

Reece continued to be 'taught' separately from the rest of the school and continued to become frustrated and angry. Despite the review of his statement and the promise of change, nothing appeared to alter. At the end of each day I asked the TA – sometimes Mrs Morrison and sometimes Mrs Curtis (who was also doing some half-days as well as lunchtimes) – if Reece had been in the classroom. I always got the same reply: 'Not yet, but we are working towards it,' whatever that meant. Reece appeared not to be learning anything as the TAs struggled to keep him amused in the canteen, which was still acting as his classroom. I didn't blame the TAs: they weren't at liberty to instigate change, which had to come from the head. Often the TAs were as frustrated and upset as Reece was, and indeed as I was, and we agreed, though not overtly, that Reece would have been better off staying at home with me, where he would have at least been happy and possibly learning something.

Far from building on the learning I had begun at home, Reece was now going backwards, and the positive attitude he'd had when he first started school was all but gone. He moaned when I got him up in the morning, and he refused even to lift a pencil or turn a page in a reading book at school. The TAs spent hours reading to him and let him colour in pictures when he should have been working – anything to pass the day and contain his frustration. But although Reece had learning difficulties he certainly wasn't daft, and when he'd had enough of being in the canteen and wanted to come home, he banged a few tables, waved his fists and threatened someone, which had the desired result. The school secretary phoned me and said I had to come and collect him immediately, which I did. I didn't ask for a formal exclusion: it seemed a bit pointless. I had come to see that nothing was going to change, and the head was doing the very thing I thought he couldn't do: treading water until Reece left me and therefore the school.

The spring bank holiday came and with it a week's break from school, which was respite for us all. We made the most of the warm weather and went in the garden and to the park as much as possible. The Guardian, Wendy Payne, visited and was not pleased that she hadn't been included in Reece's review, but doubted she could have added much, as the educational psychologist's report had been very thorough. She was even less pleased when I told her that despite the review nothing had changed at school, and Reece was really just being 'babysat'. I added that I was at a complete loss to know what to do, and said that in some respects I felt as though I was treading water too, and waiting for a time when Reece would leave us, in the hope that he would then get the education he deserved.

She said she would phone the head and see if she could 'rattle his cage', but agreed that there was very little either of us could do, for it would take many months even to start the process for a change of school. Reece was in school, as the judge had ordered, but any further change than that was up to the education department, and they had made their decision and were sticking to it. Had Reece been my own child I would have found another school and possibly kept him at home until I had what I wanted, but the judge would not have been happy if I had simply stopped sending Reece to school. I knew there were other schools in the area with much better special needs provision, but frustratingly, being his carer, there was nothing I could do.

Wendy asked me how Reece was doing at home and I confirmed he was still doing fine, apart from the constant dark cloud of school which hung over us. She said that Reece's aunt had formally registered a request to look after Reece permanently, if the final court hearing found that Reece couldn't return to his parents. The aunt was now being assessed as to her suitability, for although she was raising Reece's half-sister Lisa, it didn't necessarily mean that she was suitable for raising a child with Reece's high level of special needs.

Wendy asked me how often Jamey visited and I said he didn't, but that I saw him at meetings and kept him updated by email. She said it wasn't good enough and that he was supposed to visit every six weeks, which I knew. I also knew there was animosity between her and Jamey, and I could understand why, as they were opposites: Wendy was super-efficient and forthright, Jamey was laid back and ponderous. However, I wasn't going to become involved in criticizing Jamey, for I felt that both he and Wendy had Reece's best interest at heart, but worked in different ways. Wendy spent some time playing with Reece in the garden and then left with a promise to speak to the head and Jamey, and to phone me with any news.

School returned in June for the second half of the summer term. It was going to be a long half-term – seven weeks – and I was dreading it. The first three weeks proved my worst fears and Reece's behaviour deteriorated further. He screamed and shouted at his TAs, overturned tables, threw things, stopped eating his school lunch and started wetting the bed at night, which he had never done before. Finally he hit his TA, Mrs Curtis, and was excluded for the rest of the week. I told him off, and told him what he had done wrong. He said he was sorry and that he would say he was sorry to Mrs Curtis.

'You've said sorry before, Reece,' I said. 'Sorry means you won't do it again, but you keep on doing it! So sorry doesn't mean anything!'

'Sorry, Cathy,' he said. Then out of the blue asked: 'Will I be going back to my mum?'

It took me a moment to realize that we had changed direction, and quite dramatically. I had already explained to Reece why he was in care (which he had accepted), and about the final court hearing, when the judge would make a decision on where was the best place for him to live until he was an adult. But I hadn't actually discussed with him the implications of the judge's decision, or the options. Now I had to think carefully what to say. I couldn't pre-empt the judge's decision but I had to be realistic. Neither could I mention his aunt, for her looking after him permanently was far from certain yet.

'Reece,' I said, sitting next to him on one of the little stools in the conservatory-cum-playroom. 'Remember we talked about the judge, who is a very wise person and makes good decisions for lots of children?'

He nodded.

'Well, the judge will want to make sure that while you are a child you are looked after very well.'

He nodded again.

'Reece, I don't know what decision the judge will make, but I think he might say you won't be going to live with your mum and dad – not while you are a child. There were problems at home and you weren't always looked after as well as you might have been.'

'I know, Cathy,' he said quietly.

'So I think the judge will want to find you very special carers to look after you, because you are a very special boy.'

He looked at me, his large brown eyes even wider now. 'Am I a special boy, Cathy?'

'You are, very special indeed.'

'And I'll 'ave special carers?'

'You will, sweet, most definitely.'

'A special carer, like you?'

I smiled and swallowed the lump rising in my throat. 'Maybe like me, or maybe they will find you a home where there is a daddy as well.'

'Then I'll 'ave a new daddy!'

'In a way you will.'

'That's good,' he said, then quite matter-of-factly: 'I will love my new daddy.'

Although Reece had never shown much bonding with his parents (particularly his mother), and seemed to view contact as a chance for the cola drink that was prohibited with me, his acceptance of being in care and his future still seemed a lot easier than I would have expected. Often when children have been living away from their parents for a while, they – even those with little attachment – forget all the bad things that happened and start to view their parents as angels, and pine for them. Not so with Reece: he never mentioned his parents, unless he had a threatening message from his mum to deliver to me when he returned from contact.

'Is there anything else you want to ask me, pet?' I said.

He thought. 'Will my mum come to me school, like she done the others?'

I looked at him carefully. 'What, the school you go to now?'

He nodded.

'No, she doesn't know which school you go to.' I assumed this was so. As far as I knew she hadn't appeared outside the school gates.

'And the judge won't tell her? And he won't send me home?' Reece asked.

'No, the judge certainly won't tell her which school you go to, and I'm pretty sure you won't be going home.'

'Good, Cathy,' he said, jumping up and rushing to the toy box with the building bricks. 'That's OK. Thank you for being my carer. I love you.'

'I love you too, sweet, very much.'

I've no idea whether the reassurance I gave Reece in this conversation was responsible, perhaps removing a fear of his mum going to the school and creating trouble as she had done before, or whether he'd been worrying that he might be sent home to live, but something must have sealed itself in Reece's mind, for his behaviour at school began to alter, almost miraculously.

When we returned to school the following Monday, Reece apologized to Mrs Curtis, who was with him for the morning. He said he was sorry and that he wouldn't be bad again. Having heard Reece's apology and promises of good behaviour countless times before, Mrs Curtis took his words with a 'pinch of salt', as in fact I did.

But at the end of the day when I met Reece, now with Mrs Morrison, she said that not only had Reece had a good afternoon with her, but he'd also had a very good morning and lunchtime with Mrs Curtis. We both praised Reece immensely and Mrs Morrison asked me jokingly what I had given him, while I secretly wondered if he was ill and sickening for something. But when the following day passed without incident, and Reece had actually done some writing and number work, we began to believe that it possibly wasn't a fluke, and that Reece, for whatever reason, was beginning to turn a corner. On Friday, after five clear days, when Reece was not only tantrum free but cooperative and actually learning, Mrs Morrison said that she would speak to the head about slowly reintroducing him back into the classroom for short periods.

'Yes, please,' I said to Mrs Morrison, and then to Reece, who was standing beside me in reception and listening intently, 'Well done! That is good news.'

Reece beamed and nodded vigorously, and I thought if Mrs Morrison didn't persuade the head to start the reintroduction then I would, in no uncertain terms. Reece had proved himself and he needed to see the rewards of his labour.

However, there was no need for me to go in and see the head because on Monday morning Mrs Curtis confirmed they were 'trying Reece in the classroom'. When I met Reece at the end of the day, now with Mrs Morrison she said that he had spent an hour with his class, working alongside Troy, who, bless him, like most children was willing to forgive and forget.

During that week the one hour in the classroom gradually extended to the whole afternoon, and on Friday when I collected Reece the head was in reception with Mrs Morrison and Reece.

'Don't worry, Mrs Glass' he said, for my face had dropped at seeing him there. 'He hasn't done anything wrong – far from it.' Mr Fitzgerald took me aside and, while Mrs Morrison and Reece looked at the children's artwork on the walls, he asked me: 'Has anything changed at home?'

'No. Nothing,' I said. 'Except Reece has a clearer understanding of his future: that it is highly unlikely he will live with his parents again, and that mum won't be coming to this school to create.'

'And that's all?'

'Yes.'

'Well, something has changed him. I wouldn't have thought it possible.'

I agreed, and then a nasty thought struck me. 'Mr Fitzgerald, the change in Reece may be due to the reassurance I gave him. We are heading towards the final court hearing in September and feelings will be running high. If the judge makes the decision that Reece will not be going back to his mother, Tracey would have nothing to lose by coming here and creating. If she were to come to the school, you would make sure that she was dealt with without Reece knowing? It is essential that Reece continues to feel school is a safe place for him.'

'Yes, of course,' he agreed. 'It would make sense for us to have a photograph of her so that I can alert the staff next term. Do you have one?'

'No, but you could ask his social worker – he might. Although if my dealings with Tracey are anything to go by you will hear her before you see her.'

Reece continued to improve throughout the rest of the term. Gradually, bit by bit, and thanks to his TAs, he was reintroduced into the classroom and normal school life. He ate his lunch in the canteen and played in the playground, and although sometimes he had to be reminded about being too loud or overexcited, there was no anger or aggression. The other children made allowances for his over-zealous ways, having now lost their fear of being kicked or hit.

Three days before the end of the summer term the children put on a little play which parents and carers were invited into school to watch. Reece was given a line to learn, printed on a card, and he quickly learnt it off by heart. So too did Lucy, Paula and I, from having it chanted endlessly every evening: 'And the magic wind came from the north and blew all the badness away.' I didn't know if his lines had been purposely hand-picked for him by his teacher or if it was pure chance, but certainly the words epitomized what had happened to Reece in the last half-term – it was as though a magic wind had blown his anger and frustration away.

On the morning of the school play I sat proudly in the audience with the other parents and carers and had to swallow back the tears as Reece walked on to the stage. He was dressed in a white cloak, which was supposed to represent the wind. In his loudest voice (for they had all been told to speak up), he looked straight into my eyes and said his one line perfectly: 'And the magic wind came from the north and blew all the badness away.' Before he left the stage I had time to take a photograph of him, although I wouldn't need it, for that moment would be sealed in my mind for ever.

* * *

And as if to make the day complete, when I arrived home from watching the assembly I found Adrian, my son, unpacking his car, having just driven back from university for the summer recess.

'Surprise!' he yelled, seeing me draw up outside the house. I knew he was coming home at some point but I didn't know when. We hugged each other and then I gave him a hand unloading the rest of his things from the car. He had passed his driving test in January and had told me on the phone he'd bought an old Renault, which he was just about managing to run on the income from his student jobs.

'You did take it slowly on the motorway?' I asked him. Now he had 'wheels' I worried myself sick that he would do what some lads do and show off.

'Yes, don't worry. It won't go over a hundred,' he laughed.

Although Adrian and I had spoken to each other on the phone every other week, I hadn't seen him since Christmas, as he had gone away with his friends to Spain at Easter. It was strange having this big strapping lad in the house again. He was over six feet tall and broad-shouldered like his father, and seemed to fill any room he stood in.

When I collected Reece from school that afternoon and told him he would meet Adrian at last, he was beside himself with excitement. For the rest of the evening Adrian had a shadow who followed two feet behind him until Adrian said he was going out to 'catch up with some local mates'.

'Are you going to the pub?' I asked as he came into the living room to say goodbye.

'Probably, why?'

'You won't drink and drive, will you?'

'Mum!' he said with a sigh, and I knew I had to shut up.

The term finished for Lucy, Paula and then Reece. It was great having the family together and home for the summer, and of course the 'icing on the cake' was that I wouldn't spend the weeks dreading Reece returning to school in September as I had done before the previous term.

I hadn't booked a summer holiday because Reece's contact arrangements were still in place, and the same constraints applied as they had done at Easter. I found it was impossible to book a short break at the height of the season, so I told the girls and Adrian (if he wanted to come) that as soon as Reece's case had been to court for the final hearing, when the contact would certainly be reduced, I would book a holiday for us all abroad. Possibly in the October half-term week. If Reece were still with us, which I assumed he would be, the social worker (then with full parental responsibility) would be able to get a passport for Reece. I could have taken a holiday without Reece in the summer – he could have stayed with respite carers – but with all the changes he'd had I didn't want to run the risk of unsettling him. The girls understood. We would have days out, and Adrian, Lucy and Paula would be working for some of the time anyway.

Jill visited, as she did every four to six weeks, and was obviously as pleased as I was by the successful end of the summer term for Reece. Jill also wondered if the conversation I'd had with Reece had cemented his feelings of safety and caused the change in his behaviour, but we would never know for certain. Jill said that Jamey had finished his report for the court and had asked her to tell me that I could go into the office to read it. He felt I should read it, as it contained 'significant new information' which might help me in my care of Reece. I said I would, and when Jill left I phoned Jamey to make an appointment to go into the office.

'It's the first time anyone has brought the family's history together,' he said on the phone. 'I compiled the report from five different files which I found in five different locations. They are all on the system now. It took me ages. I'll warn you now: my report is not pleasant reading, but it does explain a lot.'

I thanked him, and then asked Lucy and Paula if they would mind looking after Reece for a couple of hours the day after tomorrow, which they were happy to do. And 'not pleasant reading' was to prove to be a gross understatement!

Chapter Eighteen:

Cycle of Abuse

Two days later I sat in the swivel chair with the file containing the report balanced on Jamey's desk and turned the pages, as Jamey, to my right, took the third phone call from Tracey that morning – and it was only 10.30. I didn't look up as his steady relaxed tone patiently deflected her anger, which I could hear coming down the phone. 'I understand, Tracey ... Yes ... I will ... Yes ... I was told ... No ... I understand.' His mellow voice and laid-back manner had found its purpose – in soothing her. After ten minutes I heard him say goodbye, then a little sigh, followed by his fingers tapping on his keyboard as he once again worked on his computer.

I still didn't look up as, transfixed, mesmerized and horrified by what I was reading, I continued to turn the pages of his report. Although it was primarily about Reece, Jamey had used the information he had gathered from all the files to place Reece in the context of the larger and wider family background, which the judge would require for the final hearing.

There were extracts from reports dating back to when Tracey had first come to the notice of the social services seventeen years before, when Sharon, her first child, had been one year old. It was noted at that time that there were concerns about Tracey's ability to look after the child as a single parent, and she and the baby were being monitored by the social services. It was also noted that Tracey could be threatening and aggressive to the professionals who were trying to help her. There was no father present, and Tracey said that Sharon's father had never seen the child and he didn't even know he was a father. She told a social worker at this time that she had been beaten and sexually abused by her own father throughout her childhood and even into adulthood.

When asked where her father was, and if he was still seeing her and had access to the baby, Tracey had become aggressive and threatened the social worker. The social worker had subsequently made a note on the file stating that she had been told by a neighbour that Tracey's father was still in the area. Tracey's mother had been ill with cancer for most of Tracey's teenage years and had died two years before Sharon had been born. Another social worker had noted in the file that because of Tracey's alleged abuse by her father, and because he had been seen in the area, there were concerns that Tracey's child, Sharon, could be at risk of abuse by the grandfather if he visited the family home. However, these appeared to remain only concerns. Tracey refused to give any more details, and then said she hadn't seen her father in years.

At this time Tracey was claiming all the benefit allowances she was entitled to but was still going into the social services' offices almost on a daily basis to demand more payments. She brought her baby daughter, Sharon, with her and said she had no money to feed her. It was noted that often the child had no socks or shoes and her clothes were dirty, although Tracey had been given extra grants for clothing. It was also noted that Tracey had learning difficulties and was functioning at a much younger level than that of her age.

The social services continued to monitor Tracey and Sharon, who was two years old when Brad was born. Again, there was no father present, but Tracey did say her own father had a new partner and that lady was helping her, though there was never any evidence of this when the social worker made a visit. By now Sharon was showing signs of being developmentally delayed and a paediatrician's assessment at the time confirmed this. Brad was a difficult baby and Tracey spent all her time seeing to the baby; Sharon became badly neglected and was taken into care at the age of three. The baby, Brad, who seemed to be thriving, was left with Tracey, although they were being carefully monitored. Tracey then moved suddenly, without notifying the social services of where she was going, and disappeared from the records. When she reappeared again, in a neighbouring county, she was pregnant again. She demanded to be rehoused, as she was living in a bed and breakfast, and she claimed again that her father had physically assaulted her. It was noted on the records that she had a black eye and swelling to her neck and upper arm.

She was rehoused and monitored, although she often denied the social services access. One social worker who did gain access had written that she thought there was a man staying. Tracey was visiting the social services' offices again and demanding more money. On each occasion she was given an emergency payment and Brad, now a toddler, was observed. A paediatric report at that time said that Brad too was suffering from delayed development. When Sean was born Brad was two and it soon became clear that Tracey wasn't coping. Brad was taken into care for six months and then returned to Tracey, who had persuaded the judge she could provide a stable home.

During the next year Tracey, Sean and Brad were monitored by the social services as much as was possible. Tracey was often abusive and aggressive when a social worker visited and sometimes denied them access. Tracey claimed again that her father had assaulted her but didn't want to press charges. She was still appearing regularly in the social services' offices for additional payments. There was a period when Sharon was returned to Tracey's care after Tracey had taken the social services to court, and for eighteen months Tracey had the three children with her, but the situation deteriorated and all three children were taken into care.

During this period Tracey presented at the social services and said she had been raped by a taxi driver and was pregnant. On examination she was found to be six months pregnant, but when interviewed by the police she withdrew the rape allegation, although she claimed to know who the perpetrator was. Tracey had been given money for the taxi fare so that she could attend contact to see the children, and although the social services and police made enquires about the taxi firm there was no evidence and no suspicion fell on anyone.

It was noted at this time that Sean too was showing signs of developmental delay. Tracey said she didn't want to keep the baby she was expecting because it had 'bad blood', and when baby Lisa was born she was placed with foster carers at three days old. The baby thrived and Tracey's sister – who had normal intelligence, was married and had limited contact with Tracey – offered to look after the baby permanently, as she had done since. Tracey never visited Lisa, still saying she had 'bad blood' and 'the devil in her'. It was noted that Lisa was thriving and developing normally, and appeared to have normal intelligence.

For no obvious reason Tracey attempted suicide at that time by swallowing pills but immediately rang for an ambulance. It was noted that Sharon, Brad and Sean were still developmentally delayed. Tracey had applied to have the children back again, but the court granted a full care order and the three children were placed in long-term foster homes. Tracey left the flat she had been living in and disappeared from view again. When she reappeared in this county she was pregnant again. She was housed in a flat and subsequently gave birth to Susie, whom she was allowed to take home because the father of the baby was also parenting the child. This new family was carefully monitored.

The records showed that at this time Tracey's own father was also spending time at the flat, sometimes living there. Tracey denied she had ever made allegations about her father and accused the social services of lying so that they could take her children into care. Baby Susie also showed signs of developmental delay and a report concluded that it was most likely a genetic predisposition being passed on through Tracey's side of the family, as all the children – Sharon, Brad, Sean and now Susie – had learning difficulties but different fathers. The unusual front teeth Tracey shared with these children were also mentioned as a sign of a dominant gene being responsible. Susie's father remained at the family home, although he spent a lot of time away.

Tracey had another baby, a girl, who suffered a cot death at 11 weeks, then Reece was born two years later. At the same time Susie's father moved out, claiming he was not the father of Reece. About that time the police were called to the family home on a number of occasions and Tracey accused Susie's father of assault, although she never pressed charges. The police noted that there were two other men in the house who Tracey said were her father and the father of Reece. After Susie's father had moved out he was never heard of again and lost contact with Susie. A paediatrician confirmed that Susie was developmentally delayed, as were Sharon, Brad, and Sean. She also noted that Susie's front teeth might need orthodontic work when she was older.

When Reece was one year old and Susie was three, Reece's father, Scott, moved into the family home.

Although Scott had a criminal record for assault it was felt that the family was benefiting from his presence and that he had a positive relationship with both his son, Reece, and his stepdaughter Susie. Reece was also noted to be showing signs of developmental delay. Scott was absent from the family home on two separate occasions, having been convicted for assault, but Tracey visited him in prison and during that time the family was once again monitored.

When Scott returned to the family home after serving his last prison sentence 'a high level of disturbance' was reported in the home and the police were called on a number of occasions. Tracey was again making regular appearances at the social services' offices, demanding more payments, issuing threats and being verbally and physically aggressive. Concerns were again expressed about her mental health but she refused to see a psychiatrist for assessment. During this period it was noted that Scott had 'friends' from his time in prison who stayed at the house and one of them was a known paedophile. The family situation deteriorated very quickly and it was noted that Susie and Reece appeared uncared for and started presenting with injuries at casualty. When Susie told her teacher that her 'daddy was doing rude things to her', she and Reece were taken into care.

This had brought me up to the present, and I paused and sat back. Although there were still some pages to go, I felt drained. An hour had passed and when I glanced at Jamey I saw he was taking yet another call from Tracey. I could hear her voice swearing and cursing at him down the phone and then Jamey's tranquil tone in direct contrast, calming her. I flexed my shoulders and returned to the file to read the conclusion. It was not the summing-up I had expected.

After Reece and Susie were taken into care and Scott was arrested, Scott denied any suggestion that he had molested his stepdaughter, Susie. He did admit to 'walloping' her and Reece when they were naughty; and he agreed that a paedophile visited sometimes, but he claimed the man was cured. Scott added that they 'needed to look closer to home for the kiddie fiddler'. He also said he had found out that he wasn't Reece's father, which I could believe, because when I had first met him I had been struck by the lack of family likeness and had assumed that Tracey's genes must have dominated.

As I read on, and Jamey continued his pacifying phone call in the background, I saw that my assumption had been partially correct – Tracey's genes had dominated; but what I could never had guessed, and what I couldn't begin to get my head round even as I read the words, was Scott's statement to the police. It said that Tracey's own father had been indecently assaulting Susie, and possibly the other children when they had been at home; and, worse, that Tracey's father was also the father of Sharon, Brad, Sean, Reece and Susie. The incest of father and daughter had produced five children.

I stared at the words and re-read them, unable, unwilling, to believe what I saw. I heard Jamey wind up on the phone in the distance as I stared at the open file before me. Although Scott's accusation hadn't been proven, it made sickening sense. The five children were identical, as if they had had no genetic input from outside, which if Scott was right, they hadn't. The fact that none of the birth certificates showed a father added weight to this. Only Scott's name was on Reece's birth certificate, for at the time he had believed he was Reece's father, though he had subsequently discovered differently. A man who thought he had been Susie's father had lived with Tracey for a while, and then had suddenly moved out, severing all contact. Had he discovered the truth as well? Added to this was that Tracey had accused her father of assault on a number of occasions, although she had subsequently withdrawn the accusations. Under pressure?

'My god!' I said out loud as Jamey finally replaced the phone. 'The children's father is their grandfather.' I turned to look at him and he nodded slowly.

'I know,' he said. 'Although it will be difficult to prove. Susie has been questioned further but is still fearful of Tracey. Contact has been stopped between Susie and Tracey because it seems likely that Tracey knew her father was sexually abusing Susie, as he had abused her. Tracey may have even been complicit in it.'

I cringed, and I felt my stomach lurch. It takes a lot to shock a foster carer, but I was shocked.

'Susie is now saying that there was another "daddy" doing rude things to her,' Jamey said, 'an older daddy. We know Tracey calls her father daddy, so it's possible.'

'And Tracey's father is the father of all her children?' I asked, still not wanting to believe it.

'Apart from Lisa,' Jamey said. 'Perversely it appears that Tracey has rejected the one child who has genes from outside the family. We don't know who Lisa's father is, but we are pretty certain it's not Tracey's father. Lisa has normal development and looks completely different, and in a weird way it makes sense of why Tracey didn't put up a fight for Lisa when she did with all the other children: Lisa wasn't family.'

I thought for a moment, still trying to take it all in. I drew a deep breath to ease the tight knot in my stomach.

'Tracey's father has disappeared,' Jamey continued, 'and Tracey is not saying where he is, if she knows.' He paused. 'Cathy, obviously don't say anything to Reece but Tracey is claiming she is pregnant again.'

'Not by her father, surely?'

Jamey shrugged. 'I don't know. But the odds are stacked for it, and Scott says she is.'

Chapter Nineteen:

Normal Family

I drove home slowly 'on autopilot', my thoughts a long way from the car in front, whose break lights periodically flashed red, when I changed gear, stopping and then starting in the traffic. There are sound physiological reasons why incest is taboo: it breeds in, rather than breeds out, any genetic weakness. Lisa had escaped the learning difficulties and developmental delay of (and physical similarities to) Tracey's family simply because the gene(s) responsible had been overridden, or diluted in the gene pool, by those from outside. But what plagued my thoughts more than the physical aspects of what I had learned was the destruction of what should have been a nurturing family structure. The very fabric of family life on which society is based had been corrupted and debased in a travesty of normality. If Scott's (and Tracey's) claims were correct, Tracey's father had been abusing her since childhood, almost as the norm; probably Tracey had grown up believing it was the norm. It appeared she had even lied to the men whom she had claimed were Susie's and Reece's fathers to cover up the awful incestuous truth.

Whereas before I'd had little time for Tracey, seeing her aggressive and self-centred behaviour as responsible for everything that had happened to Reece (and the other children), she now had some of my sympathy. She was a victim as much as her own children. With her limited intelligence and ever-present predator father, what chance had she ever stood of breaking out of, and trying to stop, the cycle of abuse? Thinking over what I had just read, and what I already knew, I could see that Tracey had given feeble clues, and little cries of help, for years – the accusations she had made about her father and then withdrawn, the suicide bid – which no one had ever suspected masked the darkest of secrets.

I now remembered the inappropriate comment she'd made in the car park after contact, about cleaning Reece's 'dick'. It has been said without any embarrassment, as though it was acceptable, which of course for her incest was. I shied away from where my thoughts were now leading me: Jamey had said that Tracey might have been complicit in her father's sexual abuse of Susie; was it also possible she had been complicit in sexual abuse of Reece? Father to daughter, grandfather to grandchildren, mother to son? Anything was possible when the normal building bricks of morality were demolished.

No wonder Reece had behaved as he had done; no wonder he lived in fear of returning home, and of his mother appearing at his school. For while I felt some sympathy for Tracey the fact remained that she was a formidable woman. If I had felt intimidated by her, how much worse was it for Reece, aged seven, with learning difficulties, lost in a cruel world of sexual abuse of the worst kind – from inside the family? There was no knowing what he had seen, or had been subjected to, and possibly no one would ever know. I had thought for some time that Reece harboured secrets with all his 'Don't knows', but I could never have guessed in a million years how dark and deep those secrets were.

I drew up outside the house and switched off the engine; then I sat for a while, staring out through the windscreen, almost steeling myself for going in. I had already made the decision not to tell Adrian, Lucy and Paula what I had learned from Jamey's report: there was no need. We were already practising safe caring to keep everyone feeling safe, and I really didn't want them to have to carry this extra burden. Doubtless at some point (if they hadn't already) they would read about incest in a newspaper, but I didn't want to sully them with it now. If Reece ever said anything to them about his life at home that needed further explanation I would deal with it as it arose. But I doubted he would. Reece presumably didn't know how he or his siblings had been conceived, so the worst-case scenario (and that was bad enough) was that he would start to talk about things he had witnessed and/or been subjected to himself.

I got out of the car and let myself into the house. From the hall I could see Lucy and Paula playing with Reece in the garden. The three of them were playing catch with a large yellow plastic football. Adrian's car wasn't on the drive, so I assumed he had gone out. I went down the hall and into the living room, where I stood for some moments looking out of the French windows and watching them. Reece's skill at catching a ball was improving, as were his other skills. I knew he would continue to make improvement, little by little, and that unlike Tracey, he (and Susie) would at least have a chance of the normal life that had been denied their mother. One could only guess at what would happen to Tracey now. Possibly more of the same; or perhaps now it was out in the open she might go into therapy and begin to make something of her future. But I thought it was doubtful that she would, as the damage was so ingrained, and Jamey had said she was pregnant, carrying what was thought to be her father's incestuous sixth child.

'I'm home,' I called, going down the steps and on to the patio. 'Everything all right?'

'Yes,' they chorused as they concentrated on throwing and catching the ball.

I sat on the bench in the shade of the tree and watched their game continue. It was a beautiful day; the temperature was just right, with the heat of the August sun soothed by a light cooling breeze. I looked at Reece playing happily and naturally with his foster sisters in a normal family setting. It crossed my mind that if for any reason his aunt couldn't look after him permanently, then perhaps we could.

I would obviously have to discuss it with Adrian, Paula and Lucy, even before I approached Jamey, for it would be a huge commitment and there were many issues to consider. Reece was only seven, nearly eight, and he would need looking after for the next ten years, and with his level of learning difficulties possibly longer. It was doubtful he could ever live completely independently and I wasn't getting any younger. Also it had been mentioned that Reece would benefit from having a father figure, which I had agreed with, but couldn't offer, although Adrian was a good male role model. Then there was the locality: the constant risk of bumping into Tracey and all that might entail, or her going to Reece's school and undoing all his present progress there. I couldn't justify moving the whole family out of the area just to get away from Tracey. I finally had to admit that Reece's aunt, on all counts, sounded like the better option – younger, part of his natural family, eighty miles away and with a husband. For Reece's sake I hoped the aunt was found to be suitable, but for my sake I selfishly hoped that she wasn't. Then I caught myself, and snapped out of it.

'Does anyone fancy going for a picnic?' I called. Does a duck like water!

It was a light relief for me, after my morning's reading, that the four of us put together an impromptu picnic from what we had in the fridge, and I drove a couple of miles to a small park, which had a goldfish pond and a few swings. It was two o'clock by the time we arrived, and we sat on the grass under the shade of a huge oak tree, and ate. Then Lucy and Paula sprawled out on the grass while I played with Reece, kicking the football he had carried from home.

'It's your birthday next week,' I said to him as the ball rolled back and forth between us. 'What would you like to do?' I had already decided on a present, which I knew he would be pleased with, but I also wanted to give him a little outing to mark the day. He didn't have any close friends otherwise I would have given him a party.

'McDonald's,' he said. 'I want to go to McDonald's and 'ave burger and chips.'

I smiled. 'It's your choice, but I was thinking of going on a special outing like to the zoo. They have a restaurant there and I'm sure that you would be able to have burger and chips.'

'Zoo? With animals?' He looked at me, amazed.

'Yes. There is a zoo about an hour away in the car. You can see a tiger, snakes, ostriches, giraffes and a lot of the animals we have read about in books.'

He grinned and gave the ball a big kick. 'Yes, we go to the zoo and I 'ave burger and chips.'

Driving home, my mobile started to ring. Paula, who was in the front passenger seat, delved into my hand-bag and answered it.

'It's Jill,' Paula said.

'Can you tell her I'm driving, please, and ask her if it's urgent?'

'Mum's driving,' Paula repeated. 'She said to ask you if it's urgent.'

Paula listened and then said to me. 'Not urgent urgent, but she would like to talk to you.'

'OK, tell her to hang on and I'll pull over.' I couldn't put the mobile on handsfree because Reece would have been able to hear the conversation. I checked behind, indicated and pulled into the kerb. 'Thanks,' I said to Paula as she passed me the mobile, then, 'Hi Jill.' I put the car into neutral but left the engine running.

'Cathy, I wanted to let you know that Tracey has just been evicted from the council offices. She is threatening everyone and claiming she knows where you live. Jamey thinks it's a bluff, because she's very wound up, but you need to be extra vigilant. Fortunately it's the school holidays, so I won't need to alert the school.'

'All right. Thanks for telling me.' I couldn't say anything else with Reece in the car, and there wasn't much else to say really. I said goodbye and hung up, then returned the phone to my handbag and pulled out from the kerb. 'Heightened state of alert,' I said to the girls and nodded towards Reece in the rear. They knew what I meant.

'Not again!' Lucy said.

'Yes, although it's thought to be a bluff.' To anyone not familiar with this situation – having an irate and aggressive woman threatening to come to the house – it would probably have seemed pretty scary, as it had been to me when I'd first started fostering. Now it was par for the course. 'Heightened state of alert' was a term I had adopted with my family and it meant checking the security spy hole on the front door before opening it to anyone, and just being aware of who was in the street. The girls knew that if anyone did approach them outside, or they saw anyone hanging around the house, they were to tell me immediately. These were precautionary measures, and the only nasty incident I'd had was when a very drunk father with a large pit bull terrier had turned up on the doorstep late one night, and I'd had to call the police.

Reece's birthday on 16 August was a runaway success. He loved the bike I had bought him, although he took a number of tumbles while practising in the garden, despite the bike having stabilizing wheels. Adrian came with us to the zoo, and Reece was incredibly excited by seeing the animals that he had only ever seen before as pictures in books or on the television. And of course the climax of the outing for Reece was the burger and chips in the zoo's restaurant, followed by a huge ice-cream sundae, which not even he could finish. When we arrived home I lit the candles on his 'Postman Pat' themed birthday cake and we sang happy birthday, and managed to eat a small portion each. Reece went to bed saying he had had the best birthday ever and could he have another one tomorrow.

'I'm afraid not, sweet,' I said as I tucked him in. 'It's a year to your next birthday. Christmas and Easter come before that.'

'OK, Cathy,' he said, his eyes heavy with sleep. 'I'll 'ave Christmas and Easter tomorrow, then my birthday. Love you.'

I smiled. 'Love you too, sweet.'

* * *

Jill visited us the last week in August and she came
with news that I received with mixed feelings. She said
that Reece's aunt, May, had been approved to look after
Reece permanently if it was the court's decision that
Reece would not return to live with his parents, which
was almost certain. Apparently there had been concerns
that May might have some contact with her father, but
she had been adamant she never saw him because of
the way he had treated her and Tracey as children.

Aunt May hadn't been sexually abused by her father,
as Tracey had, but their father had beaten her throughout her childhood. May had left home as soon as she
could at sixteen to escape him, and now bitterly regretted not taking Tracey, who was two years younger,
with her. She felt that by doing what she could to help
– by giving a loving home to Lisa, and now Reece – she
was making a small recompense for leaving Tracey to
suffer further at the hands of the man she described as
a 'monster'. May had only seen her father twice since
she'd left home: once at her mother's funeral, and for a
second time when she'd gone to the house to try to get
Tracey out, but her father wouldn't let her in or even
see Tracey. May had also reassured the Guardian and
Jamey that she would keep to whatever contact arrangements were set down by the court in respect of Reece
seeing his parents. And of course there was no chance
of May and Reece bumping into Tracey and Scott
because they lived too far away.

From what Jill said, Aunt May sounded a lovely lady
and I'd half prepared myself for Reece going to live
with her, although I was still sad at the thought of

losing him, as I knew my family would be. However, I wasn't prepared for what Jill told me next: the timescale of the proposed move!

'Jamey and the Guardian feel that as soon as the judge has made his decision the introduction of Reece to his new family should begin straightaway. Reece needs to start bonding with his aunt and uncle, and Lisa, as soon as possible.'

'Oh,' I said. 'Yes, I see. The hearing is 14 September, isn't it?'

Jill nodded. 'Six days of court time have been set aside to hear the case and the judge will make his decision on the following Monday. The Guardian would like the introductions to begin that week – 22 or 23 September – with a view to moving Reece two weeks later if everything is going all right.'

'Oh,' I said again. 'That is quick.'

Jill nodded and looked at me. 'You thought Reece would be with you for Christmas, didn't you?' she asked gently.

'Yes,' I admitted, 'I did, or at least until October half-term, when I was hoping to take him abroad on holiday.'

'Sorry,' she said. 'But it is for the best.'

'Yes, I know,' I said quietly. 'I'm happy for him. Aunt May sounds lovely.' I swallowed hard and couldn't speak again for some moments for the tears welling in my eyes.

Chapter Twenty:

Forever Family

Reece returned to school the following week, where he joined his class and stayed for the greater part of each day. Because it was the start of a new academic year the whole class had gone up a year and were now in a different room with a different teacher. Reece became anxious with the changes of that first week, and I crossed my fingers and hoped he would settle again. He still had his TA, Mrs Morrison, in the classroom with him, and aware of how unsettling the start of the new academic year might be for Reece (and Troy), she took them both out of the classroom for an hour each afternoon, when she read to them in the quiet room. By the end of the first week Reece and Troy had resettled, and worked in the classroom all day. Mrs Curtis was no longer needed as relief for Mrs Morrison and she helped another child in a class the year below.

The head was aware that the final court hearing was two weeks away and asked me at the end of the first day what the position was with Reece going to a permanent home. I said it wasn't finalized yet, which it wasn't, for only when the judge had made his decision would Reece's move to his aunt be definite. I didn't know why Mr Fitzgerald was so keen to know about the plans for Reece, because Reece wasn't causing him a problem, but perhaps, given his history, he thought he might again in the future. I had far more faith in Reece and I knew that whatever had crystallized in his mind with my reassurances that he was safe at school and that he wasn't going home would continue, as long as Tracey didn't appear at the school or at home.

I won't pretend I wasn't anxious as the court date drew close. I was, and I checked the street for any sign of Tracey whenever I left or entered the house, and also at the school when I took Reece in the morning and collected him in the afternoon. It was always more difficult at the end of the day, because Reece now left at 3.20 with the rest of the school and there were lots of parents waiting. Although Jamey hadn't sent the head a photograph of Tracey he had given him a good description, which the head had circulated to the staff. But while Tracey couldn't go barging into the school because of the security gates, there was nothing to stop her waiting outside the school, which would have been just as unsettling for Reece.

Although Scott and Tracey were no longer living together there was no animosity between them during contact, and Jamey had decided to leave the contact arrangements as they were until the final court hearing. So it continued twice a week, right up to the court date. I learned from Sabrina, who was still acting as

Reece's escort to and from contact, that there were now two security guards in place at the council offices where contact continued to be held. However, Jamey stopped contact for the week of the court hearing, saying that it would be too much for Tracey to cope with, and that she wouldn't be able to stop herself from 'offloading' her anger on to Reece. It was a wise decision, for since the beginning of August Tracey had spent most of her contact time telling Reece what a 'fucking traitor' Jamey was, hoping for Reece's agreement, which he didn't give.

It was a wonder Reece didn't become very unsettled after contact, for Tracey clearly wasn't coping, but Jill assured me the situation was being carefully monitored, and that Reece spent most of the contact playing with his father. He at least knew how to relate to his 'son', albeit mostly through play-fighting. I thought it said something good about Scott that, although he was now aware who Reece's true father was, he continued to view him and treat him as a son. I sincerely hoped no one would ever tell Reece or any of the children about their true heritage, for how does a child cope knowing they are the product of incest?

I explained to Reece that contact had been stopped for the week because everyone was very busy going to court, where the judge would make his decision. Reece accepted this without any problem, but did ask if he could have the cola drink that his mum always took to contact. I didn't think cola with all its caffeine and sugar, let alone additives, was the best drink for Reece, but aware it was a 'treat' he would be missing, I bought some and gave him a glass on Tuesday and Friday when he would have seen his mother.

Reece went to school the following Monday, the day the judge was due to give his decision, unaware of the significance of that day. I was well aware! Like all the professionals involved in Reece's case I was pretty certain of the outcome, but I still breathed a sigh of relief when at 1.30 p.m. Jamey phoned from outside the court to say that the judge had granted the full care order and Reece would not be returning home. The judge had approved the care plan, which allowed Reece to live with his aunt and uncle and Lisa permanently. There would be supervised contact for Reece to see his parents four times a year. Susie and Reece would be seeing each other six times a year, and all the siblings would meet up twice a year.

It was a good judgement and I could hear the relief in Jamey's voice. Jamey said that when he'd finished speaking to me he would phone Reece's aunt and uncle to let them know, and then Marie, for although Susie's care proceedings were ongoing he wanted to let Marie know Susie would be staying with her for the time being. Jamey said the judge had agreed that the introduction of Reece to his new family should start immediately.

'I think it will be too much for Reece to continue to go to school while the introductions are taking place,' Jamey said, 'apart from the practicality of the distance – his aunt lives eighty miles away. I want to get this moving as soon as poss, so I would like you to take Reece into school tomorrow just to say goodbye.'

'Oh, I see. OK.'

'I'll email you and his aunt a copy of the proposed timetable of introductions as soon as I get into the office. If you see a problem with the arrangements, get in touch straightaway. Would you phone his aunt and uncle to finalize the times?'

'Yes.'

'And will you tell Reece of the judge's decision? He trusts you.'

'Yes, of course,' I said. Normally the social worker would explain the judgement to the child, but by asking me Jamey was acknowledging he didn't really have a close enough bond with Reece, and he was right.

Jamey paused, then suddenly asked: 'Cathy, how did you get on with the Guardian, Wendy Payne?'

'Fine,' I said. 'She is very efficient.' There was a long pause. 'Why do you ask?'

'She had a real go at me in court. She told the judge I had failed in my duty to Reece.' He stopped and awaited my comment.

'It sounds a bit harsh,' I said, 'although if I'm honest I think you could have visited Reece a bit more. I don't think Reece would recognize you if he saw you.'

There was another pause before he said: 'It has been a very complicated and difficult case. It has taken up a lot of my time, Cathy.'

'I know, and you've done a good job gathering all the information and preparing the report for the court. I'm sure the judge was very impressed. Perhaps when Reece has gone to live with his aunt and uncle and Lisa you could visit him more often, especially in the early months when he is settling in.'

'Noted,' he said. And it was left at that. Sometimes I felt that the tactful handling of social workers wasn't dissimilar from the way I handled the children.

When I collected Reece from school I gave him a drink and a snack. Then I took him through to the living room, where we sat side by side on the sofa. I began by telling him the judge had decided he wouldn't be returning to live with his mother but he would still be seeing her and his dad, at contact, as he was doing now, only not so often. Reece nodded. 'And there is a new piece of news,' I said, 'which is very exciting, and you need to listen carefully.'

Reece looked at me and his eyes lit up. 'Will I be having another birthday, Cathy?'

I smiled and took his hand between mine. 'No, love, not until next August. You've only just had the last one. But what I am going to tell you is just as exciting.' I paused, aware that how I presented this to Reece would have a far-reaching effect on how easy or how difficult the transition to his new home would be. 'You know you have lots of brothers and sisters?' He nodded. 'There is Sharon, Brad, Sean and the one you know best, Susie.' He nodded again. 'Well, you have another sister called Lisa who you have never seen. She is twelve, a big girl, nearly as big as Lucy and Paula. She lives with your Aunt May and Uncle John, who are really nice people.'

'Do I know them?' Reece sensibly asked.

'No, not yet, love, but you and I are going to get to know them very well, because Aunt May, Uncle John and Lisa want you to go and live with them. They asked the judge and he said yes. The judge, Jamey, your social worker, and the Guardian think it is a very good idea, because your aunt and uncle will make sure you are happy and keep you safe. They will look after you as I have done.'

Reece was quiet and I could see him taking all this in. It was a lot for a child to take in, even for a child without learning difficulties.

'Do you think it's a good idea?' he asked at last.

'Yes, I do, love, because they are really nice people and I know you will be very happy. You will still see Susie regularly, and also Sharon, Brad and Sean sometimes. The judge has said you will see your mum and dad, but not quite so often because Aunt May and Uncle John will be like a new mummy and daddy to you.'

Reece was quiet again, taking in and mulling over what I had said. I thought back to the child who had arrived nearly ten months before, who couldn't have sat still long enough to mull anything over, let alone think out the questions he then asked.

'You and me will get to know them first, before I go to live with them?' he said.

'Yes, and we will start getting to know them very soon.'

'And Lisa is my sister?'

'Yes, half-sister really, but it's the same. Aunt May and Uncle John and Lisa will be your forever family.'

'And aunt and uncle want a son?'

'Yes, they do, love, very much.'

'Good. I'm going to 'ave a new mummy and daddy and they will 'ave a son. And we will all live 'appily ever after.'

'Yes, you will, sweet, just like in the stories I read to you. You will live happily ever after, I promise you.'

Chapter Twenty-One:

It's sad to say goodbye

When Reece and I went into school the following morning Mrs Morrison and the head were waiting in reception. They were aware that the judgement was due and looked at me expectantly. Mrs Morrison was about to take Reece to one side so I could speak to the head without being overheard, but I stopped her, for there was no need for secrecy.

'Reece has some very important and exciting news to tell you,' I said to them both. I was holding Reece's hand and I gave it a reassuring squeeze. The head and Mrs Morrison looked at Reece.

He smiled proudly. 'I'm gonna move. The judge 'as found me a family. My own family. Aunt May and Uncle John, and my sister Lisa. I'm gonna live with 'em 'appy every after.'

The head and Mrs Morrison looked at me for confirmation and I nodded. 'That's right,' I said. It was impossible not to be moved by Reece's declaration and I saw Mrs Morrison's eyes immediately mist. She'd always had a soft spot for Reece and had built up quite a bond with him over the last year.

The head nodded and said, 'That is good news. When?'

'We have come here today only to say goodbye,' I said. 'We are going to be very busy, aren't we, Reece?' I glanced down at him again and he nodded vigorously. 'We will be spending most of the next two weeks getting to know Reece's forever family before he moves to them.'

'Oh,' Mrs Morrison said, clearly taken aback. 'Oh dear, I see. Straightaway.'

'It's important we all say goodbye,' the head said, recovering quickly from the news that he was losing his star pupil. 'Let's go through to the class now, and I'll explain to his teacher.'

Mr Fitzgerald went ahead with Mrs Morrison, while Reece and I followed them through the 'welcome' door, which at times in the past hadn't felt welcoming at all. As we went along the corridor Mrs Morrison dropped back from the head and said quietly to me. 'I would have liked to have given Reece a goodbye present. It's all happened so quickly. I'll put something in the post.'

'That's very kind of you,' I said. 'And thank you so much for all you have done for Reece. He wouldn't be where he is now in his schooling if it hadn't been for you.'

She smiled sadly. 'I'll be sorry to see him go. He really has become a little treasure.' And I knew she meant it.

The head knocked on the classroom door and went in, while Mrs Morrison, Reece and I hovered by the open door. The class was just settling for registration and Mr Fitzgerald spoke to the class teacher, Miss Jones, who then waved for us to come in. With me holding Reece's hand we walked to the front of the class as all the children stopped what they were doing and looked at us.

'I have some very important news, children,' Miss Jones said. 'It's good news, but also a bit sad for us. Reece has come here to say goodbye. He is going to live with his family in another town, so he won't be able to come to this school any more.' A little groan of dismay went up from the children and the teacher paused. 'I know,' she said, 'while we are all very pleased for Reece we are also sad, because we will miss him.' She turned to look at Reece. 'Will you write to us with all your news, Reece?'

Reece nodded. 'I will get my aunt to 'elp me, 'cos I ain't so good at writing.'

'Good,' Miss Jones said. 'We will look forward to hearing all your news. Now I think before we say good-bye we should give Reece three big cheers. Although I have only been Reece's teacher for a few weeks, Miss Broom, your last teacher, has told me how well Reece has done, and how much she liked teaching him.' She paused and then started the three cheers. 'Hip hip!'

The class responded with a loud 'Hooray!' which was repeated three times. Reece looked so pleased and proud I could have wept.

When the class was quiet again the teacher said: 'Reece, I expect you would like to say a special goodbye to Troy.'

Reece nodded. I stayed at the front of the classroom while he made his way between the tables and went up to Troy. Troy swivelled round in his seat and looked up at Reece.

'Thank you for being my friend,' Reece said. 'I 'ope I 'ave another friend like you at my new school. I'll miss you. Goodbye.'

'I'll miss you,' Troy said. 'Goodbye, buddy.' They hugged. It was very touching and all the adults looked misty eyed.

'Is there any work in your drawer you would like to take with you?' Miss Jones asked. Reece opened the table drawer at his place and took out some workbooks and sheets.

'Would you like to give his new PE kit to someone who needs it?' I said to Mrs Morrison. 'It's hardly been worn.'

'Yes, I will. Thank you.'

Reece made his way back between the tables and took hold of my hand again.

'Goodbye, Reece,' everyone called. 'Good luck! Write to us!' We left the classroom to the sound of rapturous applause. Even the head looked slightly pensive.

Mrs Morrison and Mr Fitzgerald went with us along the corridor and through to reception. 'Let me know how he is getting on, won't you?' Mrs Morrison said to me.

'Yes, of course, and thanks again for everything,' I said. 'I should really have bought you a present, but as you say there hasn't been any time.'

'Not at all. I'm happy Reece has made so much progress. I've enjoyed teaching him.' A tear fell from her eye and she quickly wiped it away. When you work with a child as needy as Reece, who has overcome so much and improved, you develop a strong bond. Mrs Morrison would never forget Reece, nor he her.

We said a final goodbye, and the head and Mrs Morrison watched us cross the playground. They returned inside as the security gate banged shut behind us. Reece and I continued, hand in hand, along the pavement and to the car.

'It's sad to say goodbye,' he said. 'It makes you want to cry.'

'I know, sweet, but very soon we will be saying lots of hellos, and that will make you very happy, won't it?'

'Yes, Cathy. I like 'ello. Tomorrow I'm gonna say 'ello to my new family. And I won't ever 'ave to say goodbye again.'

'No, you won't, love. That's right.'

I'd phoned Aunt May the evening before, in line with Jamey's timetable of introduction, and we'd spent nearly two hours talking, during which I had told her all the little things about Reece that would make his introduction and transfer easier for him, and them. Before coming to school I'd told Reece I'd spoken to May and they were all looking forward to meeting him the following day. Again in line with Jamey's timetable, his aunt, uncle and Lisa would visit us the following day but only for a couple of hours. That first meeting is usually in the carer's home, where the child feels safe and comfortable. Lisa was taking the day off school so that she could come to this all-important introduction. Then the day after that Reece and I would be going to his aunt and uncle's home to spend a couple of hours there. Reece would be able to look around the house and see his bedroom, which his uncle John had told me he had just finished decorating.

We then had a free day, and the day after that Reece and I would go again to his new home. I would leave him there for a few hours and return later to collect him and bring him home. Two days after that, provided everyone was happy that the introduction was going all right, I would pack an overnight bag and Reece would spend his first night in his new home. I would collect him the following afternoon, and this single overnight would be repeated two days later. Two days after that he would spend the weekend, and if everyone was happy he was ready I would move him.

The 'free' days in between were to give Reece time to adjust and consolidate all the new things he would be seeing and experiencing. However, these 'free' days were quickly filling, as the Guardian (her role now finished) and Jill phoned to make a time to come and say goodbye to Reece. Jamey wouldn't be saying good-bye because he would continue to be Reece's social worker and, I hoped (after our chat on the phone), would be seeing more of Reece in the future.

It was a very excited child I finally persuaded into bed at 8.30 that night, and one who was up again at the crack of dawn. When Aunt May, Uncle John and Lisa finally drew up outside the house Reece was at the bay window in the front room waiting for them.

'They're 'ere!' he yelled at the top of his voice. 'Cathy, they're 'ere! Me family.'

It was exactly eleven o'clock, the time they were due, which was good going after a two-hour drive. I went into the front room and took Reece's hand. As the two of us went to the front door I'm not sure who was more nervous. Reece was bouncing up and down as though suspended from elastic, taking my arm up and down with him, while my stomach fluttered. I opened the door I saw that May and John were far from composed either. It was a life-changing meeting for us all.

'Come in,' I welcomed. 'Lovely to meet you.' We stood awkwardly in the hall and shook hands. It was Lisa who broke the ice by giving Reece a big kiss on the cheek.

'Hello, baby brother,' she said. 'I'm your big sister.'

That was it for Reece: he was won over. Grabbing her arm, he zoomed her off to play with his toys, while I showed John and May through to the living room, where I offered them coffee. It was really strange talking to May, for she looked like Tracey – both in some of her features and colouring, but without the learning difficulties and all the anger and aggression that contorted Tracey's face. To begin with I half expected her to jab a finger at me and yell accusations. Far from it: a more placid and gently spoken woman you could never wish to meet. John was a little taller than her, about five feet eight inches, stocky, but equally gentle in his manner. I thought what a contrast to Scott and

Tracey they were, and what perfect role models for Reece. I made coffee and brought it into the living room with a plate of biscuits. Lisa and Reece had their juice in the conservatory-cum-playroom, where most of Reece's toys were.

May, John and I chatted easily and naturally, for after our initial reserve it soon became clear they were very easy to talk to, and we had a focal point for our conversation: the children's best interests. May and John talked quite a bit about Lisa, and were aware of how careful they were going to have to be in making sure she got her fair share of attention. They recognized that once the initial euphoria and novelty of having a brother wore off, Lisa was going to have to adjust to having to share John and May with Reece. Until now she'd enjoyed being an only child and having them all to herself.

I noticed that Lisa called May and John Mum and Dad, although May said Lisa was aware her natural mother was Tracey. Lisa had never met Tracey, and had no wish to do so at present, although May and John knew Lisa might grow curious as she got older. Lisa was a tall, slender, attractive girl, with no family resemblance to her mother or siblings apart from having brown eyes. John said they had explained to Lisa that her natural father had never formed part of Tracey's life, but if she ever wanted to try to trace him they would do what they could to help. And I thought that while this was pretty heavy stuff for Lisa to come to terms with it was a lot less heavy than the roots the other siblings would find out if they ever went on a journey of discovery. I didn't know how much May and John knew about the incest in the family – maybe nothing, maybe everything – but it wasn't for me to broach the subject. Clearly May and John had handled Lisa's questions about her natural family exactly right. Lisa appeared to be a happy, confident child who, as a result of her genealogy and upbringing, had none of the problems of the other children.

When Reece had finally exhausted Lisa they came into the living room and May and John spent some time playing with Reece – Snakes and Ladders, Draughts and Guess Who. I made some sandwiches at twelve o'clock and then just after one they began to make a move to go. The timescale of the introduction is always carefully planned so that all parties gradually get to know each other and no one feels overwhelmed. It is a lot for the adults to cope with as much as it is for the children. Reece and I saw them to the door, and Lisa said that she would see Reece again when he stayed overnight because she would be in school for his next two visits. Reece kissed them all goodbye and gave Lisa a big hug. John said he would email me some directions when he got home as their place was 'a bit off the beaten track'.

Later that afternoon when Lucy and Paula arrived home Reece was still excited and had lots to tell them. I could see they shared my mixed feelings, for while we were obviously all pleased for Reece to have such a loving family of his own, we were losing a member of our family. It would have helped Lucy and Paula if they could have met May and John and seen how nice they were, but I didn't think it was going to be possible with them being at school.

Paula and Lucy were both pretty subdued that evening, particularly after Reece had gone to bed, when the house was uncannily quiet and indicative of how it would be once he had left us. To lighten their spirits I told them what I was planning: 'It will be the half-term holiday ten days after Reece leaves us,' I said. 'So I thought it would be a good opportunity to take that week abroad we were talking about. Reece will be having a great time with his new family and we're not going to sit here and mope. How about Cyprus? The climate is supposed to be ideal in mid-October.'

It did help, a little, and I knew from past experience that when the time came, and Reece had successfully moved on, the holiday would help us to move on too.

The following day, with John's emailed instructions on the front passenger seat and Reece excitedly looking out of his side window, I found John and May's home first time. And I was surprised. What John and May hadn't told me was that the reason their house was 'off the beaten track' was that it was a farm, with pigs, cows, two donkeys and meadows as far as the eye could see. Reece was as amazed as I was, and almost lost for words.

'You didn't say it was a farm,' I said as May and John welcomed us at the door.

'No? I must have forgotten,' John said, winking at Reece.

'You didn't forget,' Reece said. 'You wanted it to be a surprise.'

'That's right.' And a rapport between them was immediately established.

Once we were inside John explained he had inherited the farm five years before from his father, but unlike his father he hadn't wanted to farm full time, so he had scaled it down and kept some of the residents – the pigs, cows and donkeys we had seen at the front, together with some chickens and a retired shire horse out the back. He said he employed a local man to look after the farm with May, while he continued with his main work as a telecommunications engineer. The farmhouse was 100 years old, while the two barns were even older. John and May showed us round the downstairs, which had a relaxed country feel to it, with muddy Wellingtons in the porch, waxed raincoats on the stand and an Aga in the kitchen. The kitchen was huge and I thought the gathering point for the family. At one end was a massive pine table with matching high-back chairs.

'We don't stand on ceremony,' John said. 'You'll have to take us as you find us. Make yourself at home.' I always think seeing people in their home surroundings gives a very good clue as to the type of people they are, and May and John were clearly warm, relaxed, gentle, kind-hearted country folk.

I stayed with May in the kitchen, chatting, while John took Reece to see the animals. 'How did you get to be a farmer's wife?' I asked her, for it seemed a far cry from the council estates that Tracey had spent all her years living on. May told me how after she had fled from her father at the age of sixteen she had gone through a really bad patch and then while sleeping rough had met John. He was a member of a local church group and had as it were picked her up and dusted her off, finding her lodgings with another church member. She had been nineteen then, John was five years older, and they had been together ever since. May said that although they would have liked to have had children of their own, having Lisa and now Reece more than compensated. They were both churchgoers and felt that God had taken a hand in shaping their lives and given them each other and their family. I felt that Reece's new family was so perfect for him that I too could have believed in divine intervention, for this was surely meant to be.

Reece came in with John and then spent some time playing in his bedroom, freshly decorated with Batman and Robin wallpaper and matching duvet cover and curtains. Lisa had bought some boxed puzzle games and put them on the shelves in his room, together with a big teddy which had the message 'Home Sweet Home' embroidered on its T-shirt.

When it was time to go Reece asked if we could stay longer, but the three of us said it was time to say goodbye for today, and that we would all look forward to the next visit in two days' time, when Reece would stay for most of the day while I went shopping.

'And don't forget to put your Wellington boots in,' John called from the gate as we got into the car. 'I'm taking the day off work and I'll need some help mucking out those pigs.'

'I will,' Reece called. And I knew that Reece was going to be as happy as a pig in s*** living here. 'Oink oink,' he yelled from the car.

Epilogue

Reece moved to his new family as planned, and a month later, after we'd returned from our holiday in Cyprus, I phoned as I'd promised. Lucy, Paula and I spoke to Reece and he told us all about the animals on the farm, and said that he was going to be a farmer when he grew up. He also said he had visited his new school and would be starting the following week. His teacher was called Mrs Bing and he would be sitting next to a boy called Mark, who Reece said was a bit like Troy. I kept the conversation light and short, for the purpose of the call, apart from reassuring us, was to let Reece know that we hadn't forgotten him. Any further phone calls, or meetings, would be initiated by May and John, when and if they felt it appropriate. We would write to Reece and also send him birthday and Christmas cards, but I wouldn't phone again. It was important Reece now transferred the feelings he had for us to his forever family.

After the girls and I had spoken to Reece, I spoke to May and she confirmed Reece was settling in remarkably quickly, helped she said by having the animals to care for, which was keeping him fully occupied until he started school. Although it was still early days yet, Lisa was enjoying helping to look after Reece, and in many ways mothering him rather than seeing him as a rival for her parents' affection. I asked May when Lisa's birthday was, for I would start sending a card to her too. May told me and said that once Reece was truly settled perhaps the girls and I might like to visit. I thanked her and said we would like to very much, but obviously only when she felt the time was right.

The first week in January Tracey gave birth to a baby girl and the baby was taken from the hospital straight into foster care. Sad though it was for a new mother to lose her baby, I thought that at least that child, like Lisa, would be given a chance in life. However, unlike Lisa it seemed likely the baby was a product of incest, and would almost certainly suffer from the same genetic make-up and therefore the learning difficulties the other siblings had. Only time would tell how she fared. I heard that Scott was still being investigated in relation to Susie's allegations and the police also wanted Tracey's father for questioning but he had vanished. I wasn't told any more and wouldn't be because my involvement with the family had finished when Reece had left my care. Or almost finished.

In the July of that year, while shopping in the high street, I suddenly felt a sharp tap on my shoulder. I turned to see Tracey standing behind me. My first instinct was to run. She had a man with her, and she was even more overweight and unkept than the last time I'd seen her – in the car park after contact. Her long greasy hair straggled round her shoulders and she was wearing a badly stained nylon football club T-shirt and over-stretched faded leggings. The man she was with looked about the same age as her, was thickly set and had a tattoo of what looked like barbed wire round his neck. He wore a matching football club T-shirt and they were both drawing heavily on cigarettes.

'I thought it was you,' Tracey said, clapping her hand on my shoulder. "Ow are you, girl?'

'I'm fine, thanks, Tracey,' I said. 'How are you?'

'Apart from that bleeding social worker, I'm good. He's breaving down me back the whole time and I've told 'im to piss off. So 'as Gary.'

The man she was with nodded. 'Don't you worry, Tracey,' he said. 'I'll deal with 'im. He ain't coming poking his nose round my 'ouse. He ain't got no business there. It's my kid.'

I looked at Tracey, who smiled proudly. My eyes left her face and travelled down to her swelling stomach. She gave her stomach a pat. 'That's right,' she said. 'He ain't 'aving this one. This is Gary's and mine.'

'No,' Gary agreed. 'He ain't.'

I made no comment.

They turned and walked away; then almost as an after-thought Tracey called back: 'How's Sharky boy doing?'

I cringed at the phrase from Reece's past. 'Reece's doing fantastically well,' I said, and I continued on my way.

At the beginning of December, fourteen months after Reece had left us, we received a phone call from May inviting us for Sunday dinner. We immediately fell into conversation and after half an hour, May said, 'Let's leave this catching up until your visit. Come as soon as you can.'

So a week later, I printed out John's emailed instructions again and, bearing flowers and chocolates, Lucy, Paula and I made the two-hour drive to Pine Farm. Reece must have been looking out for us, for the front door opened as we walked down the path.

'Hi,' he said shyly. 'Come in and I'll call Mum and Dad.'

Reece had grown, by at least four inches, and now came up to my shoulder. His usually pale cheeks were glowing a healthy pink from all the country air. Lucy and Paula were immediately impressed by both the farm and Reece. As we went in May, John and Lisa appeared in the hall, and although Reece had been a bit reserved on meeting us, John and May weren't. I gave them the flowers and chocolates and there were hugs all round as I introduced Paula and Lucy. Lisa was a teenager now and had become quite a young lady. She quickly formed an alliance with Lucy and Paula and the three of them went off to her laptop in the kitchen where she was downloading a music DVD. Reece came with John, May and me into the living room.

'It's so good to see you, Reece,' I said again. 'How are you? You look very well. You have grown!'

'I'm big now,' he said, grinning shyly.

'And how is school?'

'Good. I'm doing well. I have lots of friends. Can I go and play with the girls now?'

We laughed. 'Yes, of course,' I said. 'Thank you for inviting us. It really is so good to see you.' He threw me a grin and scampered off.

May, John and I stayed in the living room. It was at the rear of the house, and from where I sat I could see the chickens pecking around in their coop.

'Reece looks very well,' I said to May and John.

'Yes,' May said. 'He is, and has settled in so nicely. His school is in the village and it's small. Reece is in a class of twelve. He only has a TA half time now, and for the rest of the time he is unsupported in the class.'

'That's a huge improvement in a year,' I said. 'Fantastic.'

'We are very proud of him,' John said, and I could see that they were.

As we continued to chat May and John said that like me they were convinced Reece harboured bad secrets, but other than a few throwaway comments he still hadn't said anything to them or Lisa about his life with his mother. Calling May and John 'Mum and Dad' had been Reece's idea, although he still saw Tracey and Scott at supervised contact – three times in the last year. John and May had taken Reece to contact and had met Tracey and Scott while the supervisor and security guard had been present. Tracey had had plenty to say to them, but had been stopped by the supervisor and warned that contact would be terminated if she persisted. I guessed that John and May had experienced some of the verbal abuse that I had endured, but they were such kind souls they would never have said a bad word about anyone. We agreed it would be a long time, possibly into adulthood, before Reece gave up any of his secrets, if ever. He'd once confided in them that 'Mummy had told him not to tell.' They also said they had been through a rough patch at school when Reece had been there for three months. It was after the first contact and he had become unsettled, convinced his mother was going to go to the school and get him. But the school had handled it very well and reassured him, and since then he had gone from strength to strength.

'Does he still want to be a farmer?' I asked John, as May went to put the finishing touches to dinner, insisting she didn't want my help.

'Very much,' John said. 'If he still does when he leaves school it's a viable option. Reece's good with practical stuff, and loves the animals. I can easily expand the farm again. There would be enough work for him as well as Bob, who runs it now.'

'What a nice thought,' I said. 'Reece always did like animals.'

'He's so gentle with them. He collects the eggs from the chickens every morning and hasn't frightened them or broken an egg yet.'

'And what about Jamey? Is his social worker paying regular visits?'

John paused and gave a small smile. 'He phones every so often, but has only managed to visit us once. He's very busy with other cases, and we don't really need his support.' So it appeared that despite Jamey's assurance of more regular visits, they hadn't materialized. It wasn't about 'support' but that as Reece's (and Lisa's) social worker, Jamey should have been in more regular contact. But I guessed John felt as I had done: that it was impossible to get annoyed with Jamey for, despite his failings, his heart was in the right place. Not that I could see John ever getting annoyed with anyone.

Presently May called us in for dinner, and the seven of us sat around the massive pine table at the far end of the kitchen while she served a huge roast with all the trimmings. It was an idyllic country setting, with the room heated by the old Aga, the sound of cows mooing in the distance and us chatting and laughing as we helped ourselves from the huge china platters. In fact the setting was so pleasant and convivial that we stayed at the table talking after we had eaten ourselves to a standstill and declined second helpings of home-made bread-and-butter pudding and clotted cream.

But as the afternoon light slowly faded, and the sky outside darkened, I said we ought to think about going. I had a two-hour drive and the temperature was set to drop to freezing that night. It was quite a pull for Lucy, Paula and me to drag ourselves away from that warm kitchen with its cosy family atmosphere to go out into the cold night air.

'Thank you all so much,' I said as May and John finally helped us into our coats in the hall.

'Thank you for the flowers and chocolates,' May said. 'There was no need to do that.'

'You're welcome,' I said. 'And if ever you are down my way please drop in. We would love to see you again.'

'Will do,' they said. We all hugged and kissed each other goodbye. I gave Reece an extra hug. 'I'm very proud of you,' I said.

He grinned sheepishly.

As we finally stood at the open door ready to leave I said quietly to May and John: 'You've done a great job. Reece is so very lucky having you both.'

May smiled self-consciously. 'Nonsense,' she said. 'All we have done is give Reece what he deserved: his own family. And we thank God for giving us what we wouldn't have had without Lisa and Reece: our very own family.'

SUGGESTED TOPICS FOR
READING-GROUP DISCUSSION

Children in care often have more than one foster home. With reference to the book, what could be the reason for this? What effect could repeated moves have on a child?

Why is Daisy, 15, allowed to do more or less as she pleases? What are your views on the freedom she is given?

Cathy believes that the behaviour of young children is learned from their parents and family. How far are Reece's parents responsible for his behaviour?

What strategies does Cathy use to manage Reece's negative behaviour?

Why is it essential for foster carers to have as much information as possible about the child or children they are looking after?

Why do you think it is important for a child in care to see his or her parents working with the foster carer? What makes this so difficult in Tracey's case?

What do you understand by the term 'safer caring policy'? With reference to the book, why is it important for foster carers to practise 'safer caring'?

A mainstream school might not be appropriate for a child with Reece's high level of needs. Discuss.

Why does Cathy succeed in managing Reece's behaviour when the school does not?

While on holiday Reece nearly tells Cathy some secrets. What do you think he wanted to say?

Why might Tracey be said to be a victim?

What intervention could break the cycle of abuse in this case?

Cathy Glass

One remarkable woman, more
than **150** foster children cared for.

Cathy Glass has been a foster carer for
twenty-five years, during which time she has
looked after more than 150 children, as well
as raising three children of her own. She was
awarded a degree in education and psychology
as a mature student, and writes under a
pseudonym. To find out more about Cathy
and her story visit www.cathyglass.co.uk.

Can I Let You Go?

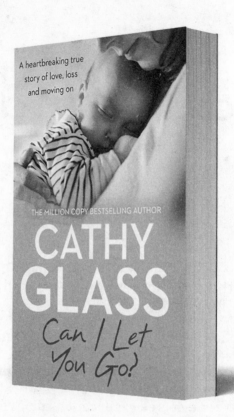

**Faye is 24 and pregnant, and
has learning difficulties as a result
of her mother's alcoholism**

Can Cathy help Faye learn enough
to parent her child?

The Silent Cry

A mother battling depression. A family in denial

Cathy is desperate to help before something terrible happens.

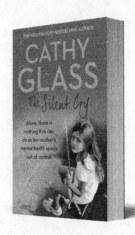

Girl Alone

An angry, traumatized young girl on a path to self-destruction

Can Cathy discover the truth behind Joss's dangerous behaviour before it's too late?

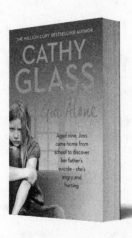

Saving Danny

Danny's parents can no longer cope with his challenging behaviour

Calling on all her expertise, Cathy discovers a frightened little boy who just wants to be loved.

The Child Bride

A girl blamed and
abused for dishonouring
her community

Cathy discovers the
devastating truth.

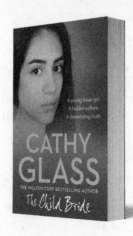

Daddy's
Little Princess

A sweet-natured girl with
a complicated past

Cathy picks up the
pieces after events take
a dramatic turn.

Will You Love Me?

A broken child desperate
for a loving home

The true story of Cathy's
adopted daughter Lucy.

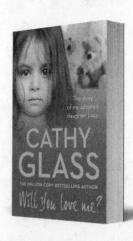

Please Don't Take My Baby

Seventeen-year-old Jade is pregnant, homeless and alone

Cathy has room in her heart for two.

Another Forgotten Child

Eight-year-old Aimee was on the child-protection register at birth

Cathy is determined to give her the happy home she deserves.

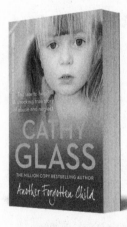

A Baby's Cry

A newborn, only hours old, taken into care

Cathy protects tiny Harrison from the potentially fatal secrets that surround his existence.

The Night the Angels Came

A little boy on the brink of bereavement

Cathy and her family make sure Michael is never alone.

Mommy Told Me Not to Tell

A troubled boy sworn to secrecy

After his dark past has been revealed, Cathy helps Reece to rebuild his life.

I Miss Mommy

Four-year-old Alice doesn't understand why she's in care

Cathy fights for her to have the happy home she deserves.

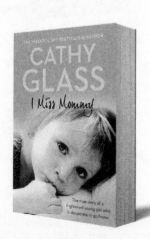

The Saddest Girl in the World

A haunted child who refuses to speak

Do Donna's scars run too deep for Cathy to help?

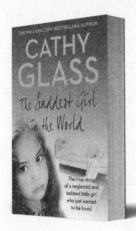

Cut

Dawn is desperate to be loved

Abused and abandoned, this vulnerable child pushes Cathy and her family to their limits.

Hidden

The boy with no past

Can Cathy help Tayo to feel like he belongs again?

Damaged

A forgotten child

Cathy is Jodie's last hope.
For the first time, this
abused young girl has
found someone
she can trust.

Inspired by Cathy's own experiences...

Run, Mommy, Run

The gripping story of a
woman caught in a horrific
cycle of abuse, and the
desperate measures she
must take to escape.

My Dad's a Policeman

The dramatic short story
about a young boy's
desperate bid to keep his
family together.

The Girl in the Mirror

Trying to piece together her past, Mandy uncovers a dreadful family secret that has been blanked from her memory for years.

Sharing her expertise...

About Writing and How to Publish

A clear and concise, practical guide on writing and the best ways to get published.

Happy Mealtimes for Kids

A guide to healthy eating with simple recipes that children love.

Happy Adults

A practical guide to achieving lasting happiness, contentment and success. The essential manual for getting the best out of life.

Happy Kids

A clear and concise guide to raising confident, well-behaved and happy children.

Be amazed
Be moved
Be inspired

—————

Discover more about Cathy Glass
visit www.cathyglass.co.uk

If you loved this book
why not join Cathy on
facebook and **twitter** ?

Cathy will share updates on the children
from her books and on those she's currently
fostering – plus, you'll be the first to know
as soon as her new books hit the shops!

Join her now

f /cathy.glass.180

t @CathyGlassUK